STUDIES IN LITERATURE AND THE HUMANITIES

George Whalley (by courtesy of William O'Neill, *Whig-Standard*, Kingston, Ontario, 1980)

STUDIES IN LITERATURE AND THE HUMANITIES

Innocence of Intent

GEORGE WHALLEY

Selected and introduced by

Brian Crick and John Ferns

McGill-Queen's University Press
Kingston and Montreal

First published 1985 by
THE MACMILLAN PRESS LTD

Published simultaneously in Canada and the United States 1985 by
McGILL-QUEEN'S UNIVERSITY PRESS
ISBN 0-7735-0535-0
Legal deposit first quarter 1985
Bibliothèque nationale du Québec

Printed in Hong Kong

Canadian Cataloguing in Publication Data
Whalley, George, 1915–
Studies in literature and the humanities.
ISBN 0-7735-0535-0.
1. Literature – History and criticism – Addresses,
essays, lectures.   2. Humanities – Addresses,
essays, lectures.   I. Crick, Brian, 1940–
II. Ferns, John, 1941–.   III. Title.
PN81.W43 1985   809   C84-099769-8

For
Elizabeth Whalley and family

It's certain there are trout somewhere
And maybe I shall take a trout
If but I do not seem to care.

W. B. Yeats, 'The Three Beggars'

Contents

Acknowledgements

For permission to reprint the essays and review article selected for inclusion here we should like to thank the following: Professor W. J. Keith, Editor of the *University of Toronto Quarterly*, for 'The Mariner and the Albatross' and 'On Translating Aristotle's *Poetics*'; Mr Robert Weaver, Editor of *Tamarack Review*, for the review of Northrop Frye's *Anatomy of Criticism*; Dr Alexander G. McKay of McMaster University, Honorary Editor of the *Transactions of the Royal Society of Canada*, for ' "Scholarship", "Research" and "The Pursuit of Truth" '; Professor Michael Fox, Editor of *Queen's Quarterly*, for ' "Research" and the Humanities', 'Birthright to the Sea: Some Poems of E. J. Pratt' and 'The Humanities in the World at Large'; Mrs Elizabeth Whalley for 'Picking Up the Thread', which first appeared in Joseph Gold's *In the Name of Language*, published by Macmillan of Canada; the Macmillan Press, London, for 'Jane Austen: Poet', which first appeared in *Jane Austen's Achievement*, edited by Juliet McMaster; President L. Harris of Memorial University of Newfoundland for 'Birthright to the Sea: Some Poems of E. J. Pratt', first published in his university's Pratt Memorial Lecture series; Professor John Baxter of Dalhousie University, Editor of *The Compass*, for 'Teaching Poetry'. 'Literature: An Instrument of Inquiry' was first delivered as the James Cappon Inaugural Lecture at Queen's University in 1977 and first appeared in the *Humanities Association Review*, xxix (1978).

Brock, McMaster and the School of Graduate Studies and Research of Queen's University deserve thanks for financial assistance towards publication of the book in Canada. We should like to thank the late George Whalley and Elizabeth Whalley for their hospitality, which we shall always remember, when we visited Hartington to discuss the present selection. Mrs Shirley Welstead of Brock University deserves our thanks for typing the manuscript. Finally, we should like to thank our families for their help and patience while the book was being prepared.

BRIAN CRICK, Brock University
JOHN FERNS, McMaster University

Introduction

'I hate everything that merely instructs me without increasing or directly quickening my activity.' These words of
Goethe, like a sincere *ceterum censeo*, may well stand at the
head of my thoughts . . . .
(Nietzsche, *The Use and Abuse of History*)

(And talking is always a *commitment* to a world.)
(Ian Robinson, *The Survival of English*)

The danger of this darkness is easily belittled by our
impoverished use of the word 'thought'. This word is
generally used as if it meant an activity necessary to scientists
when they come up against a difficulty in their research, or
some vague unease beyond calculation when we worry about
our existence. Thought is steadfast attention to the whole.
The darkness is fearful, because what is at stake is whether
anything is good.
(George Grant, *English-Speaking Justice*)

I first stumbled upon George Whalley's 'The Mariner and the
Albatross' more than twenty years ago. It certainly didn't resemble
a Brooks and Warren exercise in close textual analysis, and I doubt
whether I could have said then why I found it memorable. Those
graduate schooldays were too much taken up with an instinctive
recoil from the 'perverse, ingenious, desolate' (p.43) gospel of
Northrop Frye that held sway at the University of Western Ontario.
There was no one to direct me to Professor Whalley's wonderfully
just and prophetic review of *The Anatomy of Criticism*, from which I
borrow this judgement. Many years later, when I finally came to
teach my first course in the history of literary criticism, I knew just
enough to seek out his 'On Translating Aristotle's *Poetics*'. It served
me well as goad and guide to a fresh understanding of long familiar

1

passages I mistakenly assumed to be within my grasp. The critical rationale for this book is simply this: if these, the first three essays in the volume, have helped me find my way, then they and the balance of the selection, may do the same for a generation of students and teachers who, whether they realise it or not, desperately need an alternative to structuralism, semiotics and deconstruction. 'The urge to conform can', as Whalley warns, 'become almost compulsive if we get nervous and are afraid that we might miss a trend or a new vogue and be thought old-fashioned . . .' (p.131). For those of us who have enjoyed the privilege of teaching English in the University for a decade or more, and who now face, not without the occasional twinges of anxiety, the responsibility of another twenty years of service, there is the exhilarating example of what George Whalley achieved in the last decade before his retirement. All but the Coleridge and Frye pieces belong to that period of his life.

I

Whalley's suggestion that we adopt the same view of the *Poetics* as 'the early commentators', that it is 'acroamatic' – something to be listened to' (p.55) – recommends itself to us as the wisest way of attending to his own words. The great majority of these papers were in fact composed to be spoken aloud. The superficial signs of the lecturer's presence are readily observable: the declared pause for a sip or a nip; the reliance on certain quotations – touchstones almost – from Coleridge, Yeats or Valéry; the catalogues of student gaffes; or the aphoristic shorthand of 'news, reviews, and interviews' to characterise contemporary pop culture. These mental ticks we could have pruned out, but they are not in any event what we have in mind. We can best make that clear by urging the reader to follow the process of getting to know Whalley traced out for us in the Aristotle essay:

> For I hold the view that a piece of vigorous thinking is an activity of imagination, with its own peculiar spring and set, an action of discovery; and that its form, though overtly discursive, is yet imaginative. If so, the outcome could be expected to be not a group of 'conclusions' or doctrinal precepts, but rather the record of a feat of inventive thinking and the starting-point for fertile, elucidatory, finely controlled and

energetic reflection in response to it.

I should like a translation of the *Poetics* to disclose the *drama* of the discourse – the gesturing forth of the argument (for, as Aristotle notes in passing, *drama* means doing, acting) – so that the reader may be able to 'experience' or enter into the drama.   (p.50)

The promised translation would have sought 'to catch the sound of a voice that is good to overhear, bespeaking the grave unhurried self-possession of a man who is confident that he can think aloud coherently and inventively' (p.55).

Whalley set about the task of bringing us into direct contact with Aristotle's 'presence' – that is, 'Aristotle thinking – Aristotle making this thing' (p.50) because he assumed, and we think rightly, that

> behind every utterance there is a person. It is not simply the *words* that mean; it is a *person* who means; and what the person *means*, intends to convey or declare or conceal and for what reason, is physically imprinted into the structure and texture of his language. . . . The 'imprint' of intention is not seldom at variance with the content of the words; to the perceptive ear an utterance becomes not only a declaration *by* the writer but also a disclosure *of* the writer.
>
> Every successful utterance is a reconciliation between the needs of the speaker and the demands of language. Language is no mere instrument; and, if an instrument at all, the instrument plays on the musician as much as the musician plays on the instrument.   (p.82)

This same purpose and way of knowing informs all of Whalley's writing. For instance, at an early stage in the case he makes for recognising Jane Austen as a poet, he reveals this surprising relationship between Yeats's poetic idiom and Austen's artful composing:

> Yeats's tone-deafness steered him away from the contemporary cult of trying to write 'musical' verse, and brought him to an unmatched sense of the integrity of language – significant words rhythmically disposed, passionate hieratic utterance keyed to the inventive rhythms of the speaking voice. In the

same way, Jane Austen's incapacity for composing strong or eloquent verse seems to have endowed her with an incorruptible sense of the integrity of prose, the translucent rhythms of the speaking voice in the other harmony, the peculiar signature of breath and intelligence that identifies a person speaking and the state of mind that from moment to moment informs the voice. (p.147)

Whether it be the criticism of Aristotle, the verse of E. J. Pratt, or the prose fiction of Jane Austen, the manner and quality of Whalley's inquiring remain constant. The identical impulse and recognition also inform those marvellously integrated works of documentary fact and imaginative re-creation, *The Legend of John Hornby* and *Death in the Barren Ground*. Note the similarity between the passages we have just quoted and Professor Whalley's way of discovering their origins:

Ever since the diary was published more than 40 years ago, the imprint of that voice has proved indelible to anybody who has listened to it . . . the voice that tells of the living that went before the dying: a voice uttered in a firm round hand, the spelling insecure, the punctuation uncertain; the voice of a not-very-accomplished school boy, yet steady, generous in its admiration and in its sense of wonder for the man who had brought him to this, eloquent in its silences, confident in life right to the end. (Introduction to *Death in the Barren Ground*, pp. 19–20)

The critic, the poet and the novelist alike speak the one language if only we listen aright. What else did Wordsworth mean by the oft-quoted but rarely understood question and answer, 'What is a poet . . .?' – 'He is a man speaking to men.' The words for such making and doing and knowing are active verbs such as wondering and admiring. The first principle of such speaking-out or disclosure in writing lies in Whalley's rooted conviction that the gift of utterance is the distinctive mark of man.

II

'Language in itself does not mean, but persons can' (p.40). Keeping this aphorism in mind we can move to the 'knot or nucleus', as Whalley calls it, of his undertaking, the belief that the heart of any genuinely educative activity is to be found in language; not language as a phenomenon, nor as an object of inquiry; not language considered merely for what it says or 'means' or contains, nor even literature as examples of the use of language and ways of living; but everything that is engaged by language and in language – the thinking, the feeling, the activity of mind, the reality of experience that, in the wording of it, can be as solid as an inconsolable grief; the reality that language constantly confronts us with, of *making* as a necessary and natural human activity; language as an inventive mode of inquiry that can disclose ourselves to ourselves, discovering to us what we wanted to say; above all language that allows us to make and utter things that are not simply extensions or expressions of ourselves.   (p.133)

Or again, this equally eloquent companion passage from the same essay:

By 'a sense of language' I mean a feeling for the physique, the nerves and muscles of words, and for their textures; a feeling for what language is *doing* almost more than what it is saying or 'meaning', for what it is tracing out, acting out, gesturing forth, embodying; a feeling for the *intrinsic* qualities of words, their origins and transformations, their minute particularities as they establish themselves by context, by location, by rhythm; a feeling for their ability to declare, in precise configuration and ordered hierarchy, multiple meanings, often contrary; a feeling for the inner shaping energy that comes to the ear as shapely rhythm, as a tune often so subtle that it might seem to be on the fringes of silence. To follow this thread – a thread that leads *back* into the mind and into the source of our most inventive endowment – is to move toward the centre of articulation and initiative both in ourselves and in what we are studying.   (p.140)

Professor Whalley's 'telling over ... as a liturgy of wonder' (p.149) sounds 'a call to remembering and to loving and to thinking' (George Grant, *Time as History*, p.49). It is also his way of 'naming' the reality we have traditionally embodied in the words 'poetry' and 'the imagination':

I take it that imagination is not a 'faculty', but rather an integrated and potent state of the self – a *realising* condition, in which the self and the world are made real. I take it, correspondingly, that the word 'poetry' refers basically to a state of language, a condition qualitatively discernible but not analytically definable – or not yet; a state of language that is noticeably lucid, vivid, nervous, inventive, economical, often translucent, capable of swift movement. Incorrigibly a matter of words (and not dominantly of musical sounds), poetry is informed – or declares itself – by the inventive rhythms of a mind unfolding what cannot be known except in the uttering of it. The rhythms and tone are the indelible marks of energy and of the quality of impulse.   (p.148)

George Whalley's delight in the life of language extended to Latin and to Greek. Some of his finest insights originate in his harbouring in the mind the wordings of Aristotle. The Greek dialect Aristotle thought in, Whalley tells us, was

> extremely rich in participles, which with a fully inflected definite article offer a wide range of substantival adjectives which function like verbal nouns, preserving the active initiative of the verbs that are radical to them. This alone goes far to account for the vivid directness typical of Greek philosophical writing – the general absence of special terms and a happy restraint from abstraction. Furthermore, Greek is capable of providing a wide range of cognate words on a single root: this allows for great variety of self-expository compounds, and also adds to the range of participial nouns which by altering their terminations can refer the root to a person, a thing, a product, a process, an intention even.   (p.53)

The transmogrification of *poiēsis* and *mimēsis* into English via Latin Whalley demonstrates conclusively as the source of the modern misconceptions about Aristotle's central ideas:

> It is in words of active or indicative termination that English seems to me particularly weak for the business of translating the *Poetics* – words that *by their form* clearly imply process or continuous action. English has no words to match the processive implications that abide in the very form of the words *mimēsis*

and *poiēsis*. Too often we have to fall back on nouns formed from Latin past participles ('imitation', 'conception', 'notion', 'construction') or upon collective nouns ('poetry', for example, which has to serve far too many uses); and the present participle 'being' hovers uneasily between noun and participle (it took a Coleridge to wonder whether 'thing' could be the present participle of 'the'). Where Greek is strong, lucid, flexible and precise, and English too often, *faute de mieux*, driven to Latinism, a translator of the *Poetics* has to be crafty and unconventional, and write sentences that to an ear attuned to English philosophical writing of the last couple of centuries does not sound like philosophy at all. (p.54)

The Aristotelian sense of shaping, doing, acting, forming pervades each and every one of the passages we have selected for quotation. By locating this *dynamis* so firmly within the workings of language Whalley discovered a means for synthesising the Aristotelian emphasis on action with a Longinian concern for language. That Whalley sought the integrating of these apparently divergent strains in classical criticism is inferable from a passing comment on Frye's presumption to having done so (p.37) in rather different terms, as well as from his way of proceeding in the Austen essay (pp.146–7).

Moreover, through his use of the verb 'to realise' – to know or to recognise, as well as to make real – Whalley found his way to bringing Aristotle's *mimēsis* and the less well known *zōion ti* ('organic and living thing' – p.57) into fertile critical conjunction with Coleridge's thinking on the imagination and on the structural integrity of poetry. That 'Aristotle–Coleridge axis in criticism' (p.73) is further strengthened by the congruity Whalley intuited between Coleridge's sense of the tragic as rendered most feelingly in the narrative action of 'The Rime of the Ancient Mariner' and this Aristotelian reading of the tragic:

> tragedy is to do with the darkest and strongest issues in our experience – life and death and law and responsibility and freedom and necessity. He knows that we can betray ourselves from within, that when we take the law into our own hands we pass from freedom to mechanism and cease to be human, having cut ourselves off from the law of our inner nature; and he knows that a man can know that he is doing this and yet

do it, and watch himself doing it, capable even in his fascination of altering and reversing the action.   (p.69)

> In this view, the action of tragedy (to think of only one of the 'kinds' Aristotle has under his eye) is not a 'representation' or 'imitation' at all, but the specific delineation, within extremely fine limits, of a moral action so subtle, powerful and important that it is almost impossible to delineate it; an action self-generated that has as its end a recognition of the nature and destiny of man. (No wonder few 'tragedies' meet the specification.) In this view, mimēsis is simply the continuous dynamic relation between a work of art and whatever stands over against it in the actual moral universe, or could conceivably stand over against it.   (p.73)

Whalley learned from Coleridge and from Aristotle that the tragic is not a matter of identifying a literary genre but of living and of recognising the fundamental truths of our natures. The affinities between these two cardinal influences on Whalley's literary criticism is too large a subject to do more than point to in an introduction.

III

For our present purpose it is enough to remind the reader that Professor Whalley's thought grew out of a long tradition. Like T. S. Eliot recovering Arnold's ground or F. R. Leavis taking both Eliot and Arnold as his starting-point for the renewed exploration of the old questions, Whalley requires us to be prepared

> to take long leaps backward in search of some rare and peculiarly illuminating mind. For humanists – preoccupied with the singleness and continuity of human thought – are often vividly aware of the contemporaneity of the past, even of the distant past; their concern is not so much to preserve tradition as to nourish and enrich a continuing life.   (p.119)

In this particular formulation Whalley speaks of this discipline as simply 'humane studies', but elsewhere the designation he favours is the less familiar phrase 'heuristic'. The urgent need for this term makes itself felt in ' "Scholarship", "Research", and "The Pursuit of Truth" ', where Whalley tests traditional wordings of man's innate desire to know which have been steadily dwindling in significance until they are little more than fodder for convocation addresses. The word derives from the Greek verb *heuriskein* (see Ch.4, n.16). It makes its way into English usage somewhere about the middle of the nineteenth century: 'serving to find out or discover' (*OED*). For contemporary usage allied to Whalley's, the reader should consult Michael Polanyi's writing on science and the humanities and the later work of F. R. Leavis, *English Literature in our Time and the University* and *The Living Principle: English as a Discipline of Thought*. We offer only a single passage from each of these men to indicate the direction such a comparison might take.

> To hit upon a problem is the first step to any discovery and indeed to any creative act. To see a problem is to see something hidden that may yet be accessible. The knowledge of a problem is, therefore, like the knowing of unspecifiables, a knowing of more than you can tell. But our awareness of unspecifiable things, whether of particulars or of the coherence of particulars, is intensified here to an exciting intimation of their hidden presence. It is an engrossing possession of incipient knowledge which passionately strives to validate itself. Such is the heuristic power of a problem.
>
> But we may yet say what is usually called knowledge is structurally similar to knowledge of a problem. Knowledge is an activity which would be better described as a process of knowing. (Michael Polanyi, *Knowing and Being*, pp. 131–2)

> The nature of livingness in human life is manifest in language – manifest to those whose thought about language *is*, inseparably, thought about literary creation. They can't but realize more than notionally that a language is more than a means of expression; it is the heuristic conquest won out of representative experience, the upshot or precipitate of immemorial human living, and embodies values, distinctions, identifications, conclusions, promptings, cartographical hints and tested potentialities. (F. R. Leavis, *The Living Principle*, p. 44)

The signs of kinship here are not, as far as we can determine,

matters of influence. Whalley remains oddly silent about Leavis:
even where he brushes 'The Two Cultures' contemptuously aside,
Snow's adversary goes unnamed. Marjorie Greene, Professor
Polanyi's best-known student, is mentioned in a footnote to
the Aristotle essay, and Professor Whalley indicated to us in
conversation a familiarity with Polanyi's thought. Though there
are extensive overlaps between the third part of *Knowing and Being*
and an essay such as 'Humanities in the World at Large',
Whalley's inquiries into the modes of discovery common to poet
and scientist derive from an awareness of underlying similarities
in Bacon's and Coleridge's thinking. Reconciling ostensibly
antipathetic ways of getting to know associated with these writers
came increasingly to occupy Professor Whalley in the final months
of his life. What Bacon and Coleridge meant by the words
'method' (see pp.76, 207) and 'philosophical' (see p.204) Whalley
gathers up in his varied expositions of heuristic thought. In fact
his earliest comments on the need for such a term are enforced
by an illustration from Coleridge that Whalley comes back to
repeatedly. Coleridge, he insists, 'catches well the heuristic spirit
not only by his description but by the way he writes'.

> There is no way of arriving at any sciental End but by finding
> it at every step. The End is in the Means: or the Adequacy of
> each Mean is already its End. Southey once said to me: You
> are nosing every nettle along the Hedge, while the Greyhound
> (meaning himself, I presume) wants only to get sight of the
> Hare, and Flash – straight as a line! he has it in his mouth! –
> Even so I replied, might a Cannibal say to an Anatomist,
> whom he had watched dissecting a body. But the fact is – I
> do not care two pence for the *Hare*; but I value most highly
> the excellencies of scent, patience, discrimination, free Activity;
> and find a Hare in every Nettle I make myself acquainted
> with.   (Quoted in Ch.4, n.16)

An inkling of the thread of correspondences Whalley was still in
the process of unravelling may be picked up by comparing the
Coleridge passage just quoted (or the symbolising habit of mind
Whalley glosses for us in 'The Mariner and the Albatross', p.29,
with the following passage by Bacon:

> But knowledge that is delivered as a thread to be spun on,

ought to be delivered and intimated, if it were possible, in the same method wherein it was invented: and so is it possible of knowledge induced. But in this same anticipated and prevented knowledge, no man knoweth how he came to the knowledge which he hath obtained. But yet nevertheless, *secundum majus et minus*, a man may revisit and descend unto the foundations of his knowledge and consent; and so transplant it into another, as it grew in his own mind. (*The Advancement of Learning*, II. xv. 4)

IV

The most telling formulations that issue from Whalley's descent into the foundations of his knowing are manifest, appropriately enough, in his accounts of the place of such thought in the univeristy and its vital importance to the well-being of our cultural life. (Here again the example of F. R. Leavis cannot be overlooked.) Even a cursory run through the titles of the papers reprinted here indicates as much. As Whalley's criticism is not of the kind one can come at according to topic or theme, our emphasis must not shift from the way of knowing or the purpose of the knowing. What he offers takes the form of fine discrimination blent with incisive judgement.

The impulse behind one side of the argument is that of diagnostic intent: the uncompromising exposure of a myriad of 'deflections' from critical responsibility. With wit (of which we have said all too little) and a moral seriousness Whalley brings to book the infirmities of the age: the will to mastery of the devotees of technique; the nauseating tautologies of projective fantasy; the love of jargon and grammatical abstractions; and the scepticism and nihilism masquerading as objectivity. As we have concentrated on the gravity of Whalley's thought, a sample of his play of mind may not be amiss. His treatment of C. P. Snow's 'class action on behalf of scientists' and its reception is as lively as any of the possibilities that spring to mind:

The transmission of ideas has its own dynamics and its own laws, which, though empirical, seem too absolute in contemporary society. The First Law is, 'If what is said is bad

enough it must be true.' According to this law, Snow's tirade –
'One up for Science' – was bound to stick like a burr, especially
when it was reinforced by the Second Law: 'Indecent exposure
is better than no exposure at all.' For a time, the Third Law
was operative: 'If anything is repeated often enough it will
certainly be taken for truth.' After a while the Fourth Law
(also known as Nixon Parallax) supervened: 'If something is
repeated often enough it will nauseate the hearer.'

The phrase 'The Two Cultures' passed out of currency (as all
vogues happily do), and now has something of the melancholy
savour of a shameful overindulgence; but in its brief heyday it
did a good deal of damage, some of it probably
irreparable.   (p.233)

The same centrality of judgement declares itself in the iterative
wording of this version of illiteracy:

To be not-illiterate is to be able to recognise the unity of the
what, the *how* and the *why* of anything that is spoken or written.
If we cannot recognise by the ring of it that an argument is
specious, or that it is no argument at all, being merely a
reiteration of emotional catchwords and sophisms; if we cannot
tell by the ear the peculiar *timbre* of a third-rate mind fumbling
with matters that he neither understands nor respects; if we
cannot sniff out the shiftiness and doublespeak, of gross
dishonesty and bland self-deception dressed up in jargonish
togs of the latest design; if we cannot by ear detect the poverty
of dull earnestness or the ponderous tautologies of degenerate
abstraction; if we can do none of these things, then we are
indeed illiterate, no matter how extensive our vocabulary, no
matter how many improving magazines we subscribe to.
(p.135)

But more impressive still than these or similar indictments are
the affirmations of the things Professor Whalley stands for. The
last essay in the volume sounds to our ears the most assured, the
most coherent, and the most moving statement of Whalley's faith
(what else can we call it?) in humane studies. We should like to
quote the last four pages *in toto* but we shall settle for this selection:

As humanists we train, support, feed, excite; we try to teach people how to *read*, so that they can enter directly into the activity of the most powerful and penetrating minds that we have record of, and so to find how miraculously complex, integrative and inventive the human mind is, and language too; and so discover themselves by losing themselves. We try to teach people how to *write*, so that their states of feeling, their sense of value, the quality and accuracy of their perception becomes clear and ordered, their awareness of all things heightened, their capacity for sustained reflection strengthened – recognising that everybody has in the end to do his own work, has to work out his own integrity and destiny in solitude. In the course of this we come to recognise how intermittent and excruciating our grasp of reality is, how hard-won and hard-sustained our integrity, how fugitive any profound occasion of knowing, how almost impossible it is to convey it to someone else. Hence the starting-point of this endeavour is delight, wonder, respect, quietness – and the sustaining of it calls for strong nerves, the rejection of short-cuts, the refusal to relax our tenuous grasp upon what matters most of all to us.

. . . To accumulate knowledge and to be able to repeat it is not the primary educational end for the humanities; rather, the purpose (which is scarcely definable) is fulfilled upon the whole person, in the secret places of the mind and memory, and is to be seen in the integrity of perception, judgement, recognition; and in the quality of action that is recognisable, but neither definable nor predictable. This process, though accelerated (if it can occur at all) in a university, can prosper anywhere; yet such is the fugitive intent needed to sustain that possibility that some people devote their whole lives to – living the values and relations that we seek to disclose, turning them over constantly in the mind, in the writing, in the critical devotion to the 'monuments of its own magnificence'.

. . . And finally, how at the root of all this we find language, and the ways of language, and our ways of using language not simply as an instrument of communication for sending messages, but as an inseparable component of our nature, indispensable to our individual development as human beings, and acting reciprocally upon us and our minds and feelings according to the reconciliation we can effect with it, the aim being fidelity to the object, and the integrity of the subject. (pp.244–7)

What is there to add to these home truths? Are they not the truths we profess to believe in, unless we have lost the capacity for belief altogether? Many will no doubt find the responsibility too exacting, but we ignore it at our peril.

V

Wherever possible we have tried to let Professor Whalley speak for himself. In doing so we kept before us the ideal he commends: bringing the reader into direct and intimate contact with the man himself (p.50). There was, too, the daunting awareness of our obligation 'to qualify', as Whalley was fond of saying, 'for a line of thinking we could not have traced out for ourselves' except 'by being perceptively in the presence of the one person who *can* think it out' (p.121). We had originally intended this volume as a tribute to his exemplary dedication to the study of language and literature. We knew he had been gravely ill in recent years, but the extraordinary quality of his most recent writing we eagerly seized upon as a sign of full recovery. In our correspondence with him and in the few meetings that were left to enjoy we found the man and the writer to be one. ('What is a Thought but another word for "I thinking"?' – see Ch.4, n.12.) Our task has proven the harder for his loss and yet we have been sustained by the accents of 'sanity and penetration' (p.167) he bequeathed us. He had 'that rarest of all gifts in a writer, a manner that nobody can fabricate'. He 'wrote with the gravity of a born humorist, out of a life that had known its own peculiar sorrows and immedicable desolations' (p.167).

The Mariner and the Albatross*

For me, I was never so affected with any human Tale. After first reading it, I was totally possessed with it for many days – I dislike all the miraculous part of it, but the feelings of the man under the operation of such scenery dragged me along like Tom Piper's magic whistle.[1]

In these words, in a letter to Wordsworth dated 30 January 1801, Charles Lamb spoke of Coleridge's 'The Rime of the Ancient Mariner'. Some readers continue to echo Mrs Barbauld's complaints that the poem is improbable and has an inadequate or distasteful moral. But these are mental reservations: poetry of the order of 'The Ancient Mariner' does not work its magic upon the mind alone; and mental afterthoughts are of little use in explaining, least of all in explaining away, the profound spiritual and emotional effect of this poem. For every sympathetic reader since Lamb has been similarly possessed and haunted by 'The Ancient Mariner'.

Lamb's criticism is remarkable in a contemporary. The incisiveness of his comment, however, lies not so much in his sensitivity to the fascination of the poem as in his immediate recognition of human feeling as being central in it. Lamb understood and loved Coleridge, and was never to free himself of the fascination of the man: 'the rogue has given me potions to make me love him';[2] "tis enough to be within the whiff and wind of his genius, for us not to possess our souls in quiet'.[3] Unfortunately we have not the means of knowing that 'provocative and baffling personality' as Lamb did. But a close and sympathetic reading of 'The Rime'

*University of Toronto Quarterly, 16 (1946–7) pp. 381–98.

will bring us much nearer to the essential Coleridge than one would expect in a poem that is professedly 'a work of pure imagination'.

'The Rime of the Ancient Mariner' is less 'a fantasticall imagination and a drowsie dreame' than 'a continued allegory, and a darke conceit'. There is an important letter of Coleridge's which confirms the allegorical interpretation of the poem: 'I have often thought, within the last five or six years, that if ever I should feel once again the genial warmth and stir of the poetic impulse, and referred to my own experiences, I should venture on a yet stranger & wilder Allegory than of yore . . . .' It is difficult to see how the missing factor in the comparative could be anything but 'The Ancient Mariner'; and the opinion is confirmed by the associated idea that follows: 'that I would *allegorize* myself, as a Rock with its summit just raised above the surface of some Bay or Strait in the Arctic Sea . . . .'[4] Although the early action of the poem and the killing of the albatross take place in the Antarctic Sea, the details derive from the literature of Arctic travel, as Lowes has shown and as Coleridge would certainly remember.

I wish to examine the poem (a) to show how and to what extent Coleridge's inner life is revealed in 'The Rime'; and (b) to show that the albatross was for Coleridge, whether consciously or unconsciously, a symbol with profound personal significance.

I

The aesthetic and poetic qualities of 'The Ancient Mariner' are impressive. Other writers have examined in the poem the elements of colour and drama, the moral, the truth and accuracy of the detail, the supple and sensitive versification. But the haunting quality of the poem does not, and cannot, grow from any of these elements, whether taken singly or in any combination. Coleridge's creative imagination has fused all these elements into a completely unified organism to express his fundamental meaning; a meaning of whose full significance he was probably unconscious at the time of composition.

Without in any way detracting from the value of the 'The Rime' as a poem, I wish to show that the 'haunting quality' grows from our intimate experience in the poem of the most intense personal suffering, perplexity, loneliness, longing, horror, fear. This experience brings us, with Coleridge, to the fringes of madness and death, and carries us to that nightmare land that Coleridge inhabited, the realm of Life-in-Death.[5] There is no other single poem in which we come so close to the fullness of his innermost suffering. The year after the composition of 'The Ancient Mariner' he gave the self-revealing image of

> some night-wandering man whose heart was pierced
> With the remembrance of a grevious wrong,
> Or slow distemper, or neglected love,
> (And so, poor wretch! filled all things with himself,
> And made all gentle sounds tell back the tale
> Of his own sorrow). . . .[6]

Many years later he told how 'from my very childhood I have been accustomed to *abstract* and as it were unrealize whatever of more than common interest my eyes dwelt on; and then by a sort of transference and transmission of my consciousness to identify myself with the Object'.[7] Whether or not he recognised this process at the time, Coleridge enshrined in 'The Ancient Mariner' the quintessence of himself, of his suffering and dread, his sense of sin, his remorse, his powerlessness. And

> Never sadder tale was heard
> By a man of woman born . . . .[8]

For it is not only a crystallisation of his personal experience up to the time of the composition of the first version, but also an appalling prophecy fulfilled to a great extent in his life and successively endorsed by his own hand as time passed.

II

Life-in-Death is a recurrent theme in Coleridge's thought. In 'The Ancient Mariner' it is luridly personified:

> *Her* lips were red, *her* looks were free,
> Her locks were yellow as gold:
> Her skin was as white as leprosy,

> The Night-mare LIFE-IN-DEATH was she,
> Who thicks man's blood with cold.

And when he summarises his life in 1833 in his own epitaph, he beseeches the passer-by to

> lift one thought in prayer for S. T. C.;
> That he, who many a year, with toil of breath
> Found Death in Life, may here find Life in Death.[9]

Life-in-Death meant to Coleridge a mixture of remorse and loneliness. Yet 'loneliness' is perhaps too gentle and human a word; let us say 'aloneness'. It is precisely this combination of remorse and aloneness with which the Mariner's experience is steeped. Remorse is an emotion easy to find in the poem. It is also broadcast throughout Coleridge's letters and later poems, and requires no detailed consideration here.

The Mariner's aloneness is directly stated:

> Alone, alone, all, all alone,
> Alone on a wide wide sea!
> And never a saint took pity on[10]
> My soul in agony.

It is thrown into relief by contrast with multiplicity:

> The many men, so beautiful!
> And they all dead did lie:
> And a thousand thousand slimy things
> Lived on; and so did I.

And it culminates in the horror of utter solitude:

> O Wedding-Guest! this soul hath been
> Alone on a wide wide sea:
> So lonely 'twas, that God himself
> Scarce seemed there to be.

The same theme recurs in smaller details. When the spirits leave the shipmates' bodies, it is with the sound of birds and 'like a *lonely* flute' (emphasis added). The 'Spirit from the south pole' is a *lonesome* spirit; and, even though there is an air of self-sufficiency in the phrase 'who bideth by himself', like so many solitary people – like Coleridge, like Dorothy Wordsworth – he loves birds:[11]

> He loved the bird that loved the man
> Who shot him with his bow.

When the spectre-bark has sailed away and the Mariner has snapped the spell of the dead seamen's eyes, he looks out over the ocean and feels a sense of foreboding

> Like one, that on a *lonesome* road
> Doth walk in fear and dread.

(emphasis added). These details have a cumulative effect in heightening the direct statement of the Mariner's desolation.

The Mariner's isolation is not 'the wages of sin' so much as the state of sin:

> I looked to heaven, and tried to pray;
> But or ever a prayer had gusht,
> A wicked whisper came, and made
> My heart as dry as dust.

Or again:

> The pang, the curse, with which they died,
> Had never passed away:
> I could not draw my eyes from theirs,
> Nor turn them up to pray.

The same aloneness haunted Coleridge and echoes like doom through his other poems, his letters, the Notebooks. And, in the passionate eloquence of his morbid remorse, he is constantly and restlessly seeking the sin at the root of the desolation; finding as alternative sins his indolence, 'abstruse research', the failure of his marriage, the opium habit.

The 'Moon gloss' forges a powerful link between the Mariner and Coleridge.

In his *loneliness and fixedness* he yearneth towards the journeying

Moon, and the stars that still sojourn, yet still move onward; and every where the *blue sky* belongs to them, and is their appointed rest, and their *native country* and their own *natural homes,* which they enter unannounced, as lords that are certainly expected and yet there is a *silent joy at their arrival.*[12]

The gloss was written some time between 1806 and 1817, and may have been under revision until the completion of the 1829 collection.[13] It is Coleridge's personal and mature comment upon 'The Ancient Mariner'. The 'Moon gloss' itself contains the essence of his loneliness and homelessness, feelings which were acutely present long before the composition of 'The Ancient Mariner'.

In 'Frost at Midnight' (1798) Coleridge recalls the sense of isolation he felt as an orphan at Christ's Hospital:[14]

> if the door half opened, and I snatched
> A hasty glance, and still my heart leaped up,
> For still I hoped to see the *stranger's* face,
> Townsman, or aunt, or sister more beloved . . .
>   For I was reared
> In the great city, pent 'mid cloisters dim,
> And saw nought lovely but the sky and stars.

In January 1796 we find him writing to the Reverend T. Edwards,

> I have got among all the first families in Nottingham, and am marvellously caressed, but to tell you the truth I am quite home-sick owing to this long long absence from Bristol. I was at the *Ball,* last night – and saw the most numerous collection of handsome men and women, that I ever did in one place; but alas! the faces of strangers are but moving Portraits . . . I feel as if I were in the long damp gallery of some Nobleman's House, amused with the beauty and variety of the Paintings, but shivering with cold, and melancholy from loneliness.[15]

Six months before the composition of 'The Rime,' we find him telling his brother that

>   at times
> My soul is sad, that I have roamed through life

Still most a stranger, most with naked heart
At mine own home and birth-place . . . .[16]

And in January 1798 he wrote, 'The first sunny morning that I
walk out, at Shrewsbury, will make my heart die away within
me – for I shall be in a *land of Strangers!*'[17] With the last important
recrudescence of his creative genius, he was to write in 1802 a
curious echo of the watersnake passage:

All this long eve, so balmy and serene,
Have I been gazing on the western sky,
　And its peculiar tint of yellow green:
And still I gaze – and with how blank an eye!
And those thin clouds above, in flakes and bars,
That give away their motion to the *stars*;
Those stars, that glide behind them or between,
Now sparkling, now bedimmed, but always seen:
Yon crescent *Moon*, as fixed as if it grew
In its own cloudless, starless lake of *blue*,
I see them all so excellently fair,
I see, not feel, how beautiful they are![18]

It is important to notice in the 'Moon gloss' the association of the
Moon, the blue sky and home. Elsewhere the same combination of
symbols, sometimes with the addition of tree(s), is associated with
the thought of home, friendship and love, or their absence.

Practically speaking Coleridge was homeless for the greater
part of his life. Remembering the number of times he must have
exhausted the patience of his hosts to the point of serious
misunderstanding and even the breach of friendship, the last part
of the 'Moon gloss' is given pathetic personal significance by
comparison with 'Youth and Age' (1823–32):

Where no hope is, life's a warning
That only serves to make us grieve,
　　When we are old:

That only serves to make us grieve
With oft and tedious taking-leave,
Like some poor nigh-related guest,
That may not rudely be dismist;

> *Yet hath outstayed his welcome while,*
> *And tells the jest without the smile.*[19]

In thinking of nature as a healer, he notes (1811) the fate of the
desolate man: again his thought turns to home, and the parallel
with the 'Moon gloss' is again striking.

> and even when all men have seemed to desert us & the Friend
> of our heart has passed on with one glance from his 'cold
> disliking eye', yet even then the *blue Heaven* spreads it out &
> bends over us, & the little Tree still shelters us under its
> plumage as a second Cope, a *domestic Firmament,* and the low
> creeping Gale will sigh in the Heath-plant and soothe us by
> sound of Sympathy till the lulled Grief lose itself in *fixed gaze*
> on the purple Heath-blossom, till the present beauty becomes
> a vision of Memory.[20]

And in October 1803 he is trying to account for his aloneness:

But yet . . . the greater & perhaps nobler certainly all the subtler
parts of one's nature, must be solitary – Man exists herein to
himself & to God alone, – yea, in how much only to God – how
much lies *below* his own Consciousness![21]

Let us see how this sense of homelessness is imaged in the
'Mariner'. When the ship finally reaches port he cries,

> Oh! dream of joy! is this indeed
> The light-house top I see?
> Is this the hill? is this the kirk?
> Is this mine own countree?

This utterance is charged with deep thankfulness of the seafarer
returned. In many a page of his travel books Coleridge had read
of the emotions aroused by sighting the home port after a long
voyage; and he is able to reproduce the feeling, mingled joy and
pathos and fear, because he has experienced it imaginatively. In
December 1796, he had anticipated in a striking manner the
Mariner's return: 'The Sailor, who has borne cheerily a
circumnavigation, may be allowed to feel a little like a coward,
when within sight of his expected and wished for port.'[22] Although

the Mariner is returning to his 'own countree', one feels sure that he does not expect anybody to be waiting for him.

> The Pilot and the Pilot's boy,
> I heard them coming fast:
> Dear Lord in Heaven! it was a joy
> The dead men could not blast.

Returned from the dead, Lazarus-fashion, he is overjoyed to see living people, to hear their voices. But there is a characteristic note of homelessness when he says

> O sweeter than the marriage-feast,
> 'Tis sweeter far to me,
> To walk together to the kirk
> With a goodly company! –
>
> To walk together to the kirk,
> And all together pray,
> While each to his great Father bends,
> Old men, and babes, and loving friends
> And youths and maidens gay!

It is an impersonal picture, pregnant with the sense of isolation. There are 'loving friends' but they do not seem to be his; the 'old men' are not his brothers or his father, the 'youths and maidens gay' are not his children. We catch an overtone of words spoken by him on a grimmer occasion:

> O happy living things! no tongue
> Their beauty might declare

– words uttered with the same sense of isolation in which Coleridge wrote some twenty-five years later,

> And I the while, the sole unbusy thing,
> Nor honey make, nor pair, nor build, nor sing.[23]

Not only are the Mariner's spiritual and emotional experiences similar to, if not identical with, those we know Coleridge to have suffered, but there is rather more than a hint that the drawing

of the Mariner is a self-portrait. The Mariner's two salient
characteristics are his glittering mesmeric eyes and his passivity.[24] The Mariner says,

> I move like night from land to land,
> I have strange power of speech . . . .

The first line is not only a reflection of Coleridge's isolation, but
also a vivid metaphor description of his imaginative wanderings
while reading 'like a cormorant' before composing 'The Ancient
Mariner'. We have Lamb's evidence for Coleridge's 'strange
power of speech' even at school. 'How have I seen the casual
passer through the Cloisters stand still, entranced with admiration
(while he weighed the disproportion between the *speech* and the
garb of the young Mirandula), to hear thee unfold, in thy
deep and sweet intonations, the mysteries of Jamblichus, or
Plotinus . . ., or reciting Homer in his Greek, or Pindar . . . .'[25]
Even the hostile Hazlitt could write, in 1818: 'That spell is broke;
that time is gone for ever; that voice is heard no more: but still
the recollection comes rushing by with thoughts of long-past
years, and rings in my ears with never-dying sound.'
    The Mariner's passivity is Coleridge's too; and the significance
of that word (as of 'pathos', 'patience', 'sympathy') is rooted, in
more than the etymological sense, in suffering. In those deeply
moving observations of the night sky noted in early November
1803,[26] all written at about two o'clock in the morning, the
elements of passivity, suffering and the moon meet; while finally,
in a similar entry made in Malta six months later, all combine
with the longing for home and for Asra: 'the glorious evening
[star] coasted the moon, and at length absolutely crested its upper
tip . . . . It was the most singular at the same time beautiful Sight,
I ever beheld / O that it could have appeared the same in
England / at Grasmere . . . .'[27] In these entries we see a man who
is waiting, capable still of feeling; and he is driving down the
intolerable suffering only by the *fixedness* with which he gazes on
the sky.[28] Sometimes there must have shaped in his mind the
blasphemy that he expunged from 'The Rime' after 1798: that
'Christ would take no pity on My soul in agony'.[29] And the
Mariner's prayer must often have been repeated in those long
nights:

O let me be awake, my God!
Or let me sleep alway.

At the height of the Mariner's suffering and loneliness, sleep
and dream become central ideas. It is noticeable that the Mariner,
like Coleridge, does not regard them as necessary concomitants.
The Mariner, it is true, hears the 'two voices in the air' while he
is asleep; but he recognises them as being merely voices so that
the tempo of the verse does not race as it did when he sighted
the spectre-bark. His prayer on entering harbour shows that the
whole voyage has been, in a real and horrible sense, a dream;
when he hears the Pilot approaching, his pulse quickens because
the dream of the voyage is broken by a breath of solid human
reality. Coleridge conceived sleep to be, in its essence, dreamless.
We have his own evidence for the fact that his life (like the
Mariner's voyage) passed in a state of dream;[30] and that there
were times, *after* the composition of 'The Ancient Mariner', when
the dream, the thing imagined, was more solid and terrible than
'the normal realities of life'.

> While I am awake, by patience, employment, effort of mind,
> and walking I can keep the fiend at Arm's length; but the
> Night is my Hell, Sleep my tormenting Angel. Three nights
> out of four I fall asleep, struggling to lie awake – and my
> frequent night-screams have almost made me a nuisance in my
> own House. *Dreams with me are no Shadows, but the very Substances
> and foot-thick Calamities of my Life.*[31]

It is the dreams which accompany his sleep that are the torment
and horror. Remove the dreams from his sleep and he would not
'fall asleep, struggling to lie awake'.[32] And the Mariner's craving
and prayer for sleep are paralleled by Coleridge before 1802, and
are more insistently repeated after that date.

The first version of 'The Ancient Mariner' was completed for
publication in *Lyrical Ballads* in 1798. In 1801 Coleridge wrote,
'The Poet is dead in me.'[33] Successive revisions of 'The Rime'
were not complete until 1815;[34] the gloss, though first published
in 1817, had not achieved its final and complete form until the
edition of 1829; and, although no important changes can be
assigned to a later date than 1817, the poem was again revised
in small points of detail for the collection of 1834. The revisions

of the poem resulted in a tightening of the texture, the omission of unnecessary archaisms, the removal of elements of horror which he recognised as gratuitous and ephemeral in their appeal, and the abbreviation of certain passages whose length endangered the balance and emphasis of their setting. But no fundamental change was made in the plan or direction of the poem. Beyond these revisions the gloss, valuable more as profound meditation than as an argument, was added. That the poem was of real personal importance to Coleridge is shown not so much by his careful revision of the text as by the additions to and revisions of the gloss. The final version of 'The Ancient Mariner' is the outcome of at least twenty years of reflection, no matter how sporadic the reflection may have been. That can only mean that the poem continued to hold for him the personal significance with which it was charged at its creation.[35]

In the course of revision the symbolism has been sharpened, not least of all by the gloss; the personal context has been clarified; and, most important of all, the whole poem has been confirmed in the light of his later life.

III

It is misleading to think of Coleridge's life as falling into three distinct phases: one of turbulent preparation, one of cloudless creation, and one of disappointment and broken imagination. The brief creative period, 1797–9, emerges from a mind more hopeful than in the later period, but it is essentially the same mind – restless, mercurial, morbid, remorseful, fearful. For a short time he was lifted up (though on no constant wings) by his marriage, by the birth of Hartley, by his intimacy with William and Dorothy Wordsworth. But even such 'fecundating' happiness, a happiness ominously stressed in the letters of the period, was not able to change the thing that was Coleridge. The early period foreshadows the later. In 1796 he had written, 'There is one Ghost that I *am* afraid of; with that I should be perpetually haunted in this same cursed Acton, the hideous Ghost of departed Hope.'[36] In the same year he observed that

> Such a green mountain, 'twere most sweet to climb,
> E'en while the bosom ached with loneliness . . . .[37]

In the spring of 1797 he told Cottle, 'On the Saturday, the Sunday, and the ten days after my arrival at Stowey I felt a depression too dreadful to be described ... Wordsworth's conversation, &c., roused me somewhat; but even now I am not the man I have been – and I think never shall. A sort of calm hopelessness diffuses itself over my heart.'[38] Early in 1797 he had anticipated 'The Ancient Mariner' by telling his brother George that 'I have roamed through life / Still most a stranger,' and that 'To me the Eternal Wisdom hath dispensed / A different fortune and more different mind.'[39] As early as 1795 he had referred to the taking of drugs;[40] and in the spring of 1798 'Kubla Khan' was conceived 'in a profound sleep, at least of the external senses'. All the elements of the later broken Coleridge are noticeably present by 1797. Coleridge was too intelligent and introspective a man to fail to notice them and understand, at least dimly, their import.

Before the date of the composition of 'The Ancient Mariner' the sense of personal doom was present to Coleridge, even though at times, and for lengthy periods, he was able to 'keep the fiend at Arm's length'. It has been shown that the acute consciousness of his aloneness and homelessness was already present, foreshadowing the 'Moon gloss' and the pitiful threnody 'Youth and Age'. 'The Rime' is the projection of his own suffering, of his sense of personal danger, his passivity, his perplexity. At first he projected himself unconsciously into the poem by the intensity with which he imaginatively experienced the Mariner's situation. During the voyage from Gibraltar to Malta he had an opportunity not only to verify his 'observations' of the sea, but also to know what it was to pass '55 days of literal Horror almost daily expecting and wishing to die'. The time in Malta was a critical, desolate period; and I believe that in Malta Coleridge realised more vividly than ever before that he trembled on the brink of inactivity, of dream, of fatal procrastination, of creative impotence. It is this realisation that he projects into the 1817 version of 'The Ancient Mariner': the personal allegory is sharpened by the gloss, and the addition of important details relates the Mariner's experience more intimately with Coleridge's experience of opium.[41]

Fundamentally it is the personal quality of the poem that accounts for its vivid haunting fascination. And that effect is much heightened when we recognise the prophetic power of the poem; when we know that Coleridge himself in later life recognised the poem for a personal allegory and endorsed its prophecy by a life of wandering loneliness and suffering.

IV

The central figure of the albatross remains to be considered; for 'the albatross . . . binds inseparably together the three structural principles of the poem: the voyage, and the supernatural machinery, and the unfolding cycle of the deed's results.'[42] Nothing less than an intensely personal symbolism would be acceptable against the background of such intense suffering. The albatross must be much more than a stage property chosen at random or a mechanical device introduced as a motive of action in the plot. [43] The albatross is the symbol of Coleridge's creative imagination, his eagle.[44]

It was Wordsworth, not Coleridge, who thought of the albatross.[45] Whether Wordsworth or Coleridge actually stumbled upon the albatross, in Shelvocke or anywhere else, does not matter. In November 1797 the final element, around which the whole poem would crystallise, was needed. As Lowes has shown, Coleridge, in all his diverse and obscure reading before 'The Ancient Mariner', read with the falcon's eye 'which habitually pierced to the secret spring of poetry beneath the crust of fact': it is as though he knew intuitively what he needed without knowing exactly what he was looking for. It would be valuable to have a verbatim record of the dialogue during that momentous walk through the Quantock Hills, rather than the retrospective and somewhat patronising report made by Wordsworth nearly fifty years after the event.

Coleridge would notice at once that the albatross was mechanically suitable: it would fit naturally into a voyage to Antarctic regions; sailors are superstitious about birds and indeed have special superstitions about the albatross; and he may even have noticed that it was amenable to rhyming in a way that other alternatives may not have been. But, apart from practical considerations of plot or versification, the albatross was exactly what Coleridge was looking for. It was a rare species of bird,[46] of exceptional size,[47] solitary, haunting a limited and strange and, for Coleridge, evocative zone, harmless yet by tradition beneficient. Some or all of these facts would, I suggest, flash through Coleridge's mind; and he at once seized upon the albatross as the

right (or, at the very lowest valuation, an adequate) symbol for
his purpose.

Coleridge was a confirmed symbolist. In 1815 he wrote, 'An
idea, in the highest sense of that word, can not be conveyed but by
a *symbol*.'[48] Ten years before, he had noted how

> In looking at objects of Nature while I am thinking, as at
> yonder moon dim-glimmering through the dewy window-pane,
> I seem rather to be seeking, as it were *asking* for, a symbolical
> language for something within me that already and for ever
> exists, than observing anything new. Even when that latter is
> the case, yet still I have always an obscure feeling as if that new
> phaenomenon were the dim Awaking of a forgotten or hidden
> Truth of my inner Nature / It is still interesting as a Word, a
> Symbol! It is Λόγος the Creator! and the Evolver![49]

The process he describes here is not a newly acquired practice,
but an innate and habitual attitude of mind. 'The Ancient
Mariner' is what it is for the reason that Coleridge has clearly
given: because in that poem he found what he was 'seeking, as it
were *asking* for', long before the date of the Notebook entry – 'a
symbolical language for something within me that already and for
ever exists'. Furthermore Coleridge was not the man to use words
or symbols without consideration or to select them carelessly. In
an entry touched with more humility than this single sentence
would suggest, he said in 1805, 'few men, I will be bold to say, put
more meaning into their words than I or choose them more
deliberately & discriminatingly'.[50]

That the link between the albatross and the creative imagination grows out of the inner necessity of the poem and of the man
can be verified by only one passage in 'The Rime'. The evidence is
extremely nebulous, but, being possibly primary evidence, should
not be overlooked. The shipmates' first judgement on the killing
of the albatross was that the Mariner had 'killed the *bird* / That
made the *breeze* to blow' (emphasis added). Late in 1806 Coleridge
connects genius and the wind:

> Tho' Genius, like the fire on the Altar, can only be kindled
> from Heaven, yet it will perish unless supplied with appropriate
> fuel to feed it – or if it meet not with the virtues, whose society
> alone can reconcile it to earth, it will return whence it came, or

at least lie hid as beneath embers, till some sudden & awakening
Gust of regenerating Grace, ἀναζωπυρεῖ, rekindles and reveals
it anew.[51]

And the symbol of the imagination, or of inspiration, is frequently,
outside Coleridge's writing,[52] a bird.

Far more important is Coleridge's reply to the celebrated
strictures of Mrs Barbauld. 'The Ancient Mariner', he said, 'ought
to have had no more moral than the Arabian Nights' tale of the
merchant's sitting down to eat dates by the side of a well, and
throwing the shells aside, and lo! a geni starts up, and says he *must*
kill the aforesaid merchant, *because* one of the date-shells had, it
seems, put out the eye of the geni's son'.[53] The tone of the retort is
jocular. If 'The Rime' had for Coleridge the personal significance
that I believe it had, it would be difficult for him to reply other
than jocularly. About seven years before the reply to Mrs
Barbauld, he tells a correspondent exactly how he reacts to a
situation of that kind.

> My sentiments on the nature of all intrusions into private
> Life, & of mere private *personalities* in all shapes I have given at
> large in the Friend, and yet more pointedly in the Literary
> Life. . . . These you know; but you cannot know, my dear
> Sir! . . . how many causes accumulating thro' a long series of
> years, and acting perhaps on constitutional predisposition,
> have combined to make me shrink from all occasions that
> threaten to force my thoughts back on *myself* personally – as
> soon as any thing of this sort is on the point of being talked of, I
> feel uneasy till I have turned the conversation, or fairly slunk
> out of the room. . . .[54]

Coleridge's facetiousness in speaking of the moral of 'The
Ancient Mariner' was misleading, as it was intended to be; but it
both hides and contains the clue we are looking for.

The nature of the Mariner's crime is thrown into high relief by
Coleridge's italics *('must', 'because')*; and, with it, the nature of
Coleridge's personal 'crime' – for so he regarded it in later life.
The identity is then complete.

The crime was at the same time wanton and unintentional.[55]
The Mariner shoots 'the *harmless* albatross', and '*inhospitably* killeth
the pious bird of good omen' (emphasis added), having no

conception of the implications of his deed. The Mariner *could* have withheld his arrow, the merchant his date-shell; but neither saw any reason for doing so. Certainly the Mariner learned a sharp lesson about killing birds before the voyage was done; but that lesson was of no service to him when, in a moment of idleness or boredom, he aimed his cross-bow at the albatross. 'But so it is! Experience, like the stern lanthorn on a Ship, casts its light only on the *Wake* – on the Track already past.'[56] There is the sternness and inexorability of Greek tragedy in the paradox that an act committed in ignorance of the laws governing albatrosses and genii *must* be punished in the most severe manner.

That Coleridge regarded his own suffering in precisely this light is clear from a poem written as early as 1803.

> Such punishments, I said, were due
> To natures deepliest stained with sin, –
> For aye entempesting anew
> The unfathomable hell within,
> The horror of their deeds to view,
> To know and loathe, yet wish and do!
> *Such griefs with such men well agree,*
> *But wherefore, wherefore fall on me?*[57]

'The Pains of Sleep' is saturated with the same confusion and perplexity that the Mariner experienced. The sin from which the suffering arose was committed in the same way: 'Tho' before God I dare not lift up my eyelids, & only do not despair of his Mercy because to despair would be adding crime to crime; yet to my fellow-men I may say, that I was seduced into the ACCURSED Habit ignorantly.'[58] Even though he may have suspected, when it was too late, what would be the outcome of his struggle with 'this body that does me most grevious wrong', Coleridge did not know, when the process began, that he was killing his eagle. The act was wanton: yes, in the sense that it was unnecessary, that it could have been avoided. And it is that very knowledge – afterwards – that the act could, perhaps easily, have been avoided, if at the very beginning he had understood the implications of his action, that makes stark tragedy both in Coleridge's life and in the Mariner's voyage.

O had I health and youth, and were what I once was – but I

played the fool, and cut the throat of my Happiness, of my genius, of my utility, in compliment to the nearest phantom of overstrained Honor![59]

Well would it have been for me perhaps had I never relapsed into the same mental disease; if I had continued to pluck the flowers and reap the harvest from the cultivated surface, instead of delving in the unwholesome quicksilver mines of metaphysic lore. And if in after-time I have sought a refuge from bodily pain and mismanaged sensibility in abstruse researches, which exercised the strength and subtility of the understanding without awakening the feelings of the heart; still there was a long and blessed interval, during which my natural faculties were allowed to expand, and my original tendencies to develop themselves; – my fancy, and the love of nature, and the sense of beauty in forms and sounds.[60]

The interval was a good deal shorter and less blessed than he was prepared to remember in 1815. And there was a great deal more in the two apparently naïve verses of moral than Mrs Barbauld could have guessed, more even than Coleridge was willing to remember when, long after their writing, he was asked for an explanation.

When the process of the atrophy of his creative imagination, foreshadowed in 'The Ancient Mariner', was far advanced and Coleridge felt that his life was sinking 'in tumult to a lifeless sea', he wrote his comment upon that process. The lines are some of the most desolate ever written.

> But now afflictions bow me down to earth:
> Nor care I that they rob me of my mirth;
>   But oh! each visitation
> Suspends what nature gave me at my birth,
>   My shaping spirit of Imagination.
> For not to think of what I needs must feel,
>   But to be still and patient, all I can;
> And haply by abstruse research to steal
>   From my own nature all the natural man –
>   This was my sole resource, my only plan:
> Till that which suits a part infects the whole,
> And now is almost grown the habit of my soul.[61]

V

'The Ancient Mariner', in addition to its other unique qualities, is both an unconscious projection of Coleridge's early sufferings and a vivid prophecy of the sufferings that were to follow. The poem was probably not originally intended to be a personal allegory; but that is what, in Coleridge's eyes, it became later as the prophecy was slowly, inexorably and lingeringly fulfilled.

As far as I know 'The Ancient Mariner' has never been interpreted as a personal allegory. To do so (and the evidence for it is weighty) not only gives a clue to the source of the poem's intensity but also explains beyond cavil its moral implications. 'The Ancient Mariner' is, however, of primary importance *as a poem*; and no specialised interest – moral, biographical, or allegorical – can be allowed to assail the integrity to which, as a poem, it is entitled. But the interpretation I have suggested does bring the reader into intimate contact with Coleridge the man. Even to attempt to understand him will induce sympathy, and from sympathy some understanding can grow.

Carlyle's judgement of Coleridge is harsh and grossly unsympathetic: 'To steal into heaven ... is forever forbidden. High treason is the name of that attempt; and it continues to be punished as such.'[62] Yet Coleridge had written:

I dare affirm, that few men have ever felt or regretted their own infirmities, more deeply than myself – they have in truth preyed *too* deeply on my mind, & the hauntings of Regret have injured me more than the things to be regretted –.[63]

... for years the anguish of my spirit has been indescribable, the sense of my danger *staring*, but the conscience of my GUILT worse, far far worse than all! – I have prayed with drops of agony on my Brow, trembling not only before the Justice of my Maker, but even before the Mercy of my Redeemer. 'I gave thee so many Talents. What has thou done with them?'[64]

... and as to what *people* in *general* think about me, my mind and spirit are too awfully occupied with the concerns of another Tribunal, before which I stand momently, to be much affected by it one way or other.[65]

Carlyle's judgement overlooks the quantity and quality of the work Coleridge did complete; overlooks the fact that Coleridge throughout his life was dogged by physical disease; overlooks the fact that Coleridge became a man tormented and haunted, at times beyond the capacities of desire or effort, by the knowledge that the eagle had visited him, that he had inhospitably killed 'the pious bird of good omen', and that it might well have been otherwise.

2   Frye's *Anatomy of Criticism**

'Anatomy' may be defined as a dissection carried out to determine the structure of an organised body. This book is a dissection of literature in an attempt to give 'a synoptic view of the scope, theory, principles, and techniques of literary criticism'. The primary aim, Professor Frye tells us, is to give his reasons for believing in such a synoptic view; the secondary aim to provide 'a tentative version' of such a view to convince readers that '*a* view is attainable'. And the whole group of suggestions is intended to be of practical use to critics and students of literature.

It has long been known – though perhaps not uniformly recognised in practice – that a critic who brings to his reading of a single work anything less than everything that can relevantly be related to it will read with partial understanding, imperfect response, distorting prejudice. In practice it is not always easy for a critic to feel sure that he is in command of all the necessary resources. Professor Frye would like to secure for criticism 'the consolidating progess which belongs to a science': that is, some way of making accessible to students of literature the accumulated resources of literary knowledge and critical procedure so that every successive critical act need not be, like the writing of some poems, 'a wholly new start, and a different kind of failure'. Criticism, the argument runs, must be 'an examination of literature in terms of a conceptual framework derivable from an inductive survey of the literary field'. 'Criticism is to art what history is to action and philosophy to wisdom', and 'the critic should be able to construct and dwell in a conceptual universe of his own'. To do so he needs some 'central hypothesis which . . . will see the phenomena it deals with as parts of a whole'. The central hypothesis is 'the assumption of total coherence' – the view of literature not as a vast accumulation of single works but

Tamarack Review, no. 8 (1958) pp. 92–101.

as a single organised body. The conjunction of this hypothesis with the desire for scientific method extends into two important assumptions. One is the assertion of the autonomy of literature, not simply as a unified whole, but as an entirely verbal universe: 'A poem is a hypothetical verbal structure'; 'Poems can only be made out of poems.' The other is the claim for the autonomy of criticism: the desire to conduct criticism in a field cleared of value-judgements and of all non-literary analytic or interpretative disciplines, and to construct for criticism a scheme of descriptive classification as unequivocal as a colour chart. The central organising principles appear to be cyclic and dialectic: the cycle of life or history, and the dialectic of desire and repugnance.

The titles of the essays show a persistent attempt to correlate structural principle with various critical methods: 'Historical Criticism: Theory of Modes', 'Ethical Criticism: Theory of Symbols', 'Archetypal Criticism: Theory of Myths', 'Rhetorical Criticism: Theory of Genres'. In the first essay five modes representing the five epochs of Western literature are distinguished and arranged in order according to the hero's power of action compared with our own: myth, romance, high mimetic, low mimetic, and ironic. The modes are then shown in relation to tragedy (isolation from society) and to comedy (integration into society) in two senses: first according to the 'internal fiction' of the hero's power of action within the fiction (fictional modes), and then according to the 'external fiction' of the poet's relation to his audience (thematic modes). Although in any single work in any period there may occur a counterpointing of historical modes, the modes may be seen as a cyclical order that tends to recur. The order of modes may also be considered in terms of a dialectic tension between myth and verisimilitude, as the 'displacement of the myth in a human direction'. This scheme, through the distinction between fictional and thematic modes and their correlation in a single system, is said to bring together the two critical approaches hitherto regarded as mutually exclusive: the Aristotelian, which regards literature as a product, with catharsis or detachment as its central conception; and the Longinian, which regards literature as process, with ecstasies or absorption as *its* central principle.

The second essay seeks to discover a small number of valid methods of analysing different levels of meaning and of combining them in a single theory. Here five phases of symbolism and meaning are distinguished, each with its appropriate phase of criticism: literal, descriptive, formal, archetypal, anagogic. Two points are important here. A symbol is defined as 'any unit of any literary structure that can be isolated for critical attention'. Again – 'Understanding a poem literally means understanding the whole of it, as a poem, and as it stands. . . . Literal understanding occupies the same place in criticism that observation, the direct exposure of the mind to nature, has in the scientific method.' In this essay Frye's predilection for the archetypal begins to emerge, with an allegiance (not here followed in any detail) to Spengler, Frazer, Jung and Matthew Arnold. 'Archetypal criticism', he says, 'rests on two organizing rhythms or patterns, one cyclical, the other dialectic'; again – 'the archetypal critic is concerned with ritual and dream'; and again – 'Archetypal criticism sees poetry as a technique of civilization.' (Dream is defined as 'not simply the fantasies of the sleeping mind, but the whole interpenetrating activity of desire and repugnance in shaping thought'.) One notices that, although Frye impatiently rejects the possibility of discovering the whole structure of criticism through one method of criticism, his central hypotheses and analogies are all here concentrated. The relation of art to reality Frye asserts to be neither direct nor negative but potential, and for this relation chooses the word 'hypothetical'. The archetype is 'A symbol, usually an image, which recurs often enough in literature to be recognizable as an element of one's literary experience as a whole.' Archetypes serve a special function in the scheme; for they are seen as connecting one poem to another and to the whole field of poetry, and also as integrating human experience. The fifth phase – the anagogic – completes the hierarchy; and here literature is seen as imitating 'the total dream of man' and as 'existing in its own universe, no longer a commentary on life or reality, but containing life and reality in a system of verbal relationships'. In this phase we reach 'the conceivable or imaginative limit of desire, which is infinite, eternal, and hence apocalyptic'; and the meaning of art is 'the Logos, the shaping word which is both reason and . . . creative act'.

The third essay is entirely devoted to archetypal criticism and the theory of myths – not myths in the sense of the first essay but *mythoi* in the sense of pregeneric archetypal narratives or plots, four 'aspects of a central unifying myth'. Three organisations of

myths and archetypal symbols are first distinguished: the two
contrasting worlds of total metaphorical identification, the desirable and the undesirable, heaven and hell; the imagery of the
one being called apocalyptic, and of the other demonic. Between
these, in terms of the displacement of myth in a human direction,
lie romance and 'realism', in which the relations are analogical
in the manner of simile. After the three kinds of imagery and
meaning have been examined in turn, the three become four by
the separation of romance from 'realism', and a cosmological
diagram or wheel by Ptolemaic complexity is constructed from
the four *mythoi* in a quadrantal arrangement informed by the
cyclic principle and by the dialectic (heaven and hell, up and
down): Spring (comedy), Summer (romance), Autumn (tragedy),
Winter (irony and satire). Furthermore, each *mythos* is shown as
disclosing itself in six phases in such a way that the last three
phases of one myth are parallel to, but not coincident with, the
first three phases of the next. The six phases in each case
correspond to a miniature life-cycle from birth to death. At the
top is the apocalyptic epiphany, at the bottom the demonic
epiphany. With triumphant persistence, though not without some
symptoms of strain, Professor Frye manages to supply illustrative
examples for each of these phases.

The fourth essay considers the literary genres according to 'the
radical of presentation' – the relation between the 'speaker' of
the work and his 'audience'. The discussion had started with art
as the middle term in a Platonic triad: history, art, science-and-
philosophy. The poetic symbol had been portrayed as 'intermediate between event and idea, example and precept, ritual and
dream'; and it was said, in Aristotelian terms, that *ethos* (human
nature and the human situation) lies between and is made up of
mythos and *dianoia* (verbal imitations of action and thought). Frye
now returns to complete his account with the other three of the
six Aristotelian elements of poetry: *melos* (music), *lexis* (language)
and *opsis* (spectacle). This is the rhetorical aspect of literature,
the 'literal' level of narrative and meaning. Four rhythms are
distinguished: Recurrence (*epos*), Continuity (prose), Decorum
(drama), association (lyric). A sequence of transformations is
then described for each of the four genres: Drama, Lyric and
Epos, Prose Fiction, and Encyclopaedic Forms.

In this book there is continuous evidence of sustained and
original thinking, of fine perception and controlled insight.

Examples and illustrations are drawn from an impressive range of reading. The sections on comedy and on prose fiction are particularly interesting; there are eloquent symptoms of a Rabelaisian delight in Rabelais; there is a memorable passage on the qualities of good swearing. Throughout there are many correct, incisive and striking judgements and observations upon literature in general and upon particular works of literature; and nothing in this review should distract a reader from recognising and savouring these. The manner of writing is taut, unelaborate, beautifully controlled, almost truculent in its accomplishment. The argument is enlivened by epigrams sometimes shockingly apposite, sometimes provocatively contentious. But not all the witty and epigrammatic matter is of this sort. At times – sometimes at crucial points – the argument is conducted rhetorically through speed and virtuosity, turning upon the adroit lectern quip or upon the verbal paradoxes that 'split into half-truths in order to sharpen their cutting edges'. Occasional gestures of rejection and distaste indicate a less than ideal catholicity of sympathy. None of these idiosyncrasies would be particularly troublesome if they did not contribute to a complex uneasiness difficult to trace to its source: a sustained posture of unhesitating authority, a persistent tone of irony, the use of a subtle rhetoric, a habit of clearing the ground by the use of invective.

   The aim of this compilation of essays, Frye tells us, is not to attack methods of criticism but to attack the barriers between the methods. This sounds like a purpose public and useful enough. But he also says that 'a book of this kind can only be offered to a reader who has enough sympathy with its aims to overlook . . . whatever strikes him as inadequate or simply wrong'. And this makes the book not public and oracular but hermetic – a document perhaps for the instruction of initiates. Yet the book has in fact been made public; its intriguing complexities and commanding tone of authority can be expected to secure for it a wide circulation. And if the present state of criticism is correctly described by Frye as 'a mystery-religion without a gospel' – whatever that means – this volume might easily come to be regarded as the gospel long awaited. This metaphor of religion is used advisedly: because the book strongly implies a tendency to find in literature a substitute for religion, and in criticism a substitute for literature. The more I try to locate and examine my doubts about this book, the more they prove to be not disagreements about matters of method in the conceptual field but centrifugal issues pointing first to the premises, and then beyond these to the reasons for choosing those particular premises. But that leads the inquiry in a direction critically irrelevant and socially impertinent.

As a work of criticism this book will be stimulating for its clear-cut if not always impeccable views on a wide range of writing, and for the illumination that will come from any attempt to classify any single work according to Frye's complex *schēmata* (once one has got round to mastering them). When one looks at the *Anatomy* as an essay in poetics one feels less confident. For one discovers that the view of language as autonomous, self-shaping, impervious to all external influences is more closely related than one would have expected to the desire to establish criticism as a science free of value-judgements.

Language in itself does not mean, but persons can. Language records a person's attempt to say what he means and what he 'sees'. This is the case whether the poet is speaking deliberately out of a prepared programme or almost automatically out of dream or trance. The alternative to Frye's view that 'Poems can only be made out of poems' is not a collapse into some crude form of the 'Intentional Fallacy'. As long as the literal meaning of a poem is the total meaning, there is no reason for excluding the poet's meaning: it at least is actual and irreducible, even if only to be discerned in the poem itself. A complete self-contained verbal universe would be a complete hollow universe incapable of the transvaluative function Frye ascribes to it. Criticism can become 'an ethical instrument' only by forcing us *out* of the verbal universe into action and 'life and reality'. But of this process and of this possibility and need the *Anatomy* gives no account.

Altogether Frye seems to want to destroy all relation between literature and experience, at least in the 'highest' forms of literature. His use of the term 'mimesis' is interesting in this respect. On the one hand, he expands the terms 'symbol', 'literature' and 'dreams' to a point of omnivalence which makes discrimination difficult. On the other hand, he restricts the terms 'experience' and 'intention' to a narrowness that with justice can scarcely be ascribed to any intelligent critic or philosopher. Yet the term 'mimesis' remains conveniently vague, is omitted from the glossary, and is normally used to imply something like the common-sense notion of 'imitation' – plausible or descriptive similarity, point-for-point resemblance. It is, however, legitimate to consider that Aristotle does not so limit his term; that he uses the word 'mimesis' to indicate the varying but indefinable connection between literature and experience. But such a view of 'mimesis' would break the self-sufficiency of Frye's verbal universe. This might be dismissed as matter of interpretative opinion if we did not notice that the appeal to science serves a similar deflective function by outlawing the value-judgements that would infringe upon the verbal universe. This book does not impress one with the scientific possibilities of criticism. To take one point only: the analogies drawn from the Ptolemaic astronomy, from Spengler and Frazer are all analogies outmoded in their own disciplines. This might not matter if the Great Wheel diagram in the third essay did not behave in the way scientific analogies do when they need to be replaced, exhibiting features of excessive complication, assymetry and rigidity.

In the Introduction Frye says that criticism could be a social science. If it were, value-judgement would have to be taken into account as a datum in any observed phenomenon; and Frye wants to banish value-judgements from criticism. Yet the *Anatomy* is an intricate web of value-judgements – not because Frye is a bad scientist, but because he is engaged in critical activity. Without value-judgement there can be no sense of fact in criticism, no sense of relevance; and I had always supposed that one of the main educative virtues of criticism was in the refinement of value-judgements. Without a sense of value, particularly in the field of archetype and myth, the critic is in precisely the position Frye assigns to the sociologist working on literary material: 'Horatio Alger and the writer of the Elsie books may well be more important than Hawthorne or Melville, and a single issue of the *Ladies' Home Journal* worth all Henry James.'

The *Anatomy* is not using scientific method; it is using 'science' as a suggestive analogy. This would account for the peculiar definition of a poem as 'a hypothetical verbal structure' – which suggests that the relation between a poem and 'experience' is the same as (or analogous to?) the relation between a tentative scientific assumption and natural phenomena. But in the Conclusion Frye finds a more promising parallel for criticism in mathematics – which is some indication of the degree of abstraction he is looking for. Here an ominous note is sounded: 'Mathematics relates itself directly to the common field of experience . . . not to avoid it but with the ultimate design of swallowing it.' Is it the aim of art to 'swallow' life, of criticism to 'swallow' art? The word is not defined: but it sounds voracious.

A final point. Frye is content to see myth as a 'structural principle of literary form'. Recurrence is one thing; organisation is another. A pattern cannot organise. And it is precisely the lack of any adequate organising energy in this scheme that makes it in the end unacceptable as a synoptic view of the field. The psychological determinism of desire and repugnance fails to give an adequate account of anagogic myth as we encounter it in literature. Myth without belief is simply either a pattern of narrative or an arrangement of symbols neutral in value. Poetic belief – a strong sense of the power and manifold meaning of a myth – is 'belief for the moment', a genuine belief very different from hypothetical acceptance 'for the sake of [poetic] argument'. Compare Wordsworth's 'Immortality' ode with Yeat's 'Leda and the Swan'. Belief is the energetic principle of myth, and it imprints itself indelibly upon whatever form it may assume. For an artist to repeat the pattern without belief will neither energise the pattern nor restore belief, much as one could wish otherwise. But Frye does not discuss this element of belief in myth.

The view of myth I am advancing is one aspect of a view of knowledge and of truth. Truth and knowledge, in any extralogical field, is not comprised of portable 'things known' or 'things known as true'. Knowledge in such a sphere is inseparable from the mode of apprehension which is also a function of the reason for wanting to know. In Frye's static and abstract morphology the only energetic principle is the dialectic of desire and repugnance. Outside the enclosed system of desire and repugnance, I am sure, vision operates as an overarching principle, redeeming both life and art from determinism and mere humanity. I cannot define vision, nor can I say precisely what is 'seen' in vision. Nevertheless my own experience of literature persuades me that there is vision beyond desire. Desire can easily be mistaken for vision, as the stylite mystics well knew; and vision can be repugnant. The artist's vision, disclosed to the reader, focused perhaps by the critic's insight, can make art a civilising force. But there are many chances of a break in continuity in that process; and to call literature a 'technique of civilization' is either to overlook that fact or to fall upon one of the most popular emotive terms of our time.

I feel personal regret at not finding this book, in its speculative and synoptic aspects, satisfactory. So much of it is brilliant, memorable, stimulating; the writing is superb and there is much excellent criticism. Yet so much of it is perverse, ingenious, desolate; at crucial points gaining rhetorical speed and assuming a sharp edge to seek safety in irony, as though desire were in perpetual conflict with vision.

3   On Translating Aristotle's *Poetics**

The obvious question is – why again? Even a select list of English translations in this century makes quite a litany: Butcher, Bywater, Hamilton Fyfe, Lane Cooper, Allan Gilbert, Preston Epps, Seymour Pitcher, L. J. Potts, George Grube, Gerald Else. I admire three or four of these, and decry none of them. While the study of English literature has – in part at least – taken the place of Greek and Latin as a central humanist discipline and literary criticism has tried to assume the role almost of an autonomous discipline, Aristotle's *Poetics* has continued to be a document of great historical and critical importance. Because almost nobody in the field of English studies *reads* Greek any more – if indeed anybody ever could read fluently and without dismay the Greek of the *Poetics* – translations have accumulated, all highly accomplished.[1] But many of them are of a marmoreal smoothness; almost, the more eloquent and stylish the translation, the farther it is from inducing the direct tactile qualities of the Greek original. For many students of English literature, even some pretty mature ones, the *Poetics* is either a doctrinaire statement that can be readily mastered from a translation, or a very limited account of poetry, interesting enough as the oldest surviving treatise on poetry but distant, foreign, and not very much to the point. Certainly the continuous reprinting of Butcher's translation in collections of critical texts has not encouraged the currency in English studies of certain important developments in Aristotelian scholarship in the past forty years.[2]

As I have worked repeatedly through the *Poetics*, trying to unfold the original to students of English who have even less Greek than Shakespeare had, I have gained an increasingly vivid sense of the activity of Aristotle's mind in this broken and intermittent little document; and have wondered whether a

University of Toronto Quarterly, vol. 39 (1970) pp. 77–106.

translation could conceivably be prepared that would bring a reader to 'the revelation . . . of the driving energy of Aristotle's thought'.[3] 'An editor in these days', Ingram Bywater wrote sixty years ago, 'can hardly hope to do much to advance the interpretation of a book which has been so carefully studied and re-studied by a long succession of editors and translators, many of them among the more illustrious names in the history of classical scholarship.'[4] To think of doing anything about the *interpretation* of the *Poetics* would make the heart even of a classical scholar quail.[5] Of interpretation there is great store, not least in the work of those Chicago scholars whose enemies have called them neo-Aristotelians – Crane, Olson, McKeon, Maclean, Weinberg, to name but a few. These know their Greek as well as their English literature; and there is no sign that as critical theory has effloresced classical scholars have failed to apprise themselves of what might conceivably be profitable in the criticism of English letters to enrich and refine the commentaries they write for classical scholars. And still I feel there is something that needs to be done that has not yet been done for students of English literature; and it would probably take more than a plain translation. My purpose is simply to recover for Aristotle's *Poetics* what Werner Jaeger said was Plato's aim in writing his dialogues: 'to show the philosopher in the dramatic instant of seeking and finding, and to make the doubt and conflict visible'. [6]

Aristotle's works, as we know from the three lists that have come down from antiquity, fall into three groups, only one of which survives. His early reputation as a writer rested on a number of dialogues in the Platonic manner, many if not all written before he founded the Lyceum; all are now lost, and what little we know about them is from a few fragments and a few comments by other writers. He also compiled very extensive memoranda and compendious collections of material put together (sometimes with the help of others, he being perhaps the first to make systematic use of research assistants) for purposes of study and as a basis for future scientific works. Beyond fragments only one of these survives – the *Athenaiōn Politeia*, notes on the constitutions of 158 states, mostly Greek, prepared for publication and stylishly written, a manuscript which was recovered almost intact from the Egyptian desert as recently as 1889. Thirdly, he wrote philosophical and scientific works, still extant, about thirty in number, to which are attached two doubtful works and some seventeen spurious works. None of the works in this group was prepared for publication, and as a group they show varying degrees of finish; the *Nicomachean Ethics* is one of the most finished, the *Poetics* one of the least.

There are few indications even of the relative order of the works, though some of them have evidently been worked at over a period of time – the *Politics*, for example, and the *Poetics*. Most of them are too elaborate and detailed to be regarded as mere lecture notes. Cicero speaks of Aristotle's works in two classes: 'esoteric' works and 'commentaries'. The esoteric works were presumably the 'published' dialogues whose style Cicero praised and which he sought to imitate in his own dialogues. The word 'commentaries' (*hypomnēmata*) is not a very specific term: it could mean anything from rough notes to 'such sophisticated works as Caesar's records of his campaigns',[7] and so could cover both the encyclopaedic collections and the treatises that now survive. What we now have would be called 'esoteric' in Cicero's terms; meaning, not that they were secret or available only to initiates, but simply that they were for use 'inside', in the school. The early commentators – but not Aristotle – referred to these as '*acroamatic*' – 'works for listening to'. Though nothing is now known about the way these were actually used in the Lyceum, it is generally agreed by scholars that they were used in oral instruction and were not intended to be widely circulated outside the school. The *Poetics* is one of these – and a very small one. It takes up only fifteen pages (thirty columns) in Bekker's Berlin Academy edition (1830–1) compared with the ninety-eight pages of the *Nicomachean Ethics* and 114 pages of the *Metaphysics*. The *Poetics* runs to about 10,000 words – that is, about one-hundredth of Aristotle's extant writings.

A translator has to make up his mind about the primary document he is working with. Aristotle was, as we know, the inventor of what we now call a library, but we have no way of telling whether his successors regarded his working-manuscripts as sacrosanct in the way we now regard even the scribblings of some very minor writers: they were not, after all, drafts for finished written work. Plato's disciples prepared a sort of Academy edition of his works; Aristotle's successors seem not to have done so, and indeed we are lucky to have even the text of the *Poetics* as we have it. If the original *Poetics*, as a group of materials to be used in oral instruction, was the property of the school (as there is no reason to doubt) and remained in use after Aristotle's death, the manuscript could well – for successive uses – have been revised, cut down, altered and added to. It is impossible to deny on theoretical grounds that whatever Aristotle had originally set down *could* have been altered and revised entirely out of existence, leaving behind a manuscript ostensibly Aristotelian (and certainly Peripatetic) that contains nothing of Aristotle's beyond transmitted echoes. My own view, however, is that what has been passed down to us is genuinely Aristotle's; that a primary text – or part of it – is preserved; that the text as we have it includes revisions, additions, and afterthoughts by Aristotle, and that at least some of these can be detected with varying degrees of confidence; that a number of spurious glosses have wandered into the text (perhaps from later marginal and interlinear notes) and that these can also be identified with some certainty, without working to the high-minded principle that everything inconsistent, paradoxical, unexpected or difficult is not Aristotle's. I believe further that the substantial nucleus around which these accretal activities have occurred is distinct, coherent and shapely enough to give impressive evidence, at first hand, of Aristotle's intelligence and imagination at work.

This is an expression of faith, but not on that account a shot in the dark; for it arises from many detailed considerations, not least the minutiae of the text itself. But when we cry, 'Back to the Greek text', the question arises '*What* – or which – Greek text?' If the style were less terse and abrupt, if the state of the text were less problematical than it is, and the line of transmission of the text more direct than we know it can have been, there would be fewer difficulties in translating, and fewer chances of being deflected into anachronistic misreadings.

Although the *Poetics* first came to the Western world in the Latin translation of Giorgio Valla in 1498 (from a good manuscript), the only readily available Greek text was the Aldine edition of 1508 (in *Rhetores Graeci*, for it was not included in the great Aldine edition of Aristotle of 1495–8), which, though poorly edited from an inferior manuscript, reigned for more than 300 years. In the Renaissance, when the authority of Aristotle's philosophy was already in decline, interest in the *Poetics* was widespread; through the commentaries of Robortello and Castelvetro it assumed a menacing and authoritarian aspect and gathered to itself some non-Aristotelian doctrine. By the end of the seventeenth century the wave of doctrinaire–expository enthusiasm had subsided, leaving the Greek text in an unpurified form, even though some of Castelvetro's emendations are still worthy of consideration. The Greek text reaches us along a very shadowy route. With Aristotle's other manuscripts bequeathed to his friend and successor Theophrastus it came eventually to Rome in 84 BC after the sack of Athens and must have been included in the edition (long ago lost) made a few years later by Andronicus – the basis for our present Aristotelian corpus. But the *Poetics*, unlike the other works, received no commentary and so was not submitted to early detailed textual examination, and for a time seems to have disappeared. No passage from it is certainly quoted before the fourth century AD; the earliest manuscript with which we have any direct connection was of about the ninth century, and the link is very tenuous; the earliest authoritative Greek manuscript is dated on palaeographical evidence as having been written at the end of the tenth century. The history of the modern text of the *Poetics* begins in 1867, when Johann Vahlen established that MS Parisinus 1741 (MS A) – already known to Victorius, Tyrwhitt and Bekker – was the best and oldest surviving manuscript. Three important discoveries followed: the identification of MS B (in MS Riccardianus 46) as independent of MS A but deriving directly from a common source from which MS A derived at second remove; the discovery of the Arabic version of a Syriac version older than the common source of MSS A and B; and the discovery of a thirteenth-century Latin version of a manuscript closely related to MS A. Butcher's text of 1894 was the first attempt to combine MS A with other texts then available. In the light of successive discoveries, other editions have followed – Bywater (1909), Gudeman (1934), Rostagni (1937, 1945), Daniel de Montmollin (1951) – all of which are superseded by Rudolph Kassel's edition of 1965.[8]

This can be said with confidence: the best Greek text a translator can now work from is a great deal better than any we have had before, not only for the reliability of the central text but for the variety of carefully examined considerations it brings to bear upon the many cruces. Nevertheless it is a long way away – in time and space – from whatever it was that Aristotle wrote down and bequeathed to Theophrastus. That does not necessarily mean, however, that what we have is a wildly distorted or truncated relic of the original. The second 'book' of the *Poetics* – the whole section on 'iambic' and comedy that balanced the long account of tragedy and epic – is lost, and must have been lost before the manuscript *lambda* from which MSS A and B derive on one side, and on the other the Syriac version; for there is no trace anywhere of the section on comedy beyond the few, partly conjectural, words in MS A which may have introduced it. If the heirs of Neleus had a cellar anything like mine it would have taken less than a century for a manuscript to suffer irremediable damage, and it is known that Aristotle's manuscripts did not survive their incarceration without physical damage. Meanwhile it is clear that a translator cannot, without serious danger of systematic distortion, ignore the textual evidence that has been examined, refined and accumulated by a succession of Greek scholars of great distinction; and in the end, for better, for worse, he will have to make a number of textual decisions on his own account.

More than forty years ago, in 1923, Werner Jaeger established effectively for the first time the principle that Aristotle's canon represents a development, and that in order to understand and interpret the individual writings it is essential to imagine as vividly as possible the man and the mind that made these writings and in what order.

> Aristotle ... was the inventor of the notion of intellectual development in time, and regards even his own achievement as the result of an evolution dependent solely on its own law. ... It is one of those almost incomprehensible paradoxes in which the history of human knowledge abounds, that the principle of organic development has never yet been applied to its originator, if we exclude a few efforts which ... have been ... without influence. ... The main reason why no attempt has yet been made to describe Aristotle's development is, briefly, the scholastic notion of his philosophy as a static system of conceptions. His interpreters were past masters of his dialectical apparatus, but they had no personal experience of the forces that prompted his method of inquiry, or of his characteristic interplay of keen and abstract apodictic with a vivid and organic sense of form. ... Everybody knew indeed, that he was a power to be reckoned with, and one of the foundations of the modern world, but he remained a tradition, for the reason, if for no other, that even after the days of

humanism and the reformation men still had far too much need of his *content*.[9]

I am concerned here, not with the development of Aristotle's work altogether, but with the *Poetics* (to which Jaeger makes only two references, one of them concealed[10]) and with the *Poetics* as Aristotle's; or, to put it in Werner Jaeger's words, I wish to disclose 'his characteristic interplay of keen and abstract apodictic with a vivid and organic sense of form'. Recognising that the *Poetics* is by Aristotle, we may be expected to adopt an attentive attitude, and even to expend a little intellectual effort; but the labour may go to gathering 'content', and our interpretation could become – like much mediaeval and Renaissance commentary – minute, immensely learned, and totally devoid of any sense of the whole conception or of the energy that imparts wholeness. I feel Aristotle's presence in the *Poetics*, and find myself saying, 'We have a given text, made by Aristotle; it has a form which implies not only why it exists, but what it is, and what energy is disposed in its realisation, and what patterns of resistance have been interposed to lead that energy into self-expository form.' But the text is in Greek, which few read; if there is to be a translation, I should want it – whatever else it did – to bring the reader to a vivid sense of the energy and shape of Aristotle's thinking, and so to bring him into the presence of Aristotle thinking – Aristotle making this thing, Aristotle inventing for his purpose a method that allows him to do what he sees he must do. This after all is a very Aristotelian way of coming at things; to accept the *poïēma* as given and made; to consider its *physis* (nature); to infer the *dynamis* (power) that realises itself in the given *poïēma*, and to work out from this why it has assumed the form it has – which is to say, simply, what it *is*.

For I hold the view that a piece of vigorous thinking is an activity of imagination, with its own peculiar spring and set, an action of discovery; and that its form, though overtly discursive, is yet imaginative. If so, the outcome could be expected to be not a group of 'conclusions' or doctrinal precepts, but rather the record of a feat of inventive thinking and the starting-point for fertile, elucidatory, finely controlled and energetic reflection in response to it.

I should like a translation of the *Poetics* to disclose the *drama* of the discourse – the gesturing forth of the argument (for, as

Aristotle notes in passing, *drama* means doing, acting) – so that the reader may be able to 'experience' or enter into that drama. If we were not dealing with Aristotle, that might not be either necessary or even much to the point.

But

> Aristotle was the first thinker to set up along with his philosophy a conception of his own position in history; he thereby created a new kind of philosophical consciousness, more responsible and inwardly complex. . . . Everywhere in his exposition he makes his own ideas appear as the direct consequences of his criticism of his predecessors, especially Plato and his school. It was, therefore, both philosophical and Aristotelian when men followed him in this, and sought to understand him by means of the presuppositions out of which he had constructed his own theories.[11]

The drama of his thinking in the *Poetics* flows out of the Platonic background, and is yet the unfolding, in an invented mode, of an energetic process of discovering and seeing quite his own;[12] a self-clarification in the presence of what he is examining – in this case certain kinds of poetry.

As for Aristotle himself, his credentials as a person to speak authoritatively about poetry are rather strange. It is known that he compiled a list of all the dramatic performances given at Athens; he wrote dialogues *On Music* and *On Poets*; in addition to the surviving acroamatic *Rhetoric*, he wrote a dialogue in three books *On Rhetoric*, a summary of rhetorical theories in two books, and a summary of Theodectes' *Handbook of Rhetoric*; he annotated or corrected a copy of the *Iliad* for his pupil Alexander (which Alexander treasured), and wrote out six books of *Homeric Problems* (some traces of which seem to survive in Chapter 25 of the *Poetics*). On the other hand, although Aristotle is known to have gained a reputation for his dialogues and wrote some verses, it is clear that he is not much interested in what we think of as 'poetry'; he does not respond to the touch and tune of poetry as Plato did; neither in the *Poetics* nor elsewhere is there any notice of lyrical poetry, nor of the choric writing that we consider the glory of Greek tragedy; and his theory of metaphor, as far as it goes, is informed more by logical considerations than by a sensitive understanding of the transfigurations language can undergo in poetry. Yet his admiration for Homer is unbounded and declares itself repeatedly in the *Poetics* and elsewhere. And, if we have any tendency to suppose condescendingly that his theory of tragedy is limited by the small number of examples he happens to have had at hand to study, we do well to recall that, out of more than 300 plays by Aeschylus, Sophocles and Euripides he could have known, only thirty-two or thirty-three have come down to us; that he could have known over a thousand plays, and that his well-known compendious habits of inquiry tempt us to suppose that he may well have done.

When we try to place the *Poetics* in the context of his other work or to trace the development of the work itself, the evidence is far from conclusive. In Aristotle's other works there are a few references to what must be the *Poetics*: one in the *Politics* (the promise of a fuller treatment of *katharsis* which has not survived), and five or six in the *Rhetoric*. We know that parts of the *Rhetoric* go back to the last few years of Aristotle's stay at the Academy, and this would not be an implausible date for the earliest elements of the *Poetics*. I am willing to hold with Gerald Else that the earliest parts of the *Poetics* could have been set down at the Academy in the last years of Plato's life, and that the document may have been worked over in the Assos–Mitylene period of his teaching and perhaps also while he was instructing Alexander, and may have been worked over again in the Lyceum.[13]

From classical scholarship a translator can take a sound Greek text, and can gain some acquaintance with Aristotle's works and his ways of thinking so that appropriate connections can be made between the *Poetics* and other works of Aristotle and of Plato. Something further is needed, and for this there is little precedent – a prose style that will remain in close and continuous contact with the details of the Greek, an English vocabulary, syntax, and rhythm that will catch the immediacy and movements of the Greek.[14]

English, with its eclectic vocabulary, a strong tradition of Latinism in its philosophical terms, and of Latinistic structures in its formal writing, is not very much like the Greek Plato and Aristotle thought in. The Attic dialect, the language of Athens at the height of her literary magnificence, is the most cultivated and refined form of Greek: this was Plato's dialect, and Aristotle had it by inheritance, even though – an Ionian by birth – his usage lies in the border country between pure Attic and the less strict, less eloquent *koinē* that was beginning rapidly to develop in the wake of the Greek empire. Attic Greek differs from English in being highly inflected, in the verb as well as in the noun, and is much more highly inflected and supple than Latin (to which in some other respects it is obviously similar). Greek is extremely rich in participles, which with a fully inflected definite article offer a wide range of substantival adjectives which function like verbal nouns, preserving the active initiative of the verbs that are radical to them. This alone goes far to account for the vivid directness typical of Greek philosophical writing – the general absence of special terms and a happy restraint from abstraction. Furthermore, Greek is capable of providing a wide range of cognate words on a single root: this allows for great variety of self-expository compounds, and also adds to the range of participial nouns which by altering their terminations can refer the root to a person, a thing, a product, a process, an intention even. *Poiein, prattein aran,* and *mimeisthai* are crucial instances in the *Poetics.* From *poiein* (to do or make) we have *poiēma (a thing made – roughly our 'poem'); poiētes* (a maker – roughly our 'poet' – but *poiētria* is not poetry but a poetess); *poiēsis* (the process or activity of making – only very roughly our 'poetry', and unhappily the eighteenth century fumbled the ball in allowing 'poesy' to become an elegant variant of 'poetry' when we badly needed a word for *poiēsis*). From the noun *poiēsis,* the adjective *poiētikos* is regularly formed (to do with making, capable of making); and, since we have allowed the word 'poetic' to become merely the adjective of 'poet' and 'poetry', I should like to be able to use both the 'poetic' (in our sense) and 'poietic' (in the Greek sense). Also, a number of compounds can be formed by attaching a noun to *–poiia* (making) and *–poios* (maker) to provide 'myth-making', 'song-making', 'a tragedy-maker', 'an epic-maker', and the like. Greek is seldom at a loss for alternative words in any verbal situation; yet it may be that the many subtle variants it can devise upon a single root accounts for the semantic clarity that Greek words preserve over a long period of time, so that, even when transliterated into Roman letters and converted into English forms, they preserve – at least to those who know even a little Greek – their pristine clarity.

It is in words of active or indicative termination that English seems to me particularly weak for the business of translating the *Poetics* – words that *by their form* clearly imply process or continuous action. English has no word to match the processive implications that abide in the very form of the words *mimēsis* and *poiēsis*. Too often we have to fall back on nouns formed from Latin past participles ('imitation', 'conception', 'notion', 'construction') or upon collective nouns ('poetry', for example, which has to serve far too many uses); and the present participle 'being' hovers uneasily between noun and participle (it took a Coleridge to wonder whether 'thing' could be the present participle of 'the'). [15] Where Greek is strong, lucid, flexible and precise, and English too often, *faute de mieux*, driven to Latinism, a translator of the *Poetics* has to be crafty and unconventional, and write sentences that to an ear attuned to English philosophical writing of the last couple of centuries does not sound like philosophy at all.

Again, Attic Greek uses a variety of enclitics and particles which impart subtle shades of emphasis and relation. These also play an important part in controlling and shaping rhythm. The best Greek prose is wonderfully sinewy and fluent – athletic in its grace and with the superb athlete's way of disposing energy in repose; by contrast, much English philosophical prose recalls the muscle-bound rigidity of the Hellenistic and Roman boxers. When the Greek is abrupt, without deliberate grace or sustained fluency – as is the case in the *Poetics*, even when the text is not corrupt – even then the rhythms still trace out the inflections of a speaking voice.

But what tune is it proper to have in the ear while translating the *Poetics*? Cicero thought well enough of Aristotle's dialogue-style to fashion his own dialogues on it; but that tells us little enough – Latin not being Greek – except that Aristotle's dialogues, as might have been expected, used more sustained discursive monologue than Plato does at his best. If, in the hands of a competent writer, prose style is the image of the mind that produces it, Aristotle's prose cannot be expected to lack force, structural strength, subtlety or complexity. To my ear there are plenty of tokens of all these qualities in the *Poetics*, even though in his later years any desire he may once have had for literary distinction had been dissolved into a preoccupation with teaching. In the *Poetics* he is probably writing with only half an ear for the sound of what he is saying; but there are some elaborate sentences there which, by the way they somehow in the end, and contrary to expectation, unravel themselves triumphantly to a close, make me wonder whether we may be dealing with an absent-minded virtuoso. Parts of the *Poetics* are admittedly broken and terse, and some parts look more like jottings than sustained writing; but the opening chapters – at least fourteen of them – are continuous enough to give an impression of style, even a hint of mannerism, certainly the distinct tune of an identifiable voice. And one thing that emerges from what Aristotle has to say about style is that nothing matters so much as clarity.[16]

All we know is that the *Poetics* was acroamatic – something to be listened to. Suppose it is lecture notes on which Aristotle would improvise and expatiate, as many lecturers do: the trouble is that we don't know how in fact Aristotle did speak from these notes, if they are notes; we have only what is set down. In translating, I have decided therefore to keep very close to the words, to add no grace, to smooth no roughness, thinking rather of Aristotle as a lecturer whose authority rests in the sustained gravity and openness of his speech; a man who chooses deliberate, even angular, plainness in preference to rhetoric, stylishness, or fine and memorable phrasing. The objection to a smooth rendering of the *Poetics* is that it will probably conceal the difficulties the text presents, and bury the fascinating and exacting cruces that often confront the reader in the Greek.

The requirements I have in mind for a translation of the *Poetics* are these. The reader must never be allowed to lose touch with the Greek, even if he does not know any Greek. Latinistic words are to be avoided as far as possible. When a suitable English word does not match a central Greek word, the Greek word can be transliterated (for example, 'mimesis', 'opsis', 'lexis', 'poietic'), not in order to introduce a technical word of invariable meaning (which is the business not of language but of mathematical symbolism), but to remind the reader of the root meaning and implied functions of the word. The writing would have a *spoken* rhythm to allow for the vigour, informality, brokenness and sudden changes of direction in the Greek; it would be easy in movement syntactically a little ramshackle, perhaps, to catch the sound of a voice that is good to overhear, bespeaking the grave unhurried self-possession of a man who is confident that he can think aloud coherently and inventively.

Even if I could manage all that, it would not in itself be enough for what I have in mind. The counterpart to the gaps in the discourse that Aristotle himself might have filled or elaborated would be some sort of commentary; and the counterpart to knowing the Greek is to jog the reader's elbow constantly (if need be) to tell him what the Greek is doing, or why at any point the English is markedly different from the Greek. I would show in square brackets in the text whatever the translator has supplied by way of elucidation or implied comment, and would draw the reader's attention away from the translation as often as and wherever necessary with editorial footnotes leading to a sparse and pointed commentary. This does not make for easy reading; but who ever thought the *Poetics* was going to be easy reading? The aim is to find Aristotle, not to miss him.

Another editorial or typographical device that seems to me important in a version of the *Poetics* is to separate out from the main text all identifiably intrusive elements. These are of two kinds. (1) Interpolations into the text by other hands, presumably at some time after the original text was consolidated. These are seldom emendations of the text itself, but are usually marginal or interlinear notes carried into the text by later copyists. The provenance of some spurious interpolations in the *Poetics* can be traced from manuscript evidence; if there are certainly some of these there may well be others. (2) Aristotle's own notes and afterthoughts, which in modern book-making would be printed as footnotes and appendixes. To identify these is not easy. A good textual critic, guided by his respect for the integrity of the Greek text, is a curious mixture of daring and conservatism. Any claim to have identified an interpolation or dislocation of the text will be narrowly scrutinised by other scholars equally fastidious, daring, and conservative; few such identifications are accepted without qualification by many scholars. But in some cases there is impressive agreement, and, as long as the motive is not to resolve intractable difficulties in interpretation by tearing up the paper the problem is written on, it is well to give distinctive treatment to Aristotle's additions. In this matter I am prepared, for pedagogic purposes, not to be excessively conservative.[17]

As an acroamatic document, the *Poetics* cannot be envisaged as a draft for a publishable treatise, with corrections, alterations, and additions written in to be accommodated to a final text. Some of Aristotle's additions look like the sort of additions that in a later draft are ballooned and arrowed into a context without final adjustment of the syntax and adjustment of the argument. Some are noticeable for their expansive and relaxed style; others are evidently later than the original because they suggest a new

> Edit and annotate the lines
> That young men, tossing on their beds,
> Rhymed out in love's despair
> To flatter beauty's ignorant ear.

So William Butler Yeats, though he was to give thanks to Grierson for his learned edition of John Donne's poems. Or witness what Robert Burton saith in his *Anatomy of Melancholy*.

> Fernelius . . . puts *study*, contemplation, and continual meditation, as an especial cause of madness: . . . *Levinus Lemnius* [saith] 'Many men come to this malady [i.e. melancholy] by continual study, and night-waking, and, of all other men, scholars are most subject to it': . . . severe, sad, dry, tetrick, are common epithets to scholars: and *Patricius* therefore, in the Institution of Princes, would not have them [i.e. princes] to be great students. For (as *Machiavel* holds) study weakens their bodies, dulls their spirits, abates their strength and courage; and good scholars are never good soldiers . . . .
>
> Two main reasons may be given of it, why students should be more subject to this malady than others. The one is, they live a sedentary, solitary life, . . . free from bodily exercise, and those ordinary disports which other men use: and many times, if discontent and idleness concur with it, which is too frequent, they are precipitated into this gulf [of melancholy] on a sudden: but the common cause is overmuch study . . . .

The traditional view of the scholar is not attractive. I know that these days not *all* scholars renounce the 'ordinary disports which other men use', and that many scholars well past the middle age are yet well protected with hair. Nevertheless, 'How doth the old instinct bring back the old names' – scholar, grammarian, pedant – at best condescending, and at worst terms of abuse almost as terrible as 'critic'.

The difficulty was not to find the right name for a known category, but to find a term – or set of terms – that would define (and defend) an ill-defined activity. 'Inquiry' may lack focus but is preferable to Burton's word 'study': at least it suggests that one might be looking forward rather than backward (important though the purity of tradition may be). Even if we could clean up the word 'scholarship' it would not serve simply to associate line of attack or use a revised vocabulary; a few seem to be blocks of material taken out of something written for other purposes but found convenient to extend the argument or to provide broader illustration. In my scheme all spurious intrusions are clearly separated out of the text, but kept in sight; Aristotle's additions are kept in the text but given distinctive typographical treatment; a few larger additions are printed as appendixes; a few paragraphs are repositioned.[18]

The point of using these distinctions in presenting the text is not to 'remove incoherencies and inconsistencies'; rather they give some hope of restoring the document to the status of an organic and living thing – *zōion ti* (a favourite phrase of Aristotle's). The purpose is to make clear 'that provisional form which, being thoroughly characteristic of Aristotle's philosophy, constitutes the inevitable starting-point for every historical understanding of it'. The *Poetics* is not chaotic: the *schēma* is beautifully direct, orderly, and elegant in its logical and thematic development. Yet, for the intelligent and strenuous reader who has no Greek and therefore has no direct access to the textual problems, there seems little point in printing the translation 'plain'; then the reader would be left to resolve or ignore problems the solution of which would heighten his dramatic sense and energise his understanding. I would therefore insist upon some typographical clarification of the textual problems short of imposing dogmatic finality upon their solution. I would also introduce paragraph-numbering for large-scale reference in place of the rather perverse chapter-numbering that tradition has carried with the manuscript, while still preserving the Bekker lineation for small-scale reference.

A few examples will illustrate the sort of translation I have in mind and the kind of details that I think would be useful in a commentary to go with the translation. The two translations that I find closest to the tone I intend are George Grube's (for its firm muscularity) and Gerald Else's literal version in his *Argument* (for its close contact with the Greek and its grave self-preoccupation). But Grube's rendering is so polished as to deflect minute inquiry; and I owe too much to Else's work to venture an open comparison. I have therefore chosen S. H. Butcher's version, as an example of received standard glyptic, and Lane Cooper's, for its relaxed and Latinistic verbosity. Let us begin in the natural way at the beginning.

Butcher, 1911:

I propose to treat of Poetry in itself and of its various kinds, noting the essential quality of each; to inquire into the structure of the plot as requisite to a good poem; into the number and nature of the parts of which a poem is composed; and similarly into whatever else falls within the same inquiry. Following, then, the order of nature, let us begin with the principles which come first.

Lane Cooper, 1913:

In this work, we propose to discuss the nature of the poetic art in general, and to treat of its different species in particular, with regard to the essential quality or function of each species – which is equivalent to the proper and characteristic effect of each upon the trained sensibilities of the judicious. Accordingly, we shall examine that organic structure of the whole which is indispensable to the production of an ideally effective poem, together with such other matters as fall within the same inquiry respecting form and function. Turning first to the conception of poetry in general, we may follow the natural order, and begin with what is fundamental, the principle of artistic imitation.

I propose to translate as follows:

The poietic [art] [1] in itself and the various kinds of it, and what [particular] effect each kind has, and how plots are to be put together if the making [2] is to prosper [3]; and how many elements it has and what kind; and likewise everything else that belongs in this area of inquiry – let us discuss all this, beginning in the natural way with first things [4].

The commentary would discuss four points.

[1]   The opening words are *peri poiētikēs* [*technēs*] – from which the book takes its title. Neither 'poetry' nor 'the art of poetry' is quite right. The root of *poiētikē* – *poiein* (to make, do, fashion, perform) – is a strongly active verb that will dominate the whole discussion in the sense 'to make'. (Emphatically, it does not mean 'to create'.) I have written

'poietic' art, rather than 'poetic' art, partly to emphasise
the sense of 'making' (and the poet as 'maker'), partly as a
reminder that Aristotle does not recognise a distinction
between 'art' and 'craft'.

[2] *Poiesis*, radically the *process* of making.

[3] *Kalōs hexein* – 'to go well with, to work out luckily'. Else
translates 'to be an artistic success', but I prefer a more
direct and idiomatic word.

[4] The way the discussion later develops in detail shows that
this sentence is neither a systematic preliminary outline nor
a statement of the programme Aristotle intends to follow.
He seems to be sidling comfortably into his discourse. But
by taking his starting-point in 'first things' he shows that he
is thinking of the poietic art as cause, or 'reason why'.

After the prefatory sentence–paragraph, the plot thickens
immediately and the difficulties are formidable.

Now epic-making and the making of tragedy [5] – and comedy
too – and the art of making dithyrambs, and most of the art
of composing to the flute and lyre – all these turn out to be,
by and large, *mimeseis* [6]. But these arts differ from one another
in three respects: for they do their mimesis [7] (a) in different
matters (in-what), (b) of different subjects (of-what), and (c)
by different methods (how) [8].

[5] In the first sentence *poiein* or some derivative of it is used
three times (even recognising that by Aristotle's day *epipoiia*
often meant 'epic' rather than 'epic-making'). Aristotle is
clearly not talking about epic, tragedy, comedy, etc., as
genres or art forms; he is talking about the *making* of them.

[6] This word, the plural of *mimesis*, is transliterated to avoid
using the word 'imitations'. *Mimēsis* is in its form a processive
word – a point of great importance for much of what follows.
A useful habit is to read 'mimesis' as 'a process – mimesis'.
'The mimetic process is the activity of *poiētikē*' (Else); its
dynamis (potentiality) works towards a *telos* (end) which is
in both a substantial and active sense, a *poiēma* (poem).
Aristotle does not define either 'the poietic art' or *mimesis*;
he leaves both open for exploration and for progressive self-
definition in the body of the discussion.

[7] In this paragraph, as in many other places, Aristotle uses
mimeisthai, the verb cognate to *mimesis*. If the verb is translated
'to imitate', the meaning is deflected towards an assumed
commonplace definition for 'imitation'. In order to keep
clear that mimesis is an activity or process and not a thing
or product, I use the phrase 'they *do* their *mimesis*' for
mimountai; 'they *make* their *mimesis*' would allow mimesis to
be thought of as a product, an 'imitation'.

[8] This sentence does what is the despair of any English
translator, and does it with Greek clarity and forthrightness
and in a manner usual with Aristotle. Literally 'they differ
in as much as they do their *mimesis* in different things, of
different things, and differently and not in the same way'.
The traditional abstract terms for these three differentiae
are 'medium', 'object' and 'mode'. I prefer 'matter', 'subject'
and 'method' for the following reasons.

Matter (in-what). Even if the word 'medium' were not now
corrupted below fastidious use, it would not be quite correct
here. In current vulgar usage 'medium' refers to various means
of public presentation – printed matter, public speech, stage,
film, radio, television: in short, 'medium [of communication]' –
whatever the question-begging term 'communication' means.
Aristotle's three 'in-what' differentiae are rhythm, melody
and speech. In our way of thinking, these three are not at the
same level: rhythm is radical to both melody and speech.
Although Aristotle seems to think of each emerging as
dominant in dance, music and (dramatic) poetry, he does not
encourage us to suppose that he thinks of any one of them
functioning in isolation from at least one other. Aristotle's 'in-
what' is the physical stuff in which the action is embodied
and assumes form – e.g. for music, patterned sound, and for
painting, patterned colour-and-line-in-space. We know too
little about Aristotle's thoughts on the work of art as 'mediat-
ing' between (say) poet and reader to use the word 'medium'
confidently. What we do know is that Aristotle has a very
strong sense of physical actuality. Since he seems to have been
the first to attempt a classification of the arts according to the
physical materials they use, the choice of a correct term for
'in-what' is important.

Subject (of-what). 'Object' is unsatisfactory because (a) it
tends to imply that the model imposes a predictable or

desirable form upon the work of art, as is sometimes naïvely assumed to be the case for painting: (b) it may be mistaken for 'aim' and become so confused with Aristotle's teleological principle that the starting-point comes to look like the 'end'. 'Subject' presents no difficulty or deflection: we commonly speak of the 'subject' of a book, play, picture or poem meaning in the most general way 'what it is about' and implicitly what it starts from.

Method (how). The usual word 'mode' (as in 'narrative mode', 'dramatic mode') is unsatisfactory because it indicates a static classification into which individual works may fall. 'Method' places the initiative in the maker and helps us to concentrate on the work as in process of making or acting – which is consonant with Aristotle's emphasis throughout the *Poetics*. Fortunately this sense of the word 'method' is familiar to us from twentieth-century critical analysis of prose fiction, drama and poetry.

Let us go on, straight through the next long paragraph which happens to include two allegedly spurious insertions, one certainly spurious word, and a passage that I treat as a discursive note or afterthought of Aristotle's.

[*Differentiation by Matter*]

You know how some people make likenesses of all kinds of things by turning them into colours and shapes – some imaginatively and some [merely] by formula – [9] and how other people do their *mimesis* with the voice [10]: well, in the same way, the arts we are thinking of all do their *mimesis* with rhythm, speech and melody [11], but using speech and melody either separately or mixed together. For example, flute-playing, lyre-playing, and any other [instrumental] arts of this sort – like playing the panpipes – use only melody and rhythm [12]; while the other [verbal] art [13] – an art that happens so far to have no name* – uses only prose [speeches] of [unaccompanied] verses, and when verses, either mixed or of only one kind.

*[*A discursive note by Aristotle*] [Speaking of lack of suitable terms] we haven't in fact even got a common term to cover

the mimes of Sophron and Xenarchus and the Socratic
dialogues; and, again, if somebody does his work in trimeters,
elegiacs, or some other such verse-form [we have no name for
it] – except of course that people get into the habit of attaching
the word 'poet' to the verse-form, and speak of 'elegiac poets'
and 'epic poets' – not because they are entitled to be called
poets for the quality of their *mimesis* but because as practitioners
they are lumped together according to the verse-form they
write in. And if a man puts together some medical or scientific
work in verse, people usually call him a 'poet'; and yet Homer
and Empedocles have nothing in common except their use of
verse, and properly speaking the one should be called a poet,
and the other not a poet but a science-writer – and the same
would apply even if he used a combination of all the verse-
forms (as Chaeremon did in his *Centaur* [14]) [15].

For these arts, then, let this be our division [according to
matter].

Looking back, a few comments are in order.

[9]   Aristotle's word is 'habit' or 'routine'. Coleridge once
      referred to Southey's verse as 'cold-blooded carpentry', but
      that is probably stronger than Aristotle intended. The word
      'imaginatively' is anachronistic, but I cannot think of a
      better here.
[10] 'Sound' will not do. *Phōnē* is specifically the human voice –
      'the most mimetic of the human faculties' (*Rhetoric* 1404^{a}21).
[11] The word is *harmonia* – the due fitting-together of musical
      sounds. For Greek music this applied horizontally –
      melodically. Our use of the word 'harmony' implies a vertical
      or chordal relation.
[12] 'And the dancer's art uses rhythms alone, without melody,
      for it is through their rhythmic figures that dancers represent
      characters, feelings, and actions.' Else in his *Argument* agreed
      with Vahlen in taking this passage for an afterthought of
      Aristotle's: it certainly disrupts the run of the sentence. In
      his *Translation*, however, Else omits the passage as spurious –
      the way it is represented here.
[13] The word 'epic' has been introduced here, probably from
      an explanatory gloss; but it is obviously wrong and is marked

as spurious by Kassel. When the phrase on dancing [12] is not allowed to interrupt the sentence, it is clear that Aristotle is making a contrast between 'bare' instrumental music (without song) and the 'bare' verbal art has no instrumental accompaniment – 'an art that happens so far to have no name'.

[14] '... a mixed epic work (*miktēn rhapsōdian*) – but he [Chaeremon] is entitled to be called a poet'. Whatever *miktēn rhapsōdian* means, Chaeremon's *Centaur* (which has disappeared except for five iambic lines) was a drama, perhaps a closet drama, possibly a tragedy but more probably a satyr-play. Yet a rhapsody is normally a portion of epic of a length that can be given at one performance. Chaeremon seems to have been a contemporary of Aristotle. Aristotle's point in any case is not that Chaeremon was not a poet but that he used a mixture of all the metres.

[15] Whether this section is to be regarded as a note or an afterthought or even a 'later' addition is probably not worth quarrelling over. To mark it off typographically draws attention to its looser rhythm and more leisurely conduct in contrast to the trenchancy of the argument so far. This difference is felt if the passage is left embedded in the text, but we may get the impression that Aristotle has lost the thread and is drifting away from his announced discussion of differentiation by *matter* (in-what). It is worth noticing that the 'art that happens so far to have no name' is not what we should call 'lyrical poetry', but prose by itself and verse without music. And what seems to have led Aristotle to complain about the lack of proper terms was his insistence that the word 'poet' should not be used sloppily.

One more passage will give an example of one of Aristotle's more complicated sentences sustained against fearful odds, and will also show what happens to the central passage about the relation between plot and character in my version. The shape of the *Poetics* is, in outline at least, straightforward and purposeful. Part I, quite short, deals with the differentiation of *mimesis* secured by the matter (in-which), the subject (of-what), and the method (in what way). In part II – also quite short – Aristotle discusses the origins and growth of the poietic art. This is not so much drawn deductively from historical evidence (if indeed much was available), but is a theory of how 'it stands to reason' the poetic art took its origins and grew towards fulfilment – a very Aristotelian way of working. The poietic art, he says, grew out of two human radicals: a flair for *mimesis* (which in this context is very much like 'imitation' in Plato's sense), and a feeling for rhythm and melody. His first and basic division for the poietic art is bravely and incontrovertibly moral: two species establish themselves according as the subjects and central figures (? and poets) are *spoudaioi* ('serious', morally superior, praiseworthy) or *phauloi* ('mean', trivial – or, as Else happily suggests, 'no-account'). Hence on the one side epic and tragedy, and on the other 'iambic' (rough lampooning) and comedy. Each species 'finds itself' discovers its own nature and form, and progressively – even inevitably – moves towards realising its own peculiar nature. He then turns in Part III (which is all the rest of the manuscript as we have it) to discuss tragedy and epic *together*, with tragedy in the forefront until the closing chapters, when epic is distinguished from and compared with tragedy and found inferior to it. And all the time he is talking not about things-made so much as about things in the making, coming into being, finding themselves.

At the beginning of Part III Aristotle sets down the famous definition of tragedy after saying 'let us pick out the emergent definition of its integral nature' – emergent, that is, according to his theoretical 'history' of the way tragedy found itself. Then he discusses the six *merē* of tragedy, literally 'parts' and often translated 'constituent elements'; but, since Aristotle is thinking of tragedy as a special instance of the *poietic* art, the *merē* must be related to the making and coming-into-existence processes of tragedy. *Merē* are not component parts, and the *Poetics* is not a do-it-yourself tragedy kit. So I translate *merē* as 'aspects' – various points of vantage from which we can examine the making and functioning of a drama. Aristotle points to six 'aspects': *opsis* (an impossible word – 'look'? 'visuals'?, but preferably not 'spectacle'[19]), *melopoiia* (song-making – both words and music), *lexis* (speech or dialogue, not 'diction'), characters, 'thought', plot.

I take up the text again at the point where he has finished with *opsis, melopoiia* and *lexis*; the syntax of the first sentence is left much as it is in the Greek.

Since [tragedy] is a *mimesis* of an action and [since] it is acted out by certain people acting and these must necessarily have a certain kind of character and cast of mind (for it is in the light of these that we say that their actions are of a certain kind, and according to [their actions] they all succeed or fail); and [since] the plot is the *mimesis* of the action (for I use 'plot' in this sense – the putting-together of the events) and the 'characters' are what allow us to ascribe certain qualities to the actors, and the 'thought' is the places where [the actors] by speaking prove some point or declare wisdom – because of all this, the [number of] 'aspects' to tragedy-[making] as a whole that account for tragedy as a distinct [species] must be exactly six: plot and characters and speech and thought and 'visuals' and song-making. . . .

But the most important of these is the putting-together (? structuring) of the events. For tragedy is a *mimesis* not of men [simply] but of an action, that is, of life.[20] That's how it is that they certainly do not act in order to present their characters: they assume their characters for the sake of the actions [they are to do]. And so the [course of] events – the plot – is the *end* of tragedy, and the end is what matters most of all. Furthermore, you can't have a tragedy without an action, but you can have it without [clearly defined] characters. . . . So it follows that the first principle of tragedy – the soul, in fact – is the plot, and second to that the characters; it is a *mimesis* of an *action* (*praxis*) and therefore particularly [a *mimesis*] of men-of-action in action.

I am aware of the uncouthness of the style in these passages, but I have retained it for a distinct purposes: to hold the English to what I feel sure the Greek is saying and doing, to the way that argument runs and the emphasis falls. I must now say what guides that purpose and encourages that confidence; but sketchily, because I am not primarily concerned here with points of interpretation but with the attitude of mind that might discover a vivid interpretation if one were wanted.

Far and away the most insistently recurring words and ideas in the *Poetics* (though not so much near the end as in earlier chapters) are 'making' and 'action/acting'. Nevertheless, the radical error (*prōton pseudos*) that is most commonly made about the *Poetics* is to suppose that Aristotle is discussing – as *we* might – tragedy, epic, comedy, and the rest as genres or as somehow things-in-themselves. This may be a valid-enough way to think of these things, but it happens not to be Aristotle's way. The second error is to suppose that Aristotle has drawn together all the literary works he can lay hands on, has classified them, and drawn certain general conclusions which he then proceeds (in the standard backward philosophical way) to explicate and 'prove'. There are a number of reasons for rejecting these two assumptions, inevitable though they may be to some mentalities and even though many translations, especially the earlier ones, imply or endorse them. The dominance of 'making', 'action' and process in the Greek text makes it plain that – whatever preliminary investigations Aristotle may have made (and we may reasonably guess that they were comprehensive and minute) – he is here not working by deduction but by inference. In short, he is working in the distinctive Aristotelian way. He is seized by the individual, the particular, as substantial. What interests him, as Jaeger puts it, is the fact, 'not that something *is coming to be*, but that *something is coming to be*':[21] something that will be final and normative is making its way into existence; when it has come into existence it will have achieved *form*, it will have become what it had to be. The form then is the final statement – assertion, if you like – of an activity seeking its own end, its own fulfilment.[22]

Aristotle sometimes uses the organic example of the seed or the developed organism.[23] It has been argued – I think convincingly – that the distinctive nisus of Aristotle's thinking is most clearly to be seen in his biological investigations: contrary to Plato's ascription of reality to the Ideas only, Aristotle's habit is to insist (as he does repeatedly in the *Metaphysics*) upon individuals – particulars – as substances, the only fully real things. His biological investigations provide commanding instances of a process that he recognises in everything he sees and everything he thinks about, embodied in the notions of potency and act. The power, potency (*dynamis*) can be latent or active; when it becomes active the *dynamis* is *energeia*, actuality, activity from within that drives towards, acts towards attaining its own end (*telos*): that is, *dynamis* is self-realising. (Coleridge, though he regarded himself as a Platonist and no Aristotelian, said that 'Every thing that lives, has its moment of *self-exposition*.'[24]) For Aristotle, everything presents itself to him in terms of motion and end; and 'in every kind of motion his gaze is fastened on the end'.[25] Whether it is a snail, an octopus or dogfish, the convolutions of a nautilus shell or the evolution of the government of a city-state, or the activity of man as a moral creature, Aristotle's fascinated and stern gaze is fixed on the inescapable mystery that this *is*, that *this* is the self-exposition of its *dynamis*, the end of its action. (Wordsworth was in this sense profoundly Aristotelian.) A 'thing' is for Aristotle never inert: it always implies its action and its power. Can it be that this central analogy for the dynamis that in many specialised aspects runs through all things as through a single hierarchical order is not the organic figure drawn from plants, fishes, and animals, but the human *dynamis*? 'For the actuality of *Nous* [intelligence, intuition] is life.'[26]

When Aristotle looks at tragedy he wants to find out the form of tragedy; that is, in his terms, what tragedy of its own nature comes to be. The pre-Socratic philosophers had tried to account for everything in terms of the distribution of chaotic matter by mechanical causes; Plato and Aristotle, each in his own way, had moved away from that position. For Aristotle, action and power, motion and form are the dynamic modes which everything discloses. The higher we ascend in the order of the cosmos, he believes, the more purely the motion expresses the form that is its end; and the highest form must be pure activity. At the human level, it may be, he sees tragedy – and perhaps all art – as pure act in the human psyche. Tragedy as the end of a certain aspect of human *dynamis*; and, if the tragic action flows from the moral centre of man, tragedy will also tell us something profound about man. Aristotle's theory of the origins and growth of art starts by identifying two causes 'deep-rooted in the very nature [of man]',[27] shows how the main literary–dramatic forms emerged and identified themselves, and concludes that tragedy 'when it had gone through many changes, stopped when it had realised its own *physis* – its integral nature'.[28] When he deals with tragedy – and we must remember that he is simultaneously thinking of epic and tragedy under the heading of those literary kinds that arise out of 'serious' people and subjects – he has to find a way of thinking positively from the given *end*; he has to be able to infer accurately the action (energy) that the end realises. The action is human, the energy is human, the tragedy is human; there can be no other assumption, no other analogy. The action is plotted and prepared by a maker, a poet; it is acted out, brought into physical existence, by actors in the theatre (it is the actors, not the poet, who do the *mimēsis* – but the poet can also be an actor and often was); and the action is traced out and realises itself before an audience (though the tragic effect *can* come about through reading). Aristotle is very much aware of the complex web of relationships between poet, actors, performance and audience, and of their interactions; he knows all about the egotism of actors too, the silliness of audiences, and the way poets can be deflected by sensational appeals to vulgar taste. It has often been said that, even among the small group of superb Greek tragedies that have come down to us, few would meet Aristotle's specification; but this, I take it, is one of the clear signs that he is *not* working deductively either from the huge corpus of plays known to him or from his own personal preference (which is known to have been questionable). He is looking for the *form* of tragedy, and needs to invent a method – a means – of finding that for himself and of disclosing it to others.

His method in the *Poetics* is brilliantly simple and appropriate. He says in effect, 'Let us *suppose* that we want to *make* a tragedy; how should we set about it?' Intensely aware of the complex and refined dynamic of tragedy, he is not content to say what tragedy is (as though that were easy anyway), but insists on showing how it works. As he advances, he concentrates on making and doing and acting – and is it not poetry-*making*, not poetry itself, that is a more serious and 'philosophical' business than history-*making*? The word *dei* (it is necessary) recurs, particularly in the later chapters, like a reiterated dominant seventh: it is necessary to do this; you must –, you should –. The Renaissance scholars took these utterances for rules, and once into that mood worked out some pseudo-Aristotelian rules of their own; in the end even Corneille, it is said, shook in his shoes at the thought of breaking the 'rules', and a little later it was said that because Shakespeare broke the rules, yet wrote passable plays, he must have invented a kind of tragedy that Aristotle – poor fellow, with his limited horizon – had never dreamed of. Such conclusions seem to me less than inevitable. I cannot seriously think of Aristotle giving a master-class in tragedy-writing. But he has thought of what is probably the only way, even now, of seriously and responsibly engaging the critical attention of a student of literature: it is a dramatic device of teaching. He says in effect, 'Just imagine that you are capable of making one of these things. Just imagine that you are capable of tracing out the right action that will realise itself in the right end, that you are capable of entering into and generating the action which, acted out by others, will ruthlessly bring about this end, an end so profound and momentous that at best we can only catch a glimpse of it. Then we shall see the *physis*, the *dynamis*, the *telos*, the *life*.' His *dei, dei, dei* is the insistent reiteration, within this dramatic supposition, of what matters most: the action, the specific action that needs to be traced out, by what conceivable means, working within the limits of what resources to what end. For every action implies its realisation in an end. But there is no formula to guarantee success, only the poet's judgement and luck and vision. The fact that no poet ever worked successfully in the way Aristotle 'recommends' does not affect the validity of his imaginative scheme. His aim is not practical, but theoretical; yet paradoxically, as far as his aim is 'critical' it is intensely practical – it helps us with our doing.

Aristotle knows certain central things from his experience of tragedy: that tragedy happens only to people of a certain kind or quality; that, if part of the horror is seeing a man broken, it must be a strong man (and that is implicit in the pleasure peculiar to tragedy); that if the issue is to do with law and man's nature, the man must be morally strong – without the strength, what we see is merely pathetic, pitiful, or revolting; that tragedy is to do with the darkest and strongest issues in our experience – life and death and law and responsibility and freedom and necessity. He knows that we can betray ourselves from within, that when we take the law into our own hands we pass from freedom to mechanism and cease to be human, having cut ourselves off from the law of our inner nature; and he knows that a man can know that he is doing this and yet do it, and watch himself doing it, capable even in his fascination of altering or reversing the action. A certain quality of moral awareness is required in the person this can happen to, and a certain degree of strength; and it can happen only over something that *really* matters, such as the defiance of blood-relationship or some other primordial human bond.

A tragic action correctly traced will lead to the end of recognising at least something about the nature of man, the values that are paramount, the vulnerable centres that we must at all costs preserve – which is the law, our law. Here, it may be, the old debate about what happens according to nature (*physei*) and what according to law (*nomoi*) comes into ironic coincidence in Aristotle's mind when he sees the form of tragedy, when the inner law simply *is* our nature – not 'natural law' or 'the law of Nature' but the law of *our* nature.

'Tragedy is a mimesis [process] not of men simply but of an action, that is, of life.' To achieve the precise end, a precise action is needed. We could think of the tragic action as a sort of trajectory traced by a projectile, implying a certain amplitude, direction, velocity, momentum, target, and that in every moment of flight all these terms are implied; and the nature of the projectile matters very much, because it is a man who, being morally strong, makes choices, determines the flight, is not simply propelled, is not a mere victim. Aristotle, I suggest, is showing us the tragic action as though it were a pure abstract motion traced out with exquisite precision, the precision that is needed to impart the force of necessity to an action that can at no point be predicted for certain because it can at any moment be altered or deflected: it will at once feel both inevitable and free. The plot, the sequence of events that specifies the action, Aristotle says, has to be conceived as a *schēma*, an abstract motion, and you put in the names afterwards; but the *schēma* is not simply a locus of dramatic points or a flight plan, for the points are not so much intersections in time and space as events, each momentous, crucial, chosen, formative. Yet the tragedy is *inside* the protagonist and is of his own doing; and, if he did not know, he could have known, perhaps should have known – which is why knowing and not-knowing is crucial to the tragic action. Recognition (*anagnōrisis*) is not a device of plot-structure, but an essential crisis in the action; and *hamartia* a mistake rather than a sin, a distinction that was clearer to Peter Abelard and other subtle Fathers than it seems to be to us – *harmartia* is an *ignorant* act, and in tragedy (as in 'The Ancient Mariner') ignorance is no excuse, for in these matters the plea is made not to a court of external law, but is argued in the inner dialogue of moral choice according to the law of our nature. And these things have to be declared outwardly, presented openly in action, so that they strike us not only with the *frisson* of horror and pity but with the shock of recognition; we too must be drawn into that intricate web of knowing and not-knowing. And that is the peculiar pleasure of tragedy.

To claim that Aristotle is simply talking about a 'tragedy of action' out of poverty, not knowing anything else, and that later dramatists discovered a 'tragedy of character' that Aristotle had never considered possible, is a radical misunderstanding of Aristotle's position. To establish the existence of a 'tragedy of character' of comparable force and incisiveness it would be necessary to show that the 'tragedy of character' does in fact trace the specific action required of tragedy and that it does so with resources not accessible to the 'tragedy of action'. The resources for tracing out the tragic action are very few: plot, characters, speech, song, the various techniques of stagecraft and acting. Language is indispensable, speech being one of the principal resources of human action, if also the most ambiguous. But things need to *happen*, not simply in sequence but in a sequence that implies the whole ineluctable trajectory and the end. The people involved have to be the sort of people that such things can happen to; at least one of them has to be capable of irreversible moral choice and yet capable of making a disastrous mistake in at least one of his moral choices, and it still has to be a *moral* choice, not just an accident or 'the will of the gods' or 'Fate'. The plot is the sequence of events that in one sense delineates the action (the action which alone can produce the end); and the persons involved in the action delineate the action by being the sort of persons that could initiate such events and have them happen to them. 'You can't have tragedy without action, but you can have tragedy that is weak in character' – that is, without persons who are shown taking strong moral choices. Aristotle cites examples, but this must be at an extreme limit of tragic possibility since the tragedy *aēthēs* – 'without characters' – throws away one of the most powerful and subtle resources for delineating tragic action; for the *praxis* (action) of the play is defined by the *praxis* of the persons in the play, and the *praxis* makes the characters what they are as well as what they are becoming and will become. When Aristotle says that 'the first principle of tragedy – the soul, if you like – is the plot, and second to that the characters', he means this quite specifically, not rhetorically: the soul is the 'form' of the person, and prior to the body – the plot is the 'form' of the tragedy, and prior to the action – the characters are the 'body' of the action (will body forth the action) and are shaped by, as well as generating, the action. The person acting does not disclose or externalise his character in action, as though the character existed before the action: the character (in Aristotle's view) is *shaped* by his actions, and in tragedy we see the protagonist, as character, being shaped by his choice and his actions.

This is why the notion of *hamartia* as a tragic or fatal 'flaw' is completely wrong-headed in Aristotelian terms, and why to insist upon such a notion erodes the austere purity of Aristotle's view of tragedy. If the protagonist had by nature a 'flaw' that steered him more or less inevitably into a fatal situation, he would be a mechanism and predictable to us, incapable of inducing terror or recognition; he would be repulsive or pathetic merely; he would no longer be a man-of-action in action shaping himself towards his *telos* in this action, but a man who – having fallen into mechanism – was no longer capable of discovering his 'form' in and through action.

And as for *katharsis* – the word occurs only once in the *Poetics*;[29] in the central definition of tragedy (Ch. 6) to be sure, but so completely unrelated to anything in the introductory chapters that some textual critics have regarded the phrase as a later insertion by Aristotle. The discussions of *katharsis* in the *politics*, and of pity and terror in the *Rhetoric*, are of questionable relevance to the *Poetics*; and the promise in the *Politics* to 'explain this further in my discussion of poetry' is not fulfilled anywhere in the surviving corpus. So the one phrase – ten words – has accumulated a massive exegetic literature.[30] *Katharsis*, as we know from experience, has its implications, in some sense, for the audience; but is it a technical word at all? And are we prepared to accept that one of the distinctive formative principles of tragedy (some seem to claim that it is the *final* cause of tragedy) is to be found not in the action but in the audience's reaction? Gerald Else, as far as I know, was the first to insist that the *katharsis* occurs primarily *inside* the action; and Kitto, I think (*pace* Lucas), settles the matter for good and all. It is the incidents within the action itself (not the emotions of the audience) that are purified, brought into a sharp focus specific to tragedy, by the *mimesis*, by the presentational action – by the *mimesis*, not by 'tragedy'. Events in the area of pity and terror are minutely defined in a kathartic process towards Unity of Action – that is, Purity of Action; and so the pleasure peculiar to tragedy, because of this refinement, is aroused by the quality of the action.[31] And comedy has its *katharsis* too, presumably, in as much as *its* action needs to be 'purified' within its proper area and only so refined will arouse the pleasure peculiar to comedy. And yet, as Kitto says in a wistful aside, 'There are times when one suspects that Aristotle's own lectures on the *Poetics* would be more valuable even than the original text.'

Few of these observations are in any way new. But these are the sort of things, as a vigorous and single guiding view, that I should want a translation of the *Poetics* to keep steadily in the reader's mind, in the final choice of each central term, in the shaping of phrases that too often and too easily recall improper connections, in a pungent running commentary that keeps the reader off his comfortable heels, in the rhythms of a speech that might conceivably be coming unguardedly but deliberately out of the intelligence of the man who was affectionately known to his contemporaries in the Academy as 'The Brain'. To do so successfully, a person would need to be pretty skilful, learned, and lucky.

In this view, the action of tragedy (to think of only one of the 'kinds' Aristotle has under his eye) is not a 'representation' or 'imitation' at all, but the specific delineation, within extremely fine limits, of a moral action so subtle, powerful and important that it is almost impossible to delineate it; an action self-generated that has as its end a recognition of the nature and destiny of man. (No wonder few 'tragedies' meet the specification.) In this view, mimēsis is simply the continuous dynamic relation between a work of art and whatever stands over against it in the actual moral universe, or could conceivably stand over against it. So mimēsis is not definable by itself, least of all as a simplistic preliminary to a subtle inquiry. For this very reason, I imagine, Aristotle does not define it except in action, by a variety of uses gradually drawing around the word the limits of its activity – which is 'definition' in another but perfectly legitimate sense.

It would follow – and I should be prepared to argue – that the notion of 'mimetic' and 'non-mimetic' *art* is a verbal fiction based on a misunderstanding of Aristotle's use of the word *technē*. I should be prepared also to challenge R. S. Crane's statement that there is a 'Coleridgean method' of criticism distinct from and diametrically opposed to Aristotle's; I begin to sense an Aristotle–Coleridge axis in criticism and poetics but am not yet prepared to speak about it.[32] And I would affirm my own strong conviction that the method of the *Poetics* provides – for those who care to explore it – a paradigm for all those critical procedures that seriously seek to discover the nature of what they are examining, that seek to release with accurate definition the energy contained within what precise shaping limits. It seems to me more than possible that what Aristotle has to say about tragedy is absolute, that his account is not limited by the number of examples that he happened to have at hand. It is the privilege of genius to make such discoveries on incomplete evidence and to make durable statements about them.

In trying to discover and disclose the driving energy of Aristotle's thought in the *Poetics*, I have addressed myself to making a translation with commentary – and have in the end come upon the clean air of Aristotle's penetrating imagination and his grave, unwinking intelligence, to find the *Poetics* a dramatic record of his profound and incisive thinking, contemplative reflection of the highest order with a brilliant method of exposition to match it. Here indeed is theory, *theoria*, vision. My exhilaration may perhaps be pardoned even if it is not universally shared. Immanuel Bekker, whose Berlin Academy edition has provided the standard system of reference to the whole Aristotelian canon, edited in all some sixty volumes of Greek texts and collated more than 400 manuscripts. Gildersleeve said of him that in company he knew how to be silent in seven languages. Less learned than Bekker and less taciturn, I did not feel that, in the matter of the *Poetics*, I could any longer – whatever the hazard – be silent, in the one language I know at all well.

4 'Scholarship', 'Research' and 'The Pursuit of Truth'*

My title is about as misleading as it could be. That it could be misleading is typical of the way language works. In a company as austere and learned as this I doubt whether I would have the temerity to discourse gravely upon the subject my title seems to point to. What in fact I want to talk about is the words contained in the title, and what trying to talk about such words involves. The address might have been called 'Notes towards the Definition of Some Vectorial Functions of Language' but that wouldn't have helped much either.

A couple of years ago, when I was helping to prepare a brief addressed to the Commission on the Universities and Government, I was amazed to find how pervasive the word 'research' was in the documents we were examining and in the discussions that followed. Everybody seemed to use the word very confidently but nobody seemed sure how to make it cover, for the sciences, social sciences and humanities, the sorts of things that the government might be persuaded to spend money on.[1] Did 'research' refer to all the various kinds of sustained and careful inquiry that can be carried out at a desk or in a laboratory? If the word meant 'investigation, inquiry into things' or 'the act of searching (closely or carefully) for or after a specified thing or person', would Proust have been eligible for a grant to write *A la recherche du temps perdu?* We were not confident that government would make a research award without first asking 'What things are to be researched? and to what socio-economic end?'

Probably the question about what the word 'research' meant would not have arisen if the humanists in the company had not noticed how the word has, in recent years, quietly taken on a

* *Transactions of the Royal Society of Canada*, Series 4, vol. 8 (1970) pp. 290–322.

colour and aura that troubles the humanist and probably troubles the 'pure scientist' just as much. (I must admit, however, that it is some time since I last heard the phrase 'the romance of research' used seriously.) We noted the following overtones. (a) Research is the apotheosis of the experimental method. (b) Research typically produces 'results', which are then published as 'a contribution to knowledge' and under certain conditions will win acclaim and be awarded prizes. (c) The product of the experimental method is at least 'knowledge', and at best 'truth'; and the more strenuous and minute the research the greater the truth. (d) 'Research' (= the experimental method?) is the only way of arriving at reliable 'results'. All other procedures are, by implication, either airborne speculations, or – if not entirely futile – productive of 'results' as ill-adapted to modern uses as a mediaeval Latin gloss on an Arabic version of Aristotle's *Metaphysics* or a treatise on the fortification of cities by Uncle Toby Shandy. These conclusions – not uncoloured themselves by parodistic distortion and certain twinges of envy – irritated us humanists because we could now see how it was that if a scholar needed money to get his work done he had a much better chance of getting it if he could persuade his benefactors that he was engaged in 'research' as sketched out above. It seemed that the word 'research' could canonise any subject – no matter how trifling or cheerless. By this time we were getting into a rather uncharitable frame of mind, and were tempted to observe that certain studies that might be expected to be 'humane' because they were concerned largely with human beings – psychology, political science, and that curious hybrid sociology – seemed to be edging with Gadarene haste in the direction of parascientific 'research' through the device of 'quantification', possibly to the neglect of the philosophical and synthesising way of mind.

Our minds, thus cast in a gloomy enough mould, then turned to wonder whether, if inquiry were limited to a single technique, the concept of *method* might itself be undermined and eventually destroyed – 'method' being the way of thinking things through, getting things done, arriving at some conclusion by means established by the matter under inquiry. We knew that 'method' was an important term for both Bacon and Coleridge; we knew that Coleridge in one of his masks regarded himself as *Heraclitus redivivus*; we recalled a fragment of Heraclitus we had read at the beginning of *The Dry Salvages* – 'the way up and the way down are one and the same'. We glossed this a little and came to the tentative conclusion that discovery, or getting to know, is an activity in which the starting-point(s) and conclusion (whether actually conceived or only glimpsed beforehand) act reciprocally upon each other; and we felt confident that the study of literature would support such a proposition, and probably also a study of the way things get discovered in the sciences. If – as humanists – we were to nourish the function that Bacon hoped his *novum organum* would serve, we must 'equip the intellect for passing beyond'. So we attempted a formula in the latest jargon: 'Beware the method-oriented problem: seek out the problem-orientated method.' We thought of some instances where this maxim had been defied – behavioural linguistics, for example. We then considered the possibility of constructing a fifth-generation computer on the analogy of language instead of mathematical logic, but decided that that might take a little time because, among other things, it would have to be a machine for wool-gathering with.

When our heads had cleared a little, we found that what made us bridle most at the word 'research', as defined, was that sometimes *we* certainly did some research and couldn't well get along without it, but that the central, guiding, and most fruitful activities in humanistic studies were not much like that. 'Research', we felt, provides building-blocks but not much architecture. So we introduced into the report the old words 'scholarship' and 'inquiry' to try to break up the monolithic and unlovely figure of 'research' that kept crossing our line of sight. (We left the word 'research' in our text out of vague deference, but reserved the right – if the occasion ever arose – to point out that the experimental method perhaps did not spring into birth like Venus Anadyomene with Francis Bacon and the founding of the Royal Society; for this we were confident of presenting learned evidence.)

Our proposed solution was too simple-minded to work. 'Inquiry' is really quite a nice clean word, and rather grand if expanded into something like 'the inquiring mind'; we could see some future for that. But the more we thought about 'scholarship', dignified and impressive though the word is (and the conception), the more desperate it looked. It trails clouds all right, but not all of them glorious.

> Bald heads forgetful of their sins,
> Old, learned, respectable bald heads

'scholarship' with the humanities and 'research' with the sciences: that did not match our experience, and might even help to endorse that barren – but for Charles Snow not unproductive – fantasy of the Two Cultures.

We noticed also that, since Poincaré, some eminent scientists (stung perhaps by veiled hints of intellectual barbarity) have pointed out (with fascinating evidence to support it) that in 'pure' science the act of discovery is near enough the same as the artist's act of discovery: that it is a feat of imagination, that it takes the same daring leap into the unknown, that it induces the same frisson of delight and exaltation. The word 'creative' is often introduced to strengthen the sense that what happens in the act of discovery is rather special: hence 'creative science', 'creative research', 'creative writing', 'creative imagination', even 'creative scholarship'. Fastidious and god-fearing writers are wary of the word 'creative'; yet the use of it is symptomatic of a need to assert that what happens at the top or at the fringes of mental activity is not much like anything else.

But the humanist and scientist are no sooner caught in a single identifying glance than they shift out of focus into the some sort of difference.[2] Is it not curious, for example, that scholars are commonly called pedants, but scientists are not? Now pedantry is not necessarily to be found in the insistent use of hard words; rather it is 'the use of words unsuitable to the time, place, and company'.[3] A good case can be made for special terms, and even for jargon if only as a temporary expedient. But some scientists and most practitioners in parasciences carry their jargon into public almost as a mark of superiority – the sort of thing the old grammarians were supposed to do: hence the grotesque currency, in a democratic age, of misapplied jargon among people unlearned and inexpert. And, apart from the way of speaking, scientists now seem to bear the physical marks that tradition ascribes to the scholar. They are as industrious as bees, these scientists; they are no less farouche in aspect than any humanist, no less given to 'a sweet disorder in the dress', no less careful to cultivate the absent-minded mannerisms that are one of the few lovable features of the totally preoccupied man. Perhaps, after all, these are not marks of the pedant, but gauges of an elite; the scientists have simply changed hats with the humanists.

These lucubrations occurred a couple of years ago; not very conclusive. Then I read Professor Wynne-Edward's report on

'The Current Status of Science Policy' in the last *Transactions* of this Society, and my feelings of uneasiness turned to alarm, and my attention shifted from the use of individual words to the use of language altogether.

Social historians of technology tell us that we have now passed into the second phase of the Industrial Revolution; that the central concern is no longer energy but control. Evidence for this is seen in the spread of computers and automation, and in the way governments have been sizing up autonomous activities and institutions with a view to taking them over. Hence the Commission on the Universities and Government; hence also the Science Council and the proposal that all scientific effort be directed by government (by means not yet completely formulated) towards the end of 'social development and economic growth'. According to Professor Wynne-Edwards's summary, the Science Council proposes a classification of 'research' into two categories: (1) basic research, defined as 'curiosity-motivated', the pursuit of new knowledge for the sake of that knowledge; (2) applied research, defined as 'mission-oriented', seeking to meet a particular problem – by definition the only acceptable ends in this scheme being 'social and economic'.[4] In tracing out 'the technological steps from an initial discovery to a marketable product or process', three steps are prescribed: (1) discovery, the acquisition of new knowledge; (2) invention, the application of this knowledge to the solution of the practical problem; (3) innovation, the assembling of resources to exploit the invention.

This is much worse than what Professor Wynne-Edwards calls 'a curious jargon'. It discloses a terrifying, because confident, assumption of unexamined analogies bizarre in their parodistic inexactness. When the jargon invokes inappropriate, and therefore blinding, analogies, the jargon must not be accepted. Talking back in the same jargon will not clear the air and may do much worse harm by establishing or stimulating the mental disarray that lurks beneath the jargon. Serious scientists, confronted with statements so spicily modern, so blandly axiomatic, so eerily irrelevant to what actually occurs in the scientific field, feel as though they had their backs to the wall. How can this be attacked except with language? And how attacked successfully if, by default, 'the enemy' are allowed to establish the rules of language? Yet the 'pure scientists', those gentle, magical people who (for so we affectionately think of them) scarcely know what to say when they go to pick up their Nobel prizes, are inclined to feel, and to say, that language is not their field and may not even be their business. It is true that Sprat said in his *History of the Royal Society* that natural philosophers should make their point 'not, by a glorious pomp of Words; but by the silent, effectual, and unanswerable Arguments of real Productions'. But that seems not to have happened. 'Productions' enough there have been, God knows, since Sprat; and their silence has not brought 'effectual . . . Arguments'. Sprat recommended a clean, unadorned prose style for reporting experiments and the results of experiments – observations, discoveries. He gave no instructions about how to describe or report the nature of acts of discovery. Major discoveries have often been widely separated from any conceivable social or economic use. It is now of paramount importance that the nature of discovery not be misunderstood. Language must somehow preclude misunderstanding. Perhaps humanists can muster for our fellow inquirers, at a crucial juncture, what we know about the chinks in the armour of language. For a start it could be pointed out that some of the most damaging misunderstandings arise from a ruthless determination to understand – a fact that one had hoped a civilised education would have established long ago, humility and wonder being important functions in fertile mental process.

Coming to my title – there is something disagreeable and pretentious about it, as there is about the Science Council classification: it is a string of free-floating abstract nouns behind each of which stand, or could stand, a variety of premises, some of them conflicting or misleading. There are three objections to using abstract nouns as instruments of careful thinking (even though we can't get along without them). (1) It is hard to prevent an abstract noun from seeming to refer to some *thing*, something definite and definable; yet many abstract nouns do not refer to anything very definite, some of them refer to nothing beyond figments (an ancient philosophical question), and most of them will drift off into confusion or deceit unless firmly prevented from doing so. (2) Nouns are static: that is, they do not impart energy or movement to an utterance. If abstract nouns are the main elements in a sentence – as usually happens in overcautious or defensive writing – the sentence will lack muscle. Only verbs have driving force. (3) Many an abstract noun can look rather like an algebraic symbol (more or less arbitrary) to which only one meaning, or a select cluster of meanings, can legitimately be assigned. Although we know that the syntax of language is quite different from the syntax of mathematical notation, and although we know that (except for a few special, technical and little-used words) no word has more than limited stability, nevertheless we are very inclined to assume that the same word used two or three times in the same sentence or paragraph is being used in the same sense. Hence concealed equivocation. The variable meanings of words are best limited and defined by the activity of a dynamic context. What we need now is not a new vocabulary (though we could use some of that too) but sound principles of muscular usage.

Anybody who has seriously tried to come to grips with language knows that language has to some extent a life of its own, that it has its own principles of coherence which we do well not to disregard. Words have lives of their own too. Yet behind every utterance there is a person. It is not simply the *words* that mean; it is a *person* who means; and what the person *means*, intends to convey or declare or conceal and for what reason, is physically imprinted into the structure and texture of his language, unless he is using language very badly. The 'imprint' of intention is not seldom at variance with the content of the words; to the perceptive ear an utterance becomes not only a declaration *by* the writer but also a disclosure *of* the writer.

Every successful utterance is a reconciliation between the needs of the speaker and the demands of language. Language is no mere instrument; and, if an instrument at all, the instrument plays on the musician as much as the musician plays on the instrument. Perhaps it is, as much as anything else, the tough and intricate resistance that language interposes that draws from us the enormous scope and variety of our linguistic competence; we need only remind ourselves of the power and virtuosity of some illiterate persons – persons, that is, who can neither read nor write. An academy or a dictionary can do something to standardise conventional usage, and so save us from getting deflected in directions we don't want to go, or save us from getting suspended in a fog; but a dictionary can do little or nothing to prescribe the dynamic shapes of utterances that are by their nature innovative, discoveries in our own minds at work. How do I know what I mean till I say it? Everybody is caught in the hazards of language; we are all responsible for language, for its good health, for the way we use it, for the effect our use of language has, for the effect we allow other people's use of language to have on us. To accept the proposition that no utterance means other than the sum of the lexical meanings of its component words is to renounce one of our gravest responsibilities and to betray our birthright of living language. Surely we must recognise that in some cases the meaning is much more than the sum of the lexical meanings – and very often much less; and that language is often used to preclude communication.

In studying highly developed pieces of writing – poems, say – we find that a necessary first step is to find some way of projecting the mind, by a sort of quantum jump, to an appropriate level of response, so that the mind will grasp the lexical meaning while it is not held entirely at the lexical level. At the lexical level a poem does not function as a poem.[5] I do not attempt here to define poetry, but affirm only that under the condition of poetry single words can have multiple meanings, that words and clusters of words can have manifold functions, and that in the best writing these are finely ordered and can be controlled with an exquisite precision. At low levels of activity in language – in much discursive and expository writing, and in everyday referential usage – the manifold functioning of language is not very active, may be little needed, and so may seem not to be functioning at all. Hence presumably the curious notion that 'simple language' is the basic form of language, in which single words have single meanings. We need only notice how suddenly, and without preparation, an unexpected word-order or an unusual choice of a word will release the energy of language; words are like little time-bombs with a very quiet tick.

The meanings of words depend much less upon lexical prescription and convention than upon actual usage. A word can shift its meaning, or even be established in an incorrect meaning, in the same way that a mispronunciation is established as standard (for example, ēgo or pōlio or lōgos) – by sheer repetition. (The 'correct' pronunciation or use can then sound 'pedantic'.) Words, in varying degrees, have intrinsic meanings that depend upon their source and history; but specific meaning depends upon how words are actually used, and upon who uses them, and in what contexts, and why. Any word can erode rapidly, usually through careless or cult repetition; but any eroded word can be restored – that depends on the user too. If a word is clear to the person

using it, the word is clear in that context no matter how it may
be elsewhere. Dictionaries help to stabilise meaning, not only by
offering 'definitions' but also by recording varieties of usage; and
they can enlarge our sense of language by recording the origins
of words and the history of the uses that have been, and are
being, made of them. To know the origin and history of a word
strengthens the identity of that word in one's mind; when we
have a strong feeling of the traces of meaning in the root of a
word, the word will not blur as easily as a word that feels like an
arbitrary symbol, and it will tend to function with appropriate
vigour. The durability of words – whatever it is that preserves
words against erosion – depends more upon the verbal sensibility
of the user than upon the words themselves; yet words from Greek
roots seem to be particularly tough survivors, less given to erosion
and much less abstractive (for example) than English words
formed on Latin roots, even though a knowledge of Greek is now
a pretty rare accomplishment.[6] Poets, because of their highly
cultivated verbal sensibility, tend to be purifiers and renewers of
language – or simply good users of language.

We recognise further that precision in using language comes
in the way words define or clarify themselves in actual contexts.
Certain possible shades of meaning are endorsed, others precluded
or made peripheral. The clarifying activity of language, however,
seems to be less a function of single words than a matter of
dynamics, of the energetic shaping of a whole utterance. If words
are to define themselves accurately in use, the usage must be
energetic enough to impart defining activity. Hence my suspicion
about using abstract nouns as key terms.[7]

The study of literature shows clearly, even if there were no
evidence for this elsewhere, that even *seeing* is qualitative; for
example, a freshman and I may see the same printed marks on
the page but we do not *see* the same poem. The quality of our
individual seeing is a direct function of what a gestalt psychologist
calls 'set' – the way the mind is habitually directed or is capable
of being directed by shifts of intention, what it knows and
remembers, what it does not know, what in the mind reverberates
to the presence of what. Like taste, 'set' is closely related to what
we know selectively, what we are concerned to know and what we
choose not to know (not-knowing being the matrix of knowing).[8]
The knowing that occurs when we 'know a poem' is different in
kind from knowing (say) that Tennyson wrote the poem; and

that too affects our 'set'. Oversimplified theories of language arise not because they derive from evidence less complex than the evidence considered in a richer theory, but because a limited response to language prevents the reader from *seeing* any evidence above the level of a limited linguistic sensibility.

The recognitions that lead to literary discrimination and judgement cannot occur unless a person can respond justly to the work he is reading; literary perception is shaped by what is being perceived, and fineness of perception depends upon the capacity of the mind to be so shaped. Successive stages of inquiry are guided by a series of value-judgements (recognition of what 'matters'); otherwise there is no way of knowing what to pay particular attention to. These activities are carried out with the attention somewhat suspended, to some degree renouncing sharp concentration until valuable foci of concentration have been identified. 'There is', as Coleridge said, 'a period of aimless activity and unregulated accumulation . . . There is a period of orderliness, of circumspection, of discipline, in which we purify, separate, define, select, arrange' – which must sound as familiar to an inquiring scientist as it does to a literary scholar. And this activity is carried out over something that moves through time and can therefore never be apprehended at a glance simply as a concrete 'thing'. What is known at the end is the poem, something made, self-contained and self-declarative, single though disposed across time. It may not be an 'expression' of the poet, though in fact we know that the poet said it; it is not primarily a 'communication' from the poet, though in fact it conveys something from the poet and may even bring us into his presence; it is uttered in a language which we all use, yet in a mode – it may be – that is seldom if ever found anywhere else; though it usually arises from 'experience' it seldom describes an experience and is usually constructed on highly stylised principles; it may use the most highly developed resources of language, yet it speaks so directly that often a child or an unsophisticated person can respond directly to it. To get comfortably into such an area of interrelated paradoxes and to stay there long enough to get to know a profound poem (not quite the same as a difficult or obscure poem) takes a state of mind that is not very biddable, even with discipline and experience. Not everybody is capable of such a sustained critical activity; not everybody needs to be capable of it. Yet we are all, being endowed with imagination and inheritors of language, capable of responding directly to highly developed language; and it is well that we should have that ability, because it is only in the developed uses of language that we can find the radical of language.

The mark of true poetry, of language in its finest use, is 'unity in multeity' – a highly complex simplicity, an intensely simple complexity – which is what a mathematician calls 'elegance'; and when we grasp language in that order we see what Einstein called 'harmony' – the sudden, just, inevitable fitting-together of a host of details in a breathtakingly simple pattern. Unless we grasp the radical of language, we shall not be aware how directly and finely we can – all of us – criticise (that is, get to know) the intention that lies behind writing of the middle order that would otherwise deceive or disarm us. 'Official' and political writing, earnest and impersonal in tone and of modest literary accomplishment, may seem to be assailable only in its 'ideas' and logical connections. Yet, couched in language, it must be criticised and analysed in terms of the way we know language functions, confident that we can see why it was written in that way and not otherwise. To be able so to criticise statements, proposals, arguments is the responsibility of every civilised person, no matter how low a value he may place on his own achievement as speaker or writer.

Now, at last, for certain vectorial functions in language.[9] A vector, I take it, indicates direction and magnitude; in physics this can be represented by an arrow pointing in a certain direction, with a length indicating magnitude. In the study of language we can use this concept figuratively but precisely: figuratively, in the sense that the directions are drawn out in 'psychic space' and the magnitudes cannot be measured (though they can be compared); precisely, in the sense that it allows us to recognise goings-on that we might otherwise miss. The notion is introduced here not to provide a calculus for language, but to heighten our awareness of the dynamic functions of language.

In any use of language there are always semantic vectors at work: single words reach out towards their 'meanings' (whether thought of as in a lexicon or in one's head), towards our personal associations with the word, and towards each other in the impulse to complete an unfolding meaningful structure. (This last I think of as 'the drama of syntax', the scheme of action that puts words together.) The semantic vectors are not of uniform magnitude in a vigorous sentence; if they are too uniform or low in magnitude the sentence will feel static, almost like an algebraic expression that we have to express in some other notation before we can see what it means. In general a noun has a weak or negligible vector unless it is a metaphor or functions in a perceptual mode; transitive verbs have strong vectors; intransitive and impersonal verbs have weak vectors; passive verbs and the verb 'to be' are weakest of all. The magnitude (force) of a semantic vector depends upon the user, not simply upon the word. If the writing is entirely impersonal and the terms (as far as possible) unmetaphorical, the magnitude of the semantic vectors is almost indistinguishable – we simply read the meaning. As soon as both speaker and reader are aware of a word as metaphor, the magnitude of its vector increases and commands the hearer's attention.[10] Our habit of grasping things as meaningful is so strong that when we read a line of gibberish –

> Twas brillig, and the slithy toves
>   Did gyre and gimble in the wabe;
> All mimsy were the borogroves,
>   And the mome raths outgrabe

(Lewis Carroll, 'Jabberwocky')

semantic vectors are noticeably at work even though they can have no lexical terminus. Where only semantic vectors are functioning, the level of language is 'low' – that is, very little linguistic capacity is at work; the sentences in a patent brief would be an extreme example. The vectors, if noticed at all, feel horizontal and the usage 'linear'; the words have no resonance, having no upper partials standing over them. Sound and rhythm are of negligible importance. Language in this state – either so written, or so read (whether written that way or not) – has tempted many to suppose (mistakenly) that language is a conventional quasi-mathematical notation in which we point to objects, state propositions, give commands and announce afflic-tion, and into which we can translate 'thoughts' or 'ideas'.[11] At a 'low' level, the *word* is the irreducible element; at higher levels the *utterance* is the irreducible element, its powerful and complex vector supervening upon the integrity of single words.

At the highest level, the level of poetry, two other kinds of vectors appear which can be noted only briefly here. (1) As single words function in a manifold way, they reverberate with, or reach out towards, other complex functions. These are often contained (as it were) within the compass of the poem; but sometimes involve other contexts which are in the poet's mind but not 'in' the poem: for example, the word 'Hebrides' in Wordsworth's 'Solitary Reaper' evokes Milton's 'Lycidas' (not as 'source' but as essential functioning element). (2) The vectorial activity of words, images, phrases can comprise – if coherent enough – the whole drama of a poem. By 'drama' I mean simply action traced out, the 'movement of mind' through psychic or imaginative space eventually coming to rest where it had to come to rest, the movement being towards an end that will not be surely recognised until it has been reached. We should not be far wrong in saying that the drama traces out *thinking*.[12] This happens, for example, in Wordsworth's 'Solitary Reaper' and in his 'Immortality' Ode, and very markedly in Keats's 'Ode to a Nightingale'; and, in a different way, in 'The Exstasie', in which Donne traces out an 'argument' that leads us ineluctably from *A* to *B* by a series of connections which are not primarily logical. This function is not peculiar to any style or period; indeed it would not be extravagant to say that it is at work in every substantial poem. If we ask what, at the end of such proceedings, we *know*, the question is difficult to answer, unless we are prepared to accept as a characteristic conclusion the close of Yeats's 'The Second Coming':

> And now I know that twenty centuries of stony sleep
> Were vexed to nightmare by a rocking cradle.
> And what rough beast, its hour come round at last,
> Slouches towards Bethlehem to be born?

(There are lots of vectors of various kinds to trace there too.)

So far by way of illustration. Let me put it this way. In highly accomplished poetry (which may be verse or prose) we find language working with a precision and manifold activity far beyond the requirements of reference, logic or description. For one thing, sound and rhythm become elements of outstanding semantic, vectorial, and shaping importance. Some call this process 'symbolising' and draw a sharp distinction between 'symbolising' and 'describing'. Poets are forced into symbolising as an act of discovery and of making, encouraged and guided by their sense of the living principles of the language they use. A poet *makes* a poem – that's what the word 'poet' means if it means anything – and the making stands for something like a vision or glimpse of (what in despair we are usually forced to call) 'reality'. And that, in a great wealth of variations for which there may be no actual precedent, is what language is for; not only in poetry but at the most humble, straightforward, and referential level (because there is an infinity of 'realities'). We notice that the 'higher' level of language encompasses, but does not supersede, the function of the 'lower' level, in the same way that Einsteinian physics encompasses and goes beyond Newtonian physics but does not supersede it. Levels of language cannot be absolutely separated except by the writer's intention; all levels are capable of interweaving, and do constantly interinanimate each other. And the metaphorical function of language includes but need not destroy or supersede the logical function.

Unfortunately not all uses of language can be divided into 'high' use (? good) and 'low' (? modest or limited). There are discreditable uses: some that defy logic when they purport to be logical, some that slyly conceal their intention, some that assail the nature of language itself. These are the sort of uses I want to discuss next. But first a word on precision and imprecision generally. In 1786–98 John Horne Tooke published a philological book called *Epea pteroenta* – a Homeric phrase meaning 'winged words': that is, words like arrows with feathers to them. (Tooke's book has not lasted, but his successful self-defence against a charge of treason, for which his enemies never forgave him, suggests that he knew a thing or two about the use of language.) The title is suggestive. The good use of words – the sort of use that keeps language vigorous and a delight to listen to and handle – is a matter of marksmanship. But marksmanship of a special sort: the missile must not only hit the target in the right place; it must be of the right size and shape (as it were) to fit an odd-shaped hole in the target – that is, the precise function it needs to serve when it gets there. The objection to clichés, vague terms and cult terms is not simply that other people use them too much, but that they show poor marksmanship; they are blanket-terms, large woolly patches that can cover a host of different-sized holes; they are too compliant, too easy to use, requiring no skill, distasteful to the keen marksman. In terms of marksmanship there is no virtue in hitting a barn-door with a blunderbuss at short range –

particularly if, as is too often the case, you are shooting at a bee at long range with the hope of changing the flavour of his honey. The standards for verbal marksmanship can be expected to be rather high, because bad marksmanship encourages imprecise thinking and a blurred perception of what one is unravelling in his thinking.[13]

The objection to loose and imprecise terms is not simply that they give too blurry an effect (though they certainly do that) or that they fall below some hypothetical standard of descriptive fidelity. The objection is much more serious. Bad usage can induce a breakdown in the energetic, shaping and clarifying functions of language itself; bad usage attacks language in its central nervous system, and can turn us into linguistic cretins or paraplegics. The breakdown can occur not only in single pieces of speech and writing, but more pervasively it can spread (by habit or fashion) through a whole range of the possible uses of language. The widespread use, as we have it now, of ill-constructed words, hybrids, arbitrarily compounded locutions, rootless abstractions, uncouth acronyms of no self-evident reference, verbs used as nouns, nouns yoked ambiguously together, the shamelessly anthropomorphic coinages of the computer people – these are all well enough for merriment, or for the dialectal specification of clubs, classes, and in-groups, or even sometimes as desperate but temporary expedients in tight corners. Used uncritically and as a matter of habit and form, however, they rapidly destroy the verbal sense, the sense that discerns and keeps alive the distinct identities of words, the clear and direct vigour of utterance, the confidence that the manifold activities of language do in fact place at our disposal a rich variety of *mental* resources that have been nourished and fertilised by language for centuries. T. S. Eliot in a memorable passage reminds us how far the sense of language is a matter of the ear, engaging a very wide and active response:

What I call the 'auditory imagination' is the feeling for syllable and rhythm, penetrating far below the conscious levels of thought and feeling, invigorating every word; sinking to the most primitive and forgotten, returning to the origin and bringing something back, seeking the beginning and the end. It works through meanings, certainly or not without meanings in the ordinary sense, and fuses the old and obliterated and the trite, the current, and the new and surprising, the most ancient and the most civilised mentality.[14]

Verbal imagination of the order Eliot describes is not needed all the time perhaps, except by poets. But when it is needed – as in our present situation – it is badly needed. Poets can be expected to have a highly cultivated verbal sense. But we can all be expected to show a fair degree of cultivation, considering how much time and attention we devote as children to mastering language; and it would seem no less than our duty to be so cultivated if Chomsky is correct – as I think he is – in seeing 'linguistic competence', our infinitely innovative use of language, as *the* distinctive human achievement, the mark of man. There can be no doubt that historically our minds have been shaped and patterned by the ways we use language. Language is constantly changing, and must change constantly. There can be no doubt that our minds are at this instant being shaped by the way we use language, and can be shaped by the way others would persuade us to use our words and accept their use of words. An uncritical acceptance of usages that, if we saw them clearly, we would certainly deplore, can make the difference between civilisation and barbarism; and if 'civilisation', it will determine what kind of civilisation.

Back to vectors. Let me consider two that occur commonly in the 'middle' level of language: (1) emotive, and (2) slanting.

(1) Emotive words are words that arouse strong emotion: 'love', 'beauty', 'death', 'grief', 'freedom', 'fulfilment', 'hope', 'joy' – words that point to the central experiences and to our most persistent desires. By 'emotion' I mean a state of feeling stable enough and personal enough to be identified by name, such as 'joy', 'sorrow', 'anger', 'hatred'. (And by 'feeling' I mean simply a change of psychic energy.) The big emotive words often occur in poetry because poetry deals largely with our central concerns of value; and it is the business of poetry to handle such themes, not in an emotional way, but in intricately patterned constructions of feeling. When the rendering of feeling is imprecise and emotional we call the writing 'sentimental' – one of the most derogatory terms in literary criticism. Emotive poems are, by definition, bad poems; sentimental writing calls up emotion that is not controlled by the writing itself. The place to look for examples of the emotive use of language is in advertising copy, in the words of popular songs, in the words of sentimental hymns (if anybody sings them any more), and in

political rhetoric. Characteristically, the emotive vector is strong, and detaches itself from its origin – the emotion loses track of what it was about, floats free, and grows into a personally centred reverie. When emotive language is used deliberately (rather than through incapacity), its purpose is to arouse strong unfocused emotion. But our emotive responses to words can be very subtle: even an experienced and scrupulous critic cannot always be certain whether he is being deflected from the poem he is examining by his feeling for something that has happened to him in the past.

(2) Slanted words are, as the name implies, more obviously vectorial than emotive words; and it is difficult sometimes to be sure whether a use is emotive or slanted, or – as is often the case – both. Slanted words and phrases normally point toward an undefined area of good/bad, acceptable/unacceptable, praiseworthy/contemptible. The slanting use, with its implied and often collusive reference to an undefined area of approval or contempt, is a little like the emotive use, and slanting is often used to arouse emotion; but slanting is different inasmuch as, instead of pointing to an area of universally accessible emotion, it points to some proposition as axiomatic or widely accepted; and this allows slanting to fit into assertive utterances with the appearance of argument. The slanting vector is, in a way, a special instance of the semantic vector: it points to a meaning, but the meaning is illicit. The usage is slanted, not the word; and a term that is commonly slanted ('freedom', 'democracy', 'right', 'representation') *can* be used in an unslanted manner – though it will take a little time for the words 'Fascist' and 'pig' to return to neutral usage. Student activists are very fond of slanting, and of the equivocations (apparently logical) that slanting readily produces. We notice how an illicit argument can be disarmed, and how the temperature drops, if we agree to refer to 'required courses' rather than 'compulsory courses', and to 'rational self-government' rather than 'participatory democracy'. Not all slanting is as obvious as this. The statement 'Language is communication' would reward close analysis; and so would the slippery declaration that 'The medium is the message.' We notice that in both cases the trouble crystallises around the word 'is' – so slack-kneed a copulative that it gives no better show of strength than the stiff upper lip of a shadowy equals-sign. The words 'problem' (especially when pronounced with the 'b' silent), 'media' (especially when used as a singular noun) and 'informa-

tion', and the cant phrases 'information explosion' and 'communications revolution' would all repay separate scrutiny. And so would all those phrases like 'the language of music', 'the language of film', 'the language of TV' (which the notions of 'syntax' and 'dialect' would help to clarify). A 'computer language' is, of course, not a language at all (all of which could be clarified by using the terms 'syntax' and 'dialect').

If we take a step back from slanting as a use of language and see it as a complex rhetorical mode of pseudo-logic, we see how easily the emotion aroused by slanting can obliterate our sense of logical relation. From habits developed in my study of the classics I assume that if an argument is conducted with scrupulous logic it is irrefutable – except in its premises. One principal use of slanting is to conceal premises. From habits developed in studying the only language I know at all well, I have learned that the reason for saying something imparts structure to what is said, and that therefore, if one is not seriously to misunderstand what is said, it is always profitable to ask, 'Why was it said that way and not otherwise?' – and not to be put off with too easy an answer. I have noticed also that even logical exposition is a sort of game or convention by which we proceed from premises to conclusion as though we were giving an account of the way we reached the conclusion – a dramatic device, no doubt, to make new things plausible. Yet we know that to come upon a new thing is a pure act, a leap, no matter what analytic or purifying preparation may have made it possible; and that the act of mind is the same whether the 'new thing' is big or very small. Once out of the area of logical demonstration, there is a much more intimate relation between conclusion and premises than logic can account for: the conclusion comes first to the mind; premises and conclusion are reciprocally adjusted, and where the thinking is weak or disorderly the premises are often a back-formation from a desired conclusion. When premises and conclusion are finely correlated we feel the inevitability or elegance of the relation; when not justly correlated, we feel uneasy. Altogether, I think we are most of us much better at spotting a fishy connection, by direct insight, than we are at seeing a logical inconsistency. With thinking, as with language, most people are capable of sharper discrimination than they are aware of.

Let us look at a few sentences from a recent authoritative statement on 'Literary Studies and the Media'. It is worth noticing that slanting depends to some extent on the pace with which a term is approached and the assurance with which it is left behind; and that slanting works most effectively when language seems to be functioning at the referential or semantic level.

> We must now accept recordings, tapes, films, and multi-media events as *documents* [1] – statements which communicate [2] – with great speed [3], and in a non-linear way [4]. . . . We face a new kind of person in our universities and high schools [5] – a person who has more information about the world [6] than his parents had in middle age [7]. . . . What he needs is training in how to find answers to the questions he is able to ask [8] . . . the old academic procedures . . . no longer serve their needs; and the comprehension of electronic media, and expertise in their use, have not yet penetrated the universities. . . . But what of the professor of literature in his new atmosphere of instant information, this vast mosaic of signals that come at us (indeed bombard us) from all directions? [9] . . . the professor or teacher will have to reveal the forms and structures of all the languages of communication [10]; and, since he cannot be a polymath [11], he must instruct students in *how to get at* the information they need [12].

A few comments may be made.

[1]   *must now accept.* As long as there have been recordings, tapes, films, they have been used, when available, for whatever purpose they seemed capable of serving.

   as documents. The emphasis gives the slant, but does not define the direction. In the radical sense a 'document' is something that imparts learning; usually these days it means something written down or recorded, and reliable unless otherwise indicated. The author is trying as hard as he can to undermine the primacy of writing, so perhaps his emphasis points to something like 'records that should be taken as seriously as people used to take writing'. Of course they always have been so taken as far as that is possible. If you want to hear a symphony and haven't an orchestra around and can't read a full score, you play a recording; if you want to remind yourself of the cut of somebody's jib you look at his picture; if you want to see him in motion, and he lived recently enough, you look at film. In each case you still have to decide about the quality of the evidence presented; the fact that the symphony is recorded on magnetic tape does not establish whether the recording is technically good or the performance artistically sound. The next word after *'documents'* is 'statements', an emphatic word which, with the italics, establishes an equivocation corresponding to the proposition that the camera never lies. Instead of 'statements' he might have said 'information', but that it is a bit neutral for this context and is reserved for honorific treatment later. An important educational consideration is being dodged here: to the trained perception, evidence ('statements', 'information') is potentially meaningful against an informed 'set'; to an untrained perception evidence is multitudinous, neutral and confusing. The dual purpose of education is to encourage an energetic 'set' and to sharpen perception: this is the basis for 'imparting knowledge'. It is important to notice how often major original theories have arisen from a study of subtle and minute anomalies. In a fog of unordered minutiae the fruitful anomaly cannot be discerned.

[2]   *communicate.* It would take too long to go into this sacred cult-word. Here it is both emotive and slanted. Why not say 'are capable of being presented to us'?

[3]   *with great speed.* Sleight of hand. Radio and TV signals and telephone and telegraph messages can indeed be transmitted 'at great speed' – about the speed of light. This makes 'information' accessible at long distance in short intervals of time. But this has no bearing upon the speed of acquiring or 'reading' the 'information'; and if what is being conveyed is not 'pieces of information' a plausible analogy begins to crumble. It takes much longer to listen to a recording of a symphony than to read the full score; a poem, even by a slow reader, can be read more readily in print than it can be listened to on a recording; film and TV are not particularly economical of time, unless the material is graphical. Each method of presentation has its peculiar characteristics; as far as speed and flexibility is concerned, the book – particularly if illustrated – takes a lot of beating. In any case, a book, unlike tape, film or recordings, is not committed to a single speed of presentation.

[4]   *in a non-linear way.* A vector towards McLuhan, who apparently would like to convince us that language is always, and nothing but, 'linear'. I have already shown that language is linear only when read exclusively at the semantic level. Tape, film, recordings, etc., are in fact *more* linear than the printed word, in the sense that they are run through at a certain speed. Whether the effect is linear or not depends on the perceiver, not the method of recording and presentation. In any medium the presentation must secure 'that willing suspension of disbelief for the moment that constitutes poetic faith', otherwise the response will be mostly linear – that is, at the semantic level. The imaginative use of language (by which I mean the radical use of language) passes through time as does any kind of coherent presentation – even an explosion – but words carry envelopes and upper partials of meaning and reference (in short, are vectorial). To print utterances in parallel lines does not make the utterances linear. Habitual rapid reading can reduce almost any writing to the semantic level, and on the whole our school training does not get us very accustomed to the 'higher' levels of lanuage. Certainly we need all the means we can get to dislodge us from a self-paralysing semantic habit, and film, tape and TV may – from their relative unfamiliarity – be useful for that purpose. But to call language 'linear' is a misleading way of making *that* point. And dangerous. To allow ourselves to be persuaded that language is 'linear' – that is, not language at all – is to renounce the civilised use of language; and I cannot see any obvious gain in that.

[5]   *a new kind of person.* Emotive and slanted towards the current and questionable cult of 'youth'. Every generation provides 'a new kind of person' in a sense that means either a great deal or nothing at all. This smacks of coloured supplements, advertisements aimed at the teenager, the 'generation gap', and the Two Cultures.

[6]   *who has more information about the world.* Or has access to more information? About what? Of what quality? Does the *amount* of information matter? 'Knowledge is infinite, truth is one.' I am sure that both Robert Southey and John Wilson Croker had more 'information' than Samuel Taylor Coleridge had; I can imagine that Vergil of Toulouse and Jan Gruter both knew more things than Einstein. Does anybody now actually

possess *more* 'information' than Erasmus or any of the great mediaeval polymaths? What matters is not the amount of information available, but the quality of the information and the quality with which it is known and related.

[7] *than his parents had in middle age.* Isn't that speeding up the generation gap a bit, and shoving the over-thirties off the mortal coil rather peremptorily? Parents of children now aged twenty are usually entering or are in their middle age and all of them have grown up within 'the electronic revolution'.

[8] *answers to the questions he is able to ask.* Why 'is *able* to ask'? Is he, by virtue of his place in time, able to ask many questions that have not been asked before? Or that persons twenty or thirty or forty or sixty years older are not capable of asking? Enlightened school and university training has always been strong on training people in finding *relevant* information. Finding *answers* is a bit more difficult. If the questions *can* be answered, the answers are often quite easy to come by. The most fruitful questions are the ones that cannot be answered but won't let us stop asking them; for these there are no classes for beginners.

[9] Surely 'in this new atmosphere of instant information, [with] this vast mosaic of signals that come at us (indeed bombard us) from all directions' we are obliged to be much more selective than before. We don't have to be indiscriminate: to the despair of the advertising industry, we all choose what to take in and what not; a prime function of the human mind is selection and arrangement, and traditional education has been strong in cultivating that function. There is no evidence to suggest that the capacity to know well is any different now from what it ever has been (except that our capacity for language develops our ability to know well); nor is there evidence that the amount of 'information' retained by any individual depends upon anything except his individual capacity to retain 'information'. What matters is not what he retains as much as what he does with what he retains.

[10] *all the languages of communication.* This loose metaphor, particularly when slanted with the word 'communication', needs to be examined very closely to see whether there is in fact any detailed similarity between the dynamics, syntax,

precision and semantics of language and the ways film, music, etc., put things coherently together: in short whether there is any language except language.

[11] *polymath*. The strong slanting-impulse seems to have pushed the author into misuse of the word. A polymath is a person learned in various fields. There have always been such persons, there are now, and presumably there always will be. The misuse of the word betrays an interesting and biased assumption: the professor cannot know everything (a statement that can be truly made of anybody), and he will probably not know what the student wants to know (the generation-gap and the professor as old fogey), and being a professor he will be familiar only with a very narrow field, and now he'll have to smarten up and show his students how to find 'information' that he himself never thought worth ferreting out and using himself.

[12] how to get at *the information they need*. See also [8] above. The last word is interestingly slanted: what students 'need' is 'information' of a kind that is being withheld (deliberately? through indolence? through insensitiveness to the 'needs' of youth?); conversely, the 'information' that professors do give to students is implicitly what they do *not* 'need' (useless? misleading? 'irrelevant'?). Professors these days cannot be expected to have any idea what students 'need', this implies; but this 'new kind of person' *knows*, with an implacable and hungry certainty.

These notes only scratch the surface, but enough to see that the burden of the song is: 'Books are finished; professors are finished. Pay attention to film, TV, records, tape – they are (or will be) important [in life? in education? in society?]. And have lots of multi-media happenings.' Some of what the author is getting at needs to be got at; but the author, by being less shrill and shifty, might well have engaged our interest and concern; he might even have set our minds fruitfully thinking.

Now we have come back to the Science Council categories: discovery, invention, innovation. The distinction between category and invention is a fine one – two figures so close together as almost to make a pun. Did the Science Council know that Coleridge had used this distinction in an ironic note of self-accusation almost 170 years ago: 'Into a *discoverer* I have sunk from an *inventor*? In terms of the implied image, Coleridge evidently found 'invent' (to come upon) sharper and 'higher' than 'discover'.[15] But the word 'invent' has now drifted irreversibly to mean putting together gadgets and gizmoes on well-established principles – telephones, radar, television, jet engines. The use is acceptable because clear and established; and that leaves 'discovery' now as the top term in a sequence. But 'innovation' looks rather odd at the end of a sequence that was supposed to have its *fons et origo* in 'new things'. Can the word be slanted – implying that the novelty is somehow illegitimate unless introduced to (or brought to bear upon) 'society' and unless it affects 'economic growth'? Perhaps the whole sequence of technological development here is slanted by seeming to limit discovery to 'new things'. Often the new thing is a relation seen between old things, or between old and new things. As in the case of the Boolean algebra there can be a long interval between the discovery of the 'new thing' and any notion of a conceivable application. We might not suspect slanting if we did not notice that the proposed classification takes the emphasis off discovery, off the source – and sure enough, as the document unfolds, it is the discovery-people who will lose their money to the innovators.

Professor Wynne-Edwards detected something 'a little derisive' in the description of 'basic research' as 'curiosity-motivated'. The phrase is indeed derisive, and no doubt is intended to be. What happens if we turn the derision through 180 degrees? If somebody walked into Rutherford's laboratory, or Dirac's, or surprised Einstein or Bohr at his chalk-board, or came on Sherrington reading Jean Fernel's *De abditis rerum causis* (1548), and asked any one of them what they were doing, I doubt whether the answer would be, 'I am presently engaged in curiosity-motivated research.' They would be much more likely to say, 'I'm looking – I don't know what for – yet.' We sadly need a philosophy of heuristics – a study of the ways we hunt for and find out things when we aren't certain what we are looking for.[16] Is there indeed (coming back to abstract nouns) any such thing as *curiosity*, except by back-formation from the fact that some people have a nagging habit of looking intently and asking questions about what they see? And is there such a thing as a *motive*, except as a hypothetical fulcrum in a causal account of the way people act? The distortion is of the order of parody, and the insult grievous. What we really need now is a second Erasmus to write us another *Moriae encomium* – in praise of folly – and a second Holbein to illustrate it.

Somehow there would have to be a section on 'The Pursuit of Knowledge' and 'The Pursuit of Truth'. These phrases, recurring in convocation addresses and in expressions of goodwill from groups whose aspect is otherwise menacing, are difficult to utter any more with the required gravity. When these phrases are used, something important no doubt is being invoked; but the image is incongruous. If knowledge is infinite, and truth is one, and, if (as Bacon held) 'knowledge is the image of existence', is 'pursuit' the right word for our way of coming at any or all of these? Matthew Arnold declared, working from the Greek, that 'excellence dwells among rocks hardly accessible, and a man must almost wear his heart out before he can reach her'. Can we *pursue* under these conditions? And when we are told that students and professors are the same because both are 'learners', both engaged in 'the pursuit of knowledge', I think (once I have recovered from the shameless equivocation) of badger-hounds vigorously scouring the countryside, happy and a little brainless, and of ferrets with their long pointed noses; and am comforted to think how far that puts me out front of the field; and wonder whether there may after all have been something in the doctrine of some early-nineteenth-century phrenologist that you could measure a man's intelligence by the length of his neck – the longer the neck, the lower the intelligence. I cannot recall his name, and my information-retrieval system has failed me, not being coded either for 'neck' or 'intelligence'. Yet there, surely, was a new thing.

The Science Council has adopted as an axiom 'That the value of any scientific enterprise to a society is determined by the social, cultural, and economic goals that the society seeks.' ('Seeking' is a rather odd verb to use with 'goals'?) I don't know how a circle can be slanted, but that one is. Is the future good of society always definable in terms of 'goals'? Is *society* capable of defining goals? And are all 'cultural and economic goals' necessarily for the good of society? There is plenty of evidence to show how the unfastidious use of language in positions of power can work cumulatively towards barbarity, suspension of acute criticism, linguistic apathy. This is very agitating to a person who – like myself – had always believed that the 'armed vision' would one day come into its own. I am no longer so sure. Much of what can be done will have to be done in language. When the issue is so critical and the trouble pervasive and baffling, one can only speak obliquely, as I have done; to propose policies and 'goals' is only to reinforce what we deplore and what we would see disarmed and discredited. But who to speak to? When I learned that by 1932 – more than thirty years ago – the Royal Society of Canada had already 'made representations to the Dominion Government at various times against pollution of Canadian waterways by sewage, and as to the dangerous qualities of certain matches and illuminating gases', I realised that the Royal Society of Canada must be an action organisation. Perhaps, I thought, I should speak to them. And I have.

5   'Research' and the Humanities[*]

Methods and object can no longer be separated.

(Werner Heisenberg)

We have to learn to think, not less but more logically, without ever forgetting that the terms we are logically combining are not labels, but that each of them in itself is a symbol that flouts, by transcending, the requirements of logic.

(Owen Barfield)

I

The word 'research' is a noun. Nouns, being functionally inert, tend to be 'thingy' – that is, they seem to stand for 'things' even when they represent abstractions. Groups of nouns often indicate conceptual distinctions that do not correspond to 'real differences'; serious error can arise from mistaking conceptual distinctions for real divisions. Yet it is difficult to avoid the assumption that a noun – simply by existing – not only 'means something' but also 'stands for something'; that 'some *thing*' stands over against it, that the noun refers to that 'thing', and that therefore the 'thing' can be readily distinguished and defined or that a 'meaning' can be uncritically assumed for it. Such an assumption is not always sound. Many nouns refer to abstract and elusive notions, yet by being nouns (and 'thingy') they beguile us into supposing that the notions they refer to are neither abstract nor elusive. Indeed it is particularly those nouns that refer to vague, abstract and ill-defined notions that, out of sheer convenience, commend

Queen's Quarterly, vol. 79 (1972) pp. 441-57.

themselves most in fashionable jargon. Jargon-words provide a handy and often unnoticed way of avoiding or concealing the need for precise definition. By a 'jargon-word' I mean, not a special or technical term (the virtue of which is its precise and single reference), but a term which *seems* to be precise when it is not, and which is attractive to use because it appears to be a special or technical term with an arcane meaning that can be grasped by 'insiders' but has to be accepted uncritically by 'outsiders'. For example, it is now a favourite device of 'human engineers' to claim to make a complex abstract notion or function 'intelligible' or manageable by providing – another depressing jargon-word – a 'model'; but they do not always notice that a 'model' constructed on Newtonian principles is a little crude for delineating functions more subtle than clockwork or the movements of billiard balls, and that an inappropriate 'model' can do momentous violence to the matter under inquiry.

When there is no accepted precise definition or agreed ambience of meaning for a term, the unexamined 'common-sense' use of an abstract noun can lead to cumulative confusion, equivocation, and even deliberate deception. The equivocation can be unintentional, yet it will occur whenever we approach the word in one sense and leave it in another. Words, by their very nature, behave in a chameleon fashion; few words have single meanings, and most words carry manifold meanings in any context except quasi-mathematical technical exposition; words define themselves in use. Influential users of language have some responsibility to make sure that they are in control of the precise implications and functions of the words they use. The use of jargon-words is often a symptom of an irresponsible or meretricious use of language. Careful discussion of the nature and purpose of learning and education does not require jargon, and is likely to be the more honest and perceptive the less it relies upon jargon and other imprecise uses of language. The fault is not with the word but with the way the word is used: the same *word* can be a 'jargon-word' in one context and an elegantly precise term in another. Our need is to recognise which terms tend to be used as 'jargon-terms' and to be careful that we use them scrupulously.

The word 'research' has been a fashionable jargon-term for quite a long time. The imprecision with which it is commonly used has ominous implications for the present discussion of the function of universities and the growth of learning and culture in

Canada. To describe the variable envelope of meaning of this one word in its loose variability is almost impossible because – being a jargon-word – it is used on the tacit assumption that 'everybody knows what it means'. It is even more difficult to discern the precise meaning of the word as used in offical reports if the tone of authority is voiced in a style that manages at once to conceal the writer's intention and to prevent the language from clarifying itself as it goes.

The *Oxford English Dictionary* offers three definitions of the word 'research' (other than the meaning 'to search again'). The first two emerge in the late sixteenth and early seventeenth centuries: 'The act of searching (closely or carefully) for or after a specified thing or person'; 'An investigation directed to the discovery of some fact by careful study of a subject; a course of critical or scientific inquiry'.[1] These two definitions together (as far as I can make out) contain the indissoluble nucleus of implication most commonly present in the unexamined use of the word 'research'; that 'research' is a matter of looking for a specific *thing* and that it is to do with discovery of demonstrable *facts*; and that consequently we can tell sooner or later whether or not the research has been 'successful' – that is, whether or not what was being looked for has indeed been found. It is in this sense alone that I intend to use the word here, both because it happens to be the latent meaning of the word as it is widely used at present, and also because it allows the word to be used with some precision. In the simplest terms we could say that, whenever it is *not* possible to say that what is sought can be identified and 'found', we are not dealing with 'research'. (Could we say, then, that Einstein's formulation of the theory of relativity was not the product of 'research', and that the formulation of the structure of the DNA molecule was?) Positively we could say (in these terms) that 'research' is cumulative, empirical and deductive, and that the inferences, lucky guesses, and insight into possibilities that from time to time guide a sustained inquiry is not properly within the field of 'research' so defined.

In the years since sputnik-panic canonised 'research' as the prime hope for the Western world, and the Canada Council was founded for rather different reasons, humanists making claims for financial support for their work have often found themselves in the strange position of pretending to carry out what is officially called 'research' when they know perfectly well that their main purpose is not research. Worse than that, they have found that their work has been misinterpreted and misunderstood by being referred to a 'model' of 'research' that humanists cannot acknowledge as representing the central nature and purpose of their work. (Which is not to say that humanists do not at times legitimately carry out research – in the strict sense – or that research is foreign or hostile to their work.) Malfunctions of the word 'research' have led to a widely accepted misunderstanding of 'the humanities'; they have also deflected an appreciable amount of intellectual energy away from the central purpose of humane studies. Since misunderstanding about 'the humanities' can have serious consequences for the health of universities and the cultural growth of the community, it is well that the two terms 'research' and 'the humanities' be closely examined without reference to the 'models' that seem to have taken root unchallenged wherever policy is being formulated at present both outside and inside the universities. It would be well to establish (a) that 'research' is indeed an activity with definable purpose and function, so that we can decide whether a person is (or should be) 'doing research'; (b) that the functions of research are specialised and limited; and (c) that the word 'research' is not a suitable term for referring to the *central* initiative and purpose of sustained inquiry in 'the humanities' – or perhaps in any field.

II

'The humanities' is what 'humanists' do; not only *what* they study, but *how* they study, and *why*.[2] The work of humanists is distinguished primarily not by what is studied but by the 'way of mind' they bring to their inquiry. For this reason it would be well to avoid the term 'the humanities': it seems to point to certain 'subjects' or kinds of material, and some unwary persons might suppose that 'the humanities' (? a plural noun) can be subdivided into a number of single areas each of which is a 'a humanity'. The less handy phrase 'humane studies' is preferable if only because it points to the quality of inquiry intended.

The humanist's way of mind is distinguished by its willingness to pay serious attention to evidence that lies beyond the normal range of what is demonstrable or veridical; it is guided by a 'sense of value', paying close attention from moment to moment to the

quality of knowing; it finds its central analogies in the functions
of the human mind and in the known capacity of human beings
to act inventively (though they may not always do so) and to act
with moral intent (that is, with a sense of the nature and
implications of their actions and relations). The humanist's
activity encompasses and often relies upon empirical,
experimental and demonstrative evidence and procedures; but it
also characteristically tends at all levels of its inquiry to engage
'imagination' – that state of the person which (in Coleridge's
phrase) 'brings the whole soul of [a] man into activity, with the
subordination of its faculties to each other, according to their
relative worth and dignity'.

The way of mind peculiar to humane studies finds its deepest
satisfaction among the clear and vivid records of human experience: records, that is, of relations between persons, between
individuals and groups of persons, between persons and 'ideas',
and between persons and the physical and moral world in which
we find ourselves. A humanist tends to be concerned with anything
to do with the actions, thoughts, desires, aspirations, feelings,
judgements and choices of human beings, and is therefore
as likely to be concerned with political institutions as with
autobiography, with the rigours of philosophy as with the textures
of poetry, with psychology as with the arts of persuasion. But a
great deal of his concern in any subject-area will be with the
use of language – the most specifically human of all human
accomplishments; and his concern for language will tend to draw
his attention particularly to those most highly developed and
elusively direct uses of language that are called 'imaginative' or
'poetic'.

Humane studies arise from life, and turn back upon life to
nourish and clarify it. For the humanist there are three typical
or ideal figures: the poet, whose purpose is to secure our sense of
delight and wonder, to engage a clear and profound insight into
life, and continuously to 'purify the language of the tribe'; the
philosopher who can gaze upon 'all things in heaven or earth' –
not least the mind and its activities – and find an intricate and
reasonable order there; and the wise counsellor whose judgements,
founded upon accurate perception, fine discrimination and
compassionate engagement, are informed by a sense of the
integrity and 'otherness' of persons and the nature and dignity
of man. Since all knowing occurs through the human senses and

in 'the mind of man', anything that arises from human activity and the quality of it, or has any bearing upon human activity, is proper to humane study. This is to say that anything that can be studied is appropriate matter for humane study; but it is not to say that all study is humanist, or that the humanist's way of mind is an 'ideal' way of mind in as much as it embraces all ways of mind. Although the humanist's way of mind is most readily induced and most finely controlled in certain areas – language and literature, philosophy, certain kinds of history – it would be incorrect to suppose that some of the subject-areas that in recent years have sought to represent themselves as separate 'disciplines' – psychology, economics, political 'science', sociology, mathematics – are closed to the humanist, or that the humanist's way of mind is outmoded in those areas of inquiry, or indeed in any area of inquiry.

In the late nineteenth century in the University of Edinburgh (where, as in other Scottish universities, the singular noun 'humanity' is still used to refer to the study of Latin language and literature) it was considered that 'humanity is the key to the history, the thoughts, and the mind itself of civilised man'. The nature and function of humane studies can be most clearly seen in its educational role. For humane studies have been the foundation of all civilised education since at least the early Middle Ages – not by historical accident but simply because 'humanity' is the only conceivable way of instructing and exercising the mind and sensibilities to discern the capacities of the individual and of mankind in their relation to their nature, circumstances and aspirations, and to affirm certain specifically human capacities of the mind and of our nature.

The educational end of humane studies is not primarily to provide 'information', or 'conclusions', or to 'add to the store of knowledge' – though incidentally they do and can do all these – but to instruct (structure and exercise) the intelligence, to refine discrimination, to educate the mind by leading it through well-defined but intricate mental processes, and to encourage initiative in such matters. Humane studies seek particularly to heighten awareness and discrimination – especially where evidence is elusive – in a way that applies not exclusively to the matter under inquiry but *mutatis mutandis* to any humane inquiry by placing emphasis firmly upon the *quality* of the mental action traced out.[3] Humanists, in their most characteristic inquiries, are less concerned with 'knowledge' than with 'knowing'; they recognise various orders of knowing, and espouse orders of awareness which certain kinds of knowing alone make sustainedly possible.

What distinguishes one kind of study from another is not simply the subject-matter under inquiry, but the reason for making the inquiry and the method adopted in order to make the inquiry serve an intended purpose. Charles Sherrington's *Man on his Nature* (1940), for example, is a humanist study even though it takes its departure from a sixteenth-century medical treatise and deals extensively with the most recent medical and biological knowledge; and even though it is written by the same distinguished neurologist who had written *The Integrative Action of the Nervous System* more than thirty years earlier. Incidentally, *Man on his Nature* is a stylistic triumph of great originality. The notion that a certain 'subject' has only one proper method of inquiry is acceptable only as long as 'method' is understood simply as 'the way of getting done what is to be done'; appropriate method can be developed only with sensitive reference to the evolving demands of the material under inquiry and the evolving perception of the inquirer. The quality of a humanist's inquiry depends not only upon the quality of the method used, but also upon the quality of the person using the method; and not only upon the quality of the person but also upon the quality of the inquirer's purpose in making the inquiry at all – all of which are salutary reminders of the virtues proper to educational purpose.

Specialised methods of inquiry emerge depending upon (a) the nature of the matter under inquiry; (b) the purpose of the inquiry (which in general for humanists is 'to see more clearly and to help others to see more clearly'); (c) the level of human reference that the inquiry is to be carried to. I suggest that specialised methods of inquiry – and they are very few in number – should properly be called 'disciplines'. The distinction between 'disciplines' (in this sense) depends primarily upon what we can do about the comparative inaccessibility of much that –in humanistic terms – we insist is important to think about. The word 'discipline' could then profitably be applied to the ways we have discovered for adjusting the mind to certain specific purposes of inquiry rather than to areas of study or alleged techniques of inquiry. Poets are probably more familiar with strange devices for getting into a proper frame of mind to do their work than (for example) psychologists – or even psychiatrists – are. Although there is a tendency for certain kinds of material to demand a certain disciplinary approach, any material examined by a humanist demands a variety of disciplines if a humanistic end is to be achieved. The habit of referring to every university faculty, or even every university department, as a 'discipline' has in it a certain amount of inflated advertising-rhetoric and the black-box mystique that the Phoenician navigators found useful in securing their monopoly. It also illustrates the process by which a respectable word gets changed into a jargon-word. The question that needs to be ruthlessly pursued today, for the health of the universities, is 'What *is* a discipline?'; and that can perhaps only be approached through a family of fundamental questions such as 'How do we know?', 'How do we feel?', 'How do we perceive, recognise, judge, choose, discriminate?' – questions that might bring some philosophers and psychologists to their humanistic and medieval senses. It is a mistake to confuse *rigour*, which is a matter of prescriptive limitation of inquiry, with *discipline*, which is a positive way of getting into an appropriate way of mind to carry out the inquiry. From a humanist's point of view it is less damaging to be determined not to misunderstand than it is to be determined to understand; and a person does well to take care of his ignorance because it is the matrix of his knowing.

III

The principal business in humane studies – which happens also to be the principal business of a university – is to explore any area of inquiry *philosophically*. The end and aim is not 'the accumulation of knowledge' – though a good deal of that must go on along the way – but to find out how to establish and adjust those 'ways of mind' that are appropriate to particular questions and inquiries and phases of inquiry. To insist upon the 'practical' results of humane studies is to undermine the scope of humanistic inquiry and progressively to depress and degenerate the philosophical habit of mind. The 'practical' value of humane studies arises from the way of mind they encourage, not from the 'products' of the study; the 'results' of humane studies are to be seen in a certain quality of perception, judgement and action.

Because humane studies are a continuous process of self-education, it is virtually impossible to separate the effect of a scholar's personal study and reflection from the effect of his formal instruction. Nevertheless, humane studies provide the basis for all human education and bring educational forces into exceptional focus for two reasons: (1) they can be carried out at a cultivated level only by using a wide *variety* of 'techniques of inquiry' which need to be subtly accommodated to the inquiry; (2) they can be carried out satisfactorily only by getting into an appropriate frame of mind. These two are inseparable because the 'techniques' can seldom be applied appropriately without adopting an appropriate way of mind; and humane study – through its own peculiar 'discipline' – proceeds by discovering (in each instance) an attitude of mind that makes the inquiry possible at all, by holding elusive, fugitive and non-veridical material (usually in functions of language) within a field of sustained attention. (It is true that instructors, as well as students, can fail to engage such momentous forces; but that is a comment on the vanity of human wishes rather than on the virtue of the humanist's discipline – and an ideal might as well be stated if it can be discerned.) University 'instruction' or 'teaching' can certainly give advice and guidance in acquiring the sort of 'knowledge' without which serious inquiry can scarcely begin. But the most valuable thing that happens in the relation between a student and a good instructor is that they engage in inquiry together, the instructor tracing out in a process of discovery the intricacies and possibilities of serious inquiry; showing that such inquiry is possible and that it is worthwhile in its own right; conveying an infectious sense that – no matter how local and specialised a university may be – the habit of philosophical inquiry is an exhilarating way of mind that can touch, enliven and illuminate any aspect of every kind of life.

The dominant emphasis in humane studies differs from the emphasis in other activities of getting-to-know in two senses: (1) the level at which essential 'facts' – or, more properly, events – are apprehended and tested; (2) the publicity or intimacy of the events crucial to the study. For example, one kind of history, concerned to study patterns of political and military causes and effects, will be concerned (depending on its scale in time and space) to relate public events to inferred private motives and concealed 'causes'. Another kind will be indistinguishable from biography, and might well find a 'causal' or 'behavioural' analogy an insensitive, or even degenerate, instrument of inquiry. The first kind may easily become doctrinaire, abstract, and unreal unless the scholar has a keen biographical sense – a sense of how individuals acted and decided in certain circumstances being-what-they-were-at-that-moment. Furthermore, the historian who is primarily a biographer will find his emotional and mental field seriously limited if he does not command both a broad social and historical perspective *and* the resources usually ascribed to an 'imaginative writer'. Indeed, in any kind of historical study, the historian's capacity for sustained and subtle revelation will be a function of his ability to write in a way appropriate to the full scope of his mental demands. (And it is to be remembered that empirical observation and testing also occur in the humanist's field.) When events can be verified in the form 'It is a fact that . . .', the event is translated into a 'fact' and the 'fact' is treated as a 'thing' or 'meter-reading' or 'photographic snapshot'. In humane studies 'facts' disclose themselves for what they are: judgements of value about events. For example, to say that 'It is a fact that it is 1.13 p.m.' is a reliable and verifiable statement of 'fact' but in itself of little or no importance; if in a matter of life and death the last aircraft from Budapest left at 1.10 p.m. the 'fact' could be of harrowing importance to the individual involved in the event. The neutrality of 'fact' and the dominance of human implication as an index of value can be readily seen in such a sequence of statements of fact as these: 'It is a fact that I am thirty-seven years old'; 'It is a fact that I am white, Anglo-Saxon, and Protestant'; 'It is a fact that I am married to this woman'; 'It is a fact that I killed that man'. For the humanist, 'events' are recognitions of relation and value; he tends to see all events as (at least potentially) events of value, because his preoccupation is with the way events hold or touch a human being in their field of relations. He tends to see events of value as clustering in emergent patterns of relation and value; even his learning is always potentially shapely. For the humanist, the crucial 'facts' for an inquiry are not at a uniform level of emphasis, and they are not equally accessible. The peculiar value of humane studies in education is to be seen in this: that the student has to 'qualify' in order to carry out his inquiry – that is, he has to assume a way of mind comparable in quality to the inquiry he is conducting. To 'qualify' is a matter not of technical accomplishment or even (in itself) of hard work, but of 'grace' and submission. Humanist teachers generously suppose that all people have a capacity for 'grace' even though most have not discovered it and many will vigorously resist the self-inquiry and self-losing that is involved in serious humane study. In the humane studies one does not 'acquire skills'; one learns to be skilful – and the onus is always on the learner.

Studies in language and literature are radical to humanist education, not only because humane studies function continuously in the field of language, but particularly because the student can easily tell, at any moment in his inquiry, whether or not he is dealing with an appropriate 'level of fact'. If the level is 'too low' he will find that he is no longer studying *literature* – events of value constructed in language – but has drifted up to the surface or out of the periphery of the matter under inquiry. Since literary inquiry, in all its aspects, involves a wide variety of orders of 'fact' and does not deal exclusively with events of value, it makes continuous demands upon the sense of relevance and relation as well as upon the sense of value. The human mind, like running water, seeks the line of least resistance and flows downhill if it is allowed to do so. Literary studies face a student squarely with the decision whether he will stay with the inquiry or run downhill into the cat-tails and swampland; it helps him to tell whether or not he is indeed staying with the inquiry; and it provides him with the means of sustaining the inquiry by placing the responsibility on his own capacity and his ability to 'qualify' for the inquiry he has taken in hand.

Literary studies in a university need to be kept under close scrutiny to be sure that they are effecting their prime educational function; they can easily get cornered in a number of specialised technical and interpretative procedures that inhibit or preclude heuristic inquiry of the kind that has the greatest educational virtue. In general, the 'greatest' writers and writings are most likely to engage us in the most valuable educational activities and to hold us to them; in the end what matters is not *what* is studied, but *how* it is studied – the choice of material to be studied turns upon the quality of mental activity the material is likely to encourage. But serious literary studies make too heavy a demand upon the personal resources of students to be regarded as an educational panacea; not all students are equally educable. And the same is true of philosophy, another study traditionally important in education. Philosophy provides means of testing and manipulating 'ideas' and propositions, and exploring their relations. By a stylised procedure called 'logic' philosophers can demonstrate the relations between statements, and the relations between statements and what the statements are 'about'; and have found ways of ordering and sustaining coherent and verifiable thinking in patterns which are in fact rather different from the patterns in which heuristic 'thinking' goes on in the mind. Here, however, excessive concentration upon something approaching mathematical precision can induce defiance of language and neglect of certain readily observed functions of language; and there is danger that in the end, even in the pursuit of profound ethical questions, one will simply ask of the philosophising (though not of the question) 'What does it matter?' The philosopher or student who for long neglects to take into account the ways we think, feel, recognise, judge and speak can find himself as far removed from 'human life' or human values as a pure mathematician working at esoteric functions that cannot be expressed in language or in any intelligible non-mathematical figure.

The success of humanist education depends upon the quality of inquiry an instructor can beguile his students into; for that, both instructor and student need to be more than a little learned and to be informed by a sense of wonder.

IV

In any complex humane study a number of fields of mental activity are engaged, and a number of subsidiary 'methods' are used in order to arrive at the comprehensive and subtle method peculiar to the study. By studying the way such things have been done by others, successfully or with distinction, a scholar often finds a clue to a good way of tackling a new piece of work. The profit that comes from one's predecessors and masters, however, is less a heritage of 'technique' than an extension and clarifying of perception, a heightened sense of possibilities. The guiding principle in the method peculiar to the humanist is the reciprocal adjustment that occurs between the inquirer and the matter to be inquired into, an adjustment that progressively brings into tune the inquirer in a knowing state and the subject in a knowable state. The variety of aims open to an inquirer in humane studies is so wide that the choice of aim has important bearings upon the forming of method, and particularly in ensuring whether or not the method will provide a state of heightened (if only momentary) awareness, or whether it will simply produce another of the nauseating tautologies that come from pursuing 'method-oriented problems' instead of 'problem-oriented method'. A humanist not only has to have a flair for asking fruitful questions; he has to have a special nose for the questions that, if answered, will deflect him from his aim.

Even given the overarching impulse of a chaste purpose, different virtues will be needed in the various phases of the larger method. If we look at the complex inquiry that a mature and imaginative scholar brings to his study of (say) a group of highly developed writings, we see that his perception and judgement fall into several different modes which may function in alternating phases or perhaps even simultaneously. (The modes are seldom separable in practice: hence the humanist's aversion from checklists and clipboards.) A literary scholar may begin by establishing the integrity of his text, guided by his experience in palaeography, in bibliography, literary history, and biography, and above all what he knows about his author's way of thinking and writing. He may also find it necessary to provide a vital context for the work he is studying – matters of biography, of social, political and cultural history, often with outrides into highly specialised areas (such as Aquinas's theology, Animal Magnetism, the theory of phlogiston, or Grimm's Law). If he is engaged in a process of literary criticism which aims to heighten his reader's awareness of a piece of writing as somehow a living thing with an existence and integrity of its own, he may need to construct – or reflect again upon – a theory of the way such writings come into existence and why, what sorts of things they say, what order of 'truth' they represent, how properly they affect us: that would be an excursus into poetics, epistemology, psychology and some of the less specialised areas of philosophy; he might also – or alternatively – make an excursus to inquire about what criticism is, or is for, or can do, and he might also reflect upon varieties of critical method and scholarly technique in a largely theoretical manner. And in the end he will engage the activity of critical reflection, at the same time inventing a means of sustaining, rendering coherent and uttering either the process or the results of the process depending upon which of these will best serve the aim he has in mind. In such matters one can seldom with much confidence stand on anybody else's shoulders; and, since a critical construct is shaped by a sequence of recognitions and judgements, the whole process may degenerate or be contaminated in any of these modes by the germ of false observation or unchaste and wilful intent (Aristotle's *proton pseudos*). In none of these modes, even the ones that look most digressive and farthest removed from 'the main design' will he be able profitably to lose sight of the matter of his main inquiry; the sense of *why* he is inquiring and *what* he is inquiring into will serve as selective and guiding impulse in all the modes of his activity and will also allow any mode to be revised by the peculiar exigencies of the particular inquiry. There is no theoretical limit to the degree of minuteness to which any inquiry can fruitfully be carried; even though for practical purposes of exposition there is always a cut-off somewhere, humane studies are characteristically icebergish. Minuteness is not pedantry; the most scrupulous regard for accuracy and precision is as much the mark of a great artist as it is of a great scholar – yet nobody has any reasonable excuse for being a bore, in speech or in writing. The only serious form of pedantry in humane studies is the emotional pedantry that purports to deal bluntly and commonsensically with matters too intricate for a blunt instrument and too fugitive to fall within the compass of common sense.

Since life is short, and since the most angelic human seldom stays long in an angelic state, a complex piece of literary inquiry is not always conducted in all detail from start to finish by the one person; and, because the particular purpose that guides an inquiry colours the results of the inquiry, a complex piece of work can go adrift from having to rely upon work done by somebody else with different qualifications and with a different aim. (In general, for example, the use of a computer to do all the donkey-work on the materials for a literary study would almost certainly deprive the scholar of the intimate and tactual sense of what his study is *about*, and might leave him like a pianist trying to play a Chopin *étude* with hockey-gloves on his hands.) In any branch of study there will be a small number of persons of first-rate sensibility and intelligence who can also develop a sustained imaginative impulse; in any branch of study there will also be a large number of 'honest toilers', less brilliantly endowed, who nevertheless work very effectively at levels where the 'quality of fact' is not crucial, where the evidential material is readily accessible and easily recognised, and where there is seldom any need to make imaginative leaps-in-the-dark. By the sweet providence that seems to guide at least some parts of human affairs, the honest toiler can often identify and correlate bodies of material that will some time provide a launching-pad for those who are better at flying; and there is no saying when an honest toiler will be transfigured from ant-like industry into a blazing vision of a wider mental landscape. Yet there is no way of securing a specialisation of function into honest toilers and fliers, the one modestly providing the fuel for the other's escapades. The flier who does not do his own groundwork thoroughly is in serious danger of becoming an Icarus or of disappearing promptly off the radar scan. This has important implications for 'research' in 'the humanities'.

Humane studies tend to engage three phases of mental activity. (1) 'Reflection': the activity of mind induced when we encounter a mental obstacle that we know we must surmount if we are able to go forward with integrity of purpose. Reflection is a matter of seeing a synthesis, catching a glimpse of possibilities, entertaining families of relations implied by those emergent possibilities. Reflection can only occur when the person is *concerned for*, rather than merely 'interested in', what he is doing. There is no way of reflecting by rote, and there is no way of reflecting perfunctorily. (2) Scholarship: the accumulating, selecting, ordering, testing, and relating of the materials germane to the study. These materials are never 'raw' in the sense that they are unstructured or all at the same level of relevance. Some studies deal with *data*; humanists, like poets, deal with *données*. Recognising and selecting – like perceiving – is itself a shaping and potentially meaningful activity and it is coloured by purpose or intention. Some scholarship does not rise very high off the ground (though that does not prevent it from finding its way into print); but scholarship at its most perceptive is guided by an acute sense of the integrity, quality, and potential of the material it is handling, and at its best is indistinguishable from any highly developed kind of sustained and disciplined thinking. (3) Philosophical utterance: a linking of judgements and recognitions into a clear synthesis (as distinct from an analytical *schēma*), an act of seeing discovered in the critical activity itself and shared with the reader as an activity rather than as a conclusion, 'result', 'interpretation', or 'matter of fact'. The utterance at its best will be 'philosophical' for its clarity and precision, and 'poetic' for the way it finds itself in the wording of it.

In a complex process of humane inquiry none of these three activities can be separated from the others. 'Philosophical utterance' is itself a process of discovering, a way of giving substantial 'outness' to the thinking. A scholar who has a limited capacity for reflection and a comparatively uncultivated power of utterance will gravitate to some technical area in which there are few if any demands for the reflective and heuristic activity that is the distinctive mark of humane studies. There is a fair chance that sooner or later any technical scholarly production will contribute to humane learning and inquiry. Some work of the most humble intention has been immensely fertile, and there is no *prima facie* reason why a work that purports to be a 'synthesising study' will be superior to the honest work of an honest toiler. There is no reason, however, why we should gravely regard all 'contributions to knowledge' as equally valuable, or indiscriminately encourage the haphazard accumulation of 'matters of fact' on the off-chance that it may eventually be 'useful'. We can be reasonably confident that providence will eventually smile on the long-range dark-horsemanship of a George Boole; but George Boole was no honest toiler.

V

'Research' – the seeking out of certain 'things' – is an essential but intermittent part of humane studies: one needs to know at least exactly what was written or said, by whom, and when, sometimes under what conditions and if possible for what reason – and in the last two phrases the chances of definitiveness begin to shade off rapidly. 'Research' as a sustained programme of systematically seeking out certain 'things' is needed for some humane inquiries but not for all; and, when it is needed, it is preliminary or ancillary to the proper business of humane inquiry. There is no guarantee that a programme of research will lead to a genuine work of humane inquiry; that depends upon the quality of person doing the 'research' and his reasons for doing it. If it is desired to encourage and stimulate works of genuine scholarship and inquiry, it is to be expected that a very strong case would have to be made for supporting '*research*' in humane studies unless the research could be seen as a necessary part of a fruitful inquiry.

Inasmuch as humanistic inquiry depends upon collecting, selecting and arranging material as the basis of some comprehensive and incisive study, some humanists do in fact engage in research from time to time, and some serious scholars need more time and assistance to get through the research phase of a large piece of work than a university is likely to provide. But research – even when it is necessary – is the beginning, or an intermittent subordinate process, not the end of a humanist's work; and the 'results' produced from research are intermediate and instrumental to the larger purpose the scholar will have in mind. Some distinguished humane studies are based on research; some are not. A granting-body, concerned to encourage genuine scholarship, is faced by the need to judge the quality of applicants rather than the plausibility of the applications. It is easier to be 'objective' about 'research projects' than it is to make right judgements about scholarship, if only because it is much easier to tell whether a person is acutally 'doing his research' than it is to say what, if anything, will come of it. The anxious desire to be 'fair', 'liberal' or 'relevant' – especially when under hostile public scrutiny – tends to invoke 'criteria' which have little bearing upon the sort of selection that is most desired, the quality of work to be encouraged, or the possible relation between the proposed work and the good health of humane studies and the pervasive though oblique influence of humane education. The questions that have to be answered are not easy. Is this application to the point? Is this man good enough to back? Is this a young man of promise who only needs slight encouragement to help him realise unusual capacities, or is this a plausible enthusiast who will never write above the level of slack banality and will use a 'research project' as an interminable self-paralysing and self-justifying cocoon? In answering such questions, an appeal to 'objectivity' – or even to 'Canadianism' – is not much help. It is my impression that a good proportion of the money available for support of 'the humanities' in recent years has been spent on abortive and futile 'research' – research certainly, but much of it to no specific end except to gratify the vague assumption that any research, no matter how trivial, will in the end be 'a contribution to knowledge'. The question is whether it has improved the quality of knowing. And indeed the questions are hard. What member of 'the public' would confidently have guessed that the most radical synthesis of Chinese grammar ever written would be achieved in the University of Toronto (and promptly pirated in Taiwan); or that one of the most fertile minds England has ever produced would be unfolded to the world at large by a Canadian scholar out of prolonged and rigorous scholarship on a scale that probably no Canadian 'granting-body' could have sustained?

VI

Humane studies depends least upon special circumstances or special equipment, but they cannot flourish for long if they do not have access to large collections of books, manuscripts and documents to provide the fine-grained detail that stimulates reflection and to bring the mind into resonance with the minds and sensibilities of others, past and present. Since humane studies concentrate upon the abiding concerns of human beings and their ways of being, knowing and acting, good humanist libraries are typically large, cumulative and comprehensive, recognising no exclusion by subject, period or language. What is sought by a humanist in the humane tradition is not merely matters of knowledge (though he needs lots of those), but qualities of thinking, perceiving, discriminating, knowing. Hence his willingness – and often his need – to take long leaps backward in search of some rare and peculiarly illuminating mind. For humanists – preoccupied with the singleness and continuity of human thought – are often vividly aware of the contemporaneity of the past, even of the distant past; their concern is not so much to preserve tradition as to nourish and enrich a continuing life.

Traditionally the humane studies have been nourished by bringing together large collections of documentary material, and by providing circumstances conducive to reflection and to sustained inquiry – particularly, but not exclusively, in universities. Universities are the life-blood of humane studies: not only do they bring together persons devoted to a life of inquiry and persons skilful in various kinds of inquiry, but they provide an opportunity for a living commerce with the developing minds and sensibilities of young persons – a wholesome reminder of what minds and sensibilities are like and what inquiry is for.

Humanists – and all kinds of scholars – need to live in a certain atmosphere of inquiry; they need time for reflection and writing and talking; they need books, and, if the books are not at hand, they need to travel to read them or to meet their intellectual peers. A good university takes care of much of this as a matter of course; and a good university sees to it that outsiders do not – out of malice or ignorant goodwill – disrupt the atmosphere or curtail the activity of inquiry. Granting-authorities could probably do more than they have done to support and secure the local ambience that stimulates humane and disinterested inquiry. The tradition comes from ideals established by the universities when they were free of social and political constraint; and that tradition is one of the most precious in our culture. If the universities have not yet made this point successfully with 'the public', intelligent representatives of 'the public' – whether elected or appointed – could do much by endorsing it with a strong affirmation.

Few universities are so richly endowed or so advantageously located that they can provide everything a scholar needs. Beyond sabbatical leave and the limitied financial resources that a university can dispose, there is always need for funds to allow scholarship to come to fulfilment in a reasonable time and to make possible the research that some scholarship requires. Public funds for nourishing humane studies, for developing libraries, for fostering scholarship and inquiry of the highest quality are always limited, despite the immense value these can have for our culture. The fruitful disposition of those funds depends upon something other than 'priorities' and 'criteria'. In the same way that (as Eric Ashby once put it) good university government depends upon 'people of good will who know each other', the just disposition of resources in humane studies depends upon the insight, judgement and experience of humanists. No scholar can be correctly judged except by his peers; and correct decisions are often daring decisions that do not easily explain themselves to the casual observer. The appeal is neither to the expert nor to the sceptical philistine, but to the persons who are qualified and willing to make a judgement and are prepared to stand by it. Since no means has yet been disclosed for translating quality into quantity, there is no alternative in these matters to making judgements of quality.

Increased funds for '*research*' in 'the humanities' will not necessarily benefit humane studies; only the judicious fostering of humane studies altogether can do that. Much of the fostering happens, and must happen, in the intellectual commerce among scholars themselves and between scholars and students. The quality of knowing embodied in distinguished works of scholarship will be forever inaccessible to a person who cannot somehow match the quality of mind that produced it. Fortunately we can sometimes 'qualify' for a line of thinking that we could not have traced out for ourselves simply by being perceptively in the presence of the person who *can* think it out; we often play our best tennis against an opponent we could never hope to match. But that is not what is usually meant by 'learning' when it is assumed that 'teaching' and 'research' can be separated and cost-accounted according to the principles of management consultancy.[4] We have not yet discovered how best to spend our money in nourishing humane studies; perhaps because we have not yet cared enough. Meanwhile, in the field of humane studies, and in the attempt to make just provision for them, it is crucial not to insist on trying to answer questions that properly should never seriously have been asked.

6   Picking Up the Thread*

Much could be said about threads, apart from their use as material for nest-building. We can, for example, get so wet that we haven't a dry thread on us; there is the thread of life which Lachesis, her cloak encrusted with stars, snips with her shears when the time's up, so that our lives can be said to hang by a thread, and our fortunes too; there is the thread of an argument which is always more tenuous than we hoped it would be; and there is the thread that led Theseus out of the labyrinth after killing the Minotaur, the thread having been laid out from inside information by his lover Ariadne. Any of these threads could serve my purpose, but it's the last one I have especially in mind – not for Ariadne's sake (though I think she deserved better from Theseus than she got on the island of Naxos) but because of the labyrinth; and not because the thread would lead us out of the labyrinth as it did Theseus, but because it could lead us back into the labyrinth where we belong. We may take heart from reliable witnesses who tell us that there is not always a voracious Minotaur at the heart of the labyrinth. I wonder whether the Delphic Oracle (who knew a thing or two about double-talk) had something labyrinthine in mind when she caused to be carved over the entrance to her cave the command 'Know thyself.' At least Coleridge and Yeats guessed that it might be so.

Three or four years ago a fashionable phrase emerged – 'The Survival of Literacy'. It was put round, I suppose, by those exponents of envious egalitarianism who make it their business to accelerate the decline of any aspect of life that cannot be shown to contribute directly to the gross national product. Although it's always a mistake to meet the enemy on his own terms, a conference of teachers of English from schools and universities met – our composure a little ruffled – to discuss this theme and its implied

*From *In the Name of Language*, ed. Joseph Gold (Toronto: Macmillan, 1975) pp. 46–70.

conclusion: that 'literacy' is holding on by the skin of its teeth for the moment but probably won't last long. It is difficult to accept this phrase 'The Survival of Literacy' very seriously, recognising it as belonging to the same rhetorical family as 'The Death of God' and 'The Two Cultures', whose poor relations are 'The Pursuit of Knowledge', 'The Just Society' and 'Peace with Honour'. But there we were, members of a vanishing species, fellows of the duck-billed platypus, the whooping crane, the sperm whale, and those delicately poised pelagic birds of the Pacific Islands that were driven from their own natural homes by pigs and rats. We addressed ourselves to the theme on the supposition that – at least for purposes of serious discussion – it was not a trendy catch-phrase, loaded and equivocal, beloved of weekend journalism and debating-societies; we tried in all charity to see if we could make some sense of it, and quickly came to the conclusion that the phrase was meant to imply something of this sort: 'The age of authorised misrepresentation has dawned. "Communications" and "the super-8 revolution" have taken over. Let there be noise above the threshold of pain. To discriminate is to be economically anti-social. Verbal is out, visual is in. Literature is not 'relevant''.'

We are inclined to bridle a little at such a declaration: we had thought that, since 'literature' is our business, 'literacy' was perhaps our peculiar business. If 'literacy' goes, our business goes. (Note the subtle but familiar shift in the word 'business'.) The more resolute among us could say, '*Professional* survival matters very little. The "great work" is all. I can, like the deposed leader Zatopek, drive a junk-cart and be content – nobody can stop me humming.' The more wary among us might be puzzled that in societies allegedly civilised the ear should suddenly be superseded by that abstractive organ the eye. Reflecting a little (which is difficult to do without words), the rather limited intellectual and emotional life of the dragonfly and the owl might suggest that to be able to see well may not be quite enough; we might even wonder whether the waters prophetically described by McLuhan are more muddy than profound, and whether the confident declarations that go with the discovery may be more collusive than illuminating. Nevertheless, there can be no doubt that the threat is aimed at us, and I think it would be well to consider whether there is any substance to the threat, and also what connection there is between 'English' and 'literacy'. What with aggressiveness on the one side and a saintly ineptitude on the other, idle rhetoric could produce an actual killing. If it did, the killing would be a suicide.

To begin with, 'literacy' is not identical with either 'the teaching of English' or 'the study of English'. I should like to move in two directions. First to look at the term 'literacy' in the hope of bringing the word to some agreeable definition. Then, if the only purpose of 'English' is to make students 'literate' (as seems to be assumed in most schools and universities), I should like to affirm the traditional view – never more poignantly relevant than it is now – that the purpose of 'English' is not simply to provide a 'literating' regimen, but to fulfil a civilising-function that has been renounced by virtually every other 'subject'.

The evolution of the word 'literacy' shows an interesting shift in emphasis: it began by referring to a quality to be admired, and has ended by becoming a low-order fact to be entered in census statistics. 'Literate' – from Latin *litteratus* (lettered) – was used in mediaeval times to refer to a person who not merely knew the letters of the alphabet but particularly who made good use of that knowledge: it meant 'learned' or 'educated'. 'Illiterate', also directly from Latin, was originally the negative form of 'literate', meaning a person who was *un*learned, *un*educated. The positive and negative forms of the same word often follow different semantic paths. By the middle of the sixteenth century 'illiterate' was sometimes used of a person who could not read or write; not until 1894 do we find 'literate' – the opposite of the negative word 'illiterate' in its new sense – used of a person who *could* read and write: it took about 250 years for that particular meaning of 'literate' to develop out of a special and limited meaning of the word 'illiterate'. The history of the nouns formed from those adjectives endorses the history of the adjectives. The noun 'illiteracy' occurs in 1660, referring to the state of being unlearned or uneducated, and in the late seventeenth century only occasionally in the special sense of the state of one who could neither read nor write; 'literacy' first occurs in 1883 as the state of being literate, presumably in all senses, but particularly in the sense of being learned or educated.

It is worth noticing that the word 'literate', coloured from its earliest use by the respect and reverence paid to those who (through being able to read and write) were learned or educated, carried over into the abstract noun 'literacy' (when it came to be coined) assumptions about the *potential* implied in the ability to read and write rather than the mere fact of being able to manage the letters of the alphabet intelligibly. Yet the word 'illiterate' is now seldom used except to refer to a person who either cannot in fact read or write, or else is so grotesquely uncivilised that you can't believe that he can do either. The abstract noun 'literacy', however, suffered no such reversal of meaning: it was coined at a time when the assumed benefits of universal education were first being advocated on a national scale in most civilising countries.[1] The undefined emotive word provided a convenient rallying-point – a procedure now well known to us from the propaganda- and advertising-industries. It is melancholy to reflect that the self-sell that drew tens of thousands of guileless but bemused young people into universities in the sixties said nothing about literacy or civilisation, but much about economic self-improvement and the gross national product; the word 'education' (equally undefined and emotive) promised a painless initiation into the mysteries of 'the good life', as specified in full colour with the molar grin of confident affluence.

Unfortunately high-mindedness does not always go hand-in-hand with a profound sense of reality. To be able to read is indeed something worth attaining; but we all know that there are different levels of reading, as there are different levels of writing; we also know that to be able to voice printed or written characters in a semblance of intelligible speech, or to be able to job together written or printed characters into a semblance of coherent writing, is a rather compassionate test of literacy. Those who say, 'I *only* want you to teach my people how to write simple plain English', never seem to understand that that is precisely what any serious writer would give his eye-teeth to be able to do.

If we place the test of literacy (of being learned or educated) at a rather high level, as I am sure we should insist, the definition of 'literacy' can be seen to vary according to the size and homogeneity of the group that can be called learned or educated. If the group is homogeneous and sizable, a knowledge of certain authors and writings can serve as indications of how learned or educated any individual is. In the first half of the eighteenth century, for example, we could assume for a literate person a reading-knowledge of Horace, Cicero, Vergil and Ovid, and some Martial or Juvenal (according to taste); Greek would be desirable but not imperative; in English, Milton and Shakespeare could be assumed, with perhaps a little Spenser. Prose fiction (as far as it existed) would be regarded as a pleasant diversion but not worthy of serious regard, yet a literate person would probably know that very civilised and dotty book *Tristram Shandy*. Certain contemporary English poets would be well known – Dryden, Pope (not least his ingenious translation of Homer) and, when they came along, Gray, Collins, James Thomson and the like. But there would also be included certain philosophers, preachers, essayists, historians, and biographers, and much literature of travel. The locus of literacy was limited pretty much to capital cities and the few university towns. The very strictness of definition and uniformity of taste gave a peculiar blend of zest and urbanity to the literate class – what Coleridge, about the time of the Reform Bill, was to call 'the clerisy', by which he meant all educated professionals. The zest of that literate complex was transplanted to North America in the early years with a sense of responsibility; unhappily little of the urbanity has survived, and not much of the zest.

In the Canadian House of Commons it is a long time since anybody quoted Horace or Martial – or even Milton or Clarendon or Swift or Harrington. I am not aware that in the last twenty-five years our elected representatives have ever quoted anything except each other's more hasty and exploitable utterances, though it is true that Mr Trudeau, a very cultivated man, has once or twice chosen phrases from *Desiderata* – which was a comfortingly democratic thing to do. In 200 years circumstances have altered in many ways, not only in the House of Commons. The number who can read and write has increased immensely in this century, and the number who can read well and write well must be rather larger than it was a century ago. Yet journalism, becoming increasingly pervasive, has on the whole set a rather low and uniform level for staple reading and everyday speech; the best-seller market (already lively 200 years ago) has turned into an organised industry that circulates a large volume of commodities of variable quality that are sometimes read and usually, for a short time, talked about. The *Reader's Digest* has, I suppose, taken the place of the *Quarterly Review*, and Andrew Tooke's *Pantheon* has been superseded by the comic strips; distinctions of class, in speech as well as in dress and deportment, have been heavily eroded; for some years the schools have been teaching methods of reading that ensure shallowness of impression. All these considerations (and many more) prevent us from conceiving of 'literacy' with the precision that could have been achieved even as late as the onset of the Second World War.

Whatever 'literacy' means now, we are forced to recognise that we must look for it under a number of different manifestations, with a large variety of indicators, and in a much more heterogeneous group that even before – not least among those who are self-taught. The concept of literacy is now very difficult to define, and statistical surveys won't help much with a definition because we don't know what questions to ask to identify a *quality*. But that does *not* mean that 'literacy' itself has declined or that it has been dissipated or even that it is in danger of disappearing. A term that was in the first place very imprecise, though for a short time stable enough to be definable, has become much more fugitive in the ninety years since it was coined. But the blurring of the field of search need not affect the fineness of the search. If we are looking for garlic in a pig-sty we can still know quite clearly what garlic looks like and smells like. It may be difficult to find a needle in a haystack, but the difficulty doesn't prevent us from knowing what a needle is and what it is used for; and, if it's a needle we want, it would be more intelligent to look for one in a pin-cushion than in a haystack.

The word 'literacy' was never intended to imply anything but a desirable or admirable *quality* of intellectual cultivation. The word was coined and borne aloft by the assumption (now largely disappointed) that given the *means* – to be able to read and write – the *quality* would naturally follow; that a person who was 'lettered' (knew his letters) would tend (other things being equal) to become *literate*, learned, educated. But the process can work very slowly. John Berryman, when he was a brash young American undergraduate before the Second World War, discovered a curious instance of provinciality in Cambridge – Cambridge being, one would have thought, a fairly civilised place, and its undergraduates moderately literate.

> These men don't know *our* poets.
> I'm asked to read: I read Wallace Stevens & Hart Crane
> in Sidney Sussex & Cat's
> The worthy young gentlemen are baffled. I explain
>
> But the idiom is too much for them.

> The Dilettante Society here in Clare
> asked me to lecture to them on Yeats
> & misspelt his name on the invitations.

This refers to a matter of elementary literacy that we run into more and more as more and more students come from a relatively unlearned background – and some teachers too. It can of course happen to anybody. How could anybody be expected to know by instinct that the name Bagehot is pronounced 'Bajut', or that Elia is pronounced 'Elïa'. Louis Arnaud Reid, studying aesthetics at Oxford about sixty years ago, thought for a whole under-graduate year that Bosanquet was two people – Bowes and Kett – like Liddell and Scott, or Lewis and Short, or Samson and Delilah. (I have met students who thought that 'jesting Pilate' was a seafaring-metaphor). I usually think it advisable at the end of a course in literature to say, 'These are some of the names we have been bandying about. This is how they are spelled; this is how they are pronounced. I can't insist that you *read* them all; but if you want to give the air of having read them, it is well to get the spelling right, and the pronunciation. It goes ill in a billiard saloon to chalk the wrong end of the cue.' But we must be patient. Some of my students still say 'Colleridge' even though I point again and again to Coleridge's own epigram on the various mispronunciations of his name (including this one). We must indeed be patient.

'Literacy', in the historical view, means to have read or heard or seen some things that made the heart leap up because they seemed to have been made especially for you; to have encountered some things that 'with the swift composure of a fish' (Virginia Woolf's phrase) entered the fibre of the mind and stayed there; to have some feeling that literature is a living tissue spread out in time, a spider's web that can, at a light touch, tremble right back to the beginnings of recorded speech or far below the levels of individual memory or experience. Literacy in that sense cannot be *taught*; but the possibility of it can be made available. To teach children – a little roughly if need be – to read and write and do sums has always been the staple of schools; this is how it all begins and this is how it all should begin, and the sooner the better.

But the formal study of 'English' in universities is a quite recent development, which began, roughly speaking, when classical studies ceased to be the central humanist discipline and the torch was handed to 'English'. Until that time – say the first quarter of the twentieth century – it seems always to have been assumed (in England at least) that a firm acquaintance with the literature of one's own language was what – given a salutary shove at school – civilised people achieved, somehow, in the dog-watches, when nobody was looking. You didn't have to 'take courses'; you were taught your own language at school and made to read a certain amount of 'what everybody reads'; after that you were on your own. (Those who clamour for a strong diet of courses in 'Canadian literature' should give a little thought to this.) Oxford considered 'English' hardly a matter worthy of serious study, compared with the classics; and when an English School was eventually established late in the nineteenth century, the emphasis was placed on philology and Anglo-Saxon (a foreign language), and after Anglo-Saxon the advance towards Milton was tentative and grudging. It was not supposed that in such a study you were meant to *enjoy* English: that was your own affair, not the University's. Cambridge was a little less stuffy, and recognised that there might have been some writing in English after 1800 that would, in educational terms, reward study.

When classics was finally edged out of its commanding position, through the neglect of those who could best have profited from those studies, 'English' found itself landed with the responsibility that classics had borne ever since the thirteenth and fourteenth centuries. Such arrangements are never made formally and are never openly acknowledged; after a decorous delay professors of English found themselves carrying the ball. But to have to turn the study of language and literature into a prime civilising-instrument is rather a tall order, and nobody knew quite how to do it; and anyway matters of this sort seem to go better when there is no apocalyptic purpose openly in mind. The New Criticism, begun in Cambridge and turned into a paedagogic technique in the United States, threw the emphasis very firmly upon the integrity of literature and single works of literature; this greatly extended the precision, depth and comprehensiveness of literary studies, and seemed for a while to have provided a way of 'teaching English' that would engage a fine range of discernment appropriate to the heart of humane studies. That was in the thirties and forties. But by about the time the last veterans of the wars had left the University and Cleanth Brooks was beginning to look theoretically a little thin and Ivor Richards's hope of a psychological calculus for literature looked more like a piece of science fiction than a real possibility, signs of fragmentation began to appear, mostly in the promotion of broad dogmatic schemes of interpretation and the representation of literature as a form of social history.

It seems to me that, at present, 'English' is not in general carrying out the function of a central humane discipline. I speak of the run-of-the-mill work both in schools and in universities – which I suppose is what most 'teaching' is.

The backwash of the New Criticism, reinforced by the nihilistic abstractions of behaviourism and scientific analysis, and fostered by a desperate desire to get in on the power-game, is to be seen in the wanhope of short cuts and technical gimmicks. There is talk of teaching 'skills' and 'techniques' (rather than of making people skilful); of the 'tools of research' and the 'tools of criticism'; of identifying 'approaches' and 'views' and 'problems'; faculties of education and institutes of education (which seem in an odd way to be busy with something other than education) refer confidently to 'the learning-experience' and 'the educational process' as though those actually existed, and urge us to establish 'objectives' and 'goals' and 'to evaluate performance by objective criteria' or by 'behavioural output', and to 'quantify the results'. This is a godforsaken and desolate zone, as deadly as uranium 235, to be avoided at all costs if what we have in mind is the civilised study of 'English'.

Yet I suppose this sort of thing is inevitable in times of desperation. Our minds are by nature idle; faced with a taxing circumstance we hope for a simple solution, an easy answer, and clutch at anything that looks 'viable'; with the instinct of a cat burglar we try the back door first; we look for a key that can be turned in one motion of the fingers rather than a clue to be followed or a thread to be patiently unravelled; and, if we can manufacture some high-sounding jargon to cover the case, rationalisation and self-deception go decorously hand-in-hand. We insist that we must *understand*, and so avoid the grace of showing that touch of respect that would make us determined *not* to *mis*understand. To insist on understanding is to be most unreasonable. Not that all that loose jargon, with its crude analogies and empty abstractions, is utterly useless; but it doesn't happen to serve our central purpose, which is to illuminate, to come upon the vigorous complex reality of language and literature and grasp it for what it is. Yet, with all the beating of drums about innovation and audio-visual technology and 'communications' and Canadianism, the noise can get a little confusing, and the urge to conform can become almost compulsive if we get nervous and are afraid that we might miss a trend or a new vogue and be thought old-fashioned – and think that we might wake one morning to find that for a whole generation most people had been talking in Arabic and we hadn't even noticed.

Thinking of language and jargon and the wide uncritical currency of catch-phrases, I should say that in my view there is no such thing as a *language* of film, or a *language* of music, or a *language* of dance or painting, even though, as loose metaphors, those phrases may not be utterly useless. The only language is the language of what we call 'words'. A true language has a grammar – that is, a description of intrinsic functions; music, painting, film and the like have only *syntax* – that is, principles of putting together. Anybody who has ever attempted criticism of music or painting or film will know what I mean. Words alone have intrinsic 'meaning' (as we call it for lack of a better word); and words alone have the intrinsic functions that shape syntax. Visual images can have quite strong implications: a smiling face is not usually an unhappy face (though it may be an empty one); a male and a female figure disposed in a certain configuration can imply an amatory, erotic, or filial relation; but not everybody finds a toad ugly, or a mouse frightening, or a snake repulsive; and not all of us 'read' the bee or the goldfinch as a symbol of chastity. The minor mode seems to close a sad relay in our emotional circuitry; a descending interval or scale is less elevating than an ascending figure. But these emotional resources, although they can in context be controlled with fine and intricate precision, cannot be articulated with the specific definition that words at a much lower level of accomplishment are capable of.

I say that words have 'intrinsic' meaning and function in order to make the point that language is not a 'medium'; it is not simply a neutral 'carrier-wave' (although under certain conditions it can be); we can push it only so far; it plays on us as much as we play on it; language even affects the physical structure of our faces. We have somehow to come to terms with it, because language – no matter how conventional it sometimes seems – is not merely a conventional notation in which we record thoughts, wishes and feelings. We spend several of the early years of our lives trying to find out how, in a rudimentary way, to use language; and since language in its very nature is always complex we often do quite well at the beginning even though we may get clumsier as we go on. Some of us spend the whole of our lives trying to use language, and only in occasional moments of elation are we confident that it is possible to advance much beyond the level of finger-pointing and vague gestures.

The implied threat to literacy is the barbarous assumption that language has decayed to such an extent that it is no longer useful for human purposes, and that a substitute must be found – anything visual or noisy (it seems) will do: film, artificial fog, fluorescent plastics, disorienting confusion of indiscriminate sound. Which brings me back to 'literacy'. The word bears in its bones the implication of 'letters', the record of what is spoken or written; it may even carry with it some feeling for the unfathomable gap between what is written and what needed to get said. As far as 'literacy' means being learned or cultivated, we should want to extend the word to include some acquaintance with (say) music, painting, sculpture, architecture, dancing, acting; but the indissoluble element of 'literacy' is language, and the use of language, and some recognition of the manifold and variable functions of language. We need to pay attention to *what* is written, but even that is difficult to pick out because of the bond between the *what* and the *how* in any writing other than semi-mathematical discursive prose. A 'literate' person is, I think, what we mean by an 'educated' person (however he comes by it). I think not of *expert* knowledge but rather of the honest and comprehensive appreciation of the keen amateur who has a reasonably well-developed and well-informed taste. His mind is not so much 'filled' or 'stocked' as ready, alert, responsive, having something to respond *with*.

Particularly, to be literate is to be sensitive to language in all its manifestations. Reading – that is, actually reading lots of books – is perhaps a specialised activity, like skiing or rock-climbing or engraving on glass; for writing there is no other way of 'Studying monuments of its own magnificence'. Short of that – but not really a substitute for it – is to speak articulately, preferably with a touch of rough and improvised eloquence; and to be able to listen to speech attentively, grasping it as the dramatic unfolding of a necessary improvisation. The breaking-up of isolated social groups, and the pressure to conform to 'standard speech' may now have deprived us almost completely of dialects, and so of impromptu virtuosity in language. But the old instinct quickly returns if we decline to ape the formulated patterns.

This, I suppose, is the keystone or knot or nucleus of my argument – if it is an argument: that 'literacy' is radically to do with language, and that the heart of any genuinely educative activity is to be found in language; not language as a phenomenon, nor as an object of inquiry; not language considered merely for what it says or 'means' or contains, nor even literature as examples of the use of language and ways of living; but everything that is engaged by language and in language – the thinking, the feeling, the activity of mind, the reality of experience that, in the wording of it, can be as solid as an inconsolable grief; the reality that language constantly confronts us with, of *making* as a necessary and natural human activity; language as an inventive mode of inquiry that can disclose ourselves to ourselves, discovering to us what we wanted to say; above all the language that allows us to make and utter things that are not simply extensions or expressions of ourselves.

It is conceivable that the sense of language may go on decaying, that the finely articulate and modulated poetic speech that English is capable of could collapse into a mutter-tongue. But language is always decaying; and also language is always renewing itself. The renewal is brought about not by tight-lipped academicians standing pale (and almost speechless) at the barricades, nor by the stern schoolteacher who has a ruler for every knuckle; it occurs through the sheer exuberance of invention and delight in invention. For language is not only the specific and distinctive mark of man, but his most naturally inventive resource. Nobody knows how we do it; and probably nobody ever will.[2]

Literacy, whether arising from formal or private study, is a by-product rather than a definable end, a spin-off rather than a product, a responsive and discerning habit of mind rather than a possession or an accomplishment. If, in our teaching, our concern is to encourage literacy, we might to well not to assume that it will come only to the most talented students. The most talented will find it anyway, somehow or other. Our concern should be to provide at every level a starting-point from which individual development and vitality can begin to discover and affirm the gift of language. Yet the literate will always be a minority because literacy depends upon a gift for language; there is no law that says that everybody must be fascinated by language (though I wish there were a law, particularly among people in positions of influence or authority, about using language in a responsible manner). The only mistake is to suppose that it could be otherwise. The ideal of teaching everybody to read and write was probably inevitable; but the risk almost outbalances the blessing. It is now very clear that universal literacy (in the elementary sense) is in danger of producing universal illiteracy (in the qualitative sense), by breeding disrespect for language and whatever can be finely spoken or written; by submerging our sense of wonder at the most remarkable of our endowments, the gift of inventive speech; by throwing doubt upon our discriminate perception of the *why* of anything that is spoken or written.

I can't remember when I last met a person who could not read printed words – except for very small children and perhaps a few psychopaths. That disability is surely much rarer now than to have only one leg, or two eyes of different colours, or to bear scars of incontinent motor-driving. Speech is a marvel enough in itself; we are perhaps most often reminded of it when we hear a five-year-old child speak fluently in a language not our own – Dutch, Hungarian, Russian. To be able to convert written characters, is yet another and different marvel; it demands a flair for imaginative projection more studied and artificial than the act of speaking. One ideal of written language is that it should sound as though spoken, even though a direct transcript of actual speech will seldom do the trick. Yet many who have 'done well at school' are (we find) utterly deaf when they read; content to 'get the message' or to 'pick up the information', they fail to hear in the writing the very qualities that in speech they would welcome and even rejoice in.

We know that in real life if we do not *listen* we miss not only *what* is said but also *why* it was said. Yet, for reasons mysterious to me, children have for many years been taught in school to 'read by eye', thereby systematically suppressing the ability to listen to what is written. This may explain why we find so many students – even some 'good' university students – who stiffen at the sight of a pen, the hand scrunching up like an arthritic old bird's claw; the writing then goes clumsily enough, often with a deadly pedantry or uncouth pretentiousness that we never hear in their speech (unless they are trying to talk like an article in a learned journal or are engaged in student politics). No doubt it's a good thing to have a quick way of getting through large quantities of printed material that 'isn't worth listening to'; but if that is our only way of reading we ensure that nothing we read will be worth listening to – that is, worth reading.

A large part of my energy and ingenuity as an instructor of English in a university goes into encouraging people to read attentively and to write as well as they can. The first is not too difficult because some have survived their early training scot-free and few have suffered irreparable damage; the second is more taxing because few are endowed to write as well as they speak, and even fewer are willing to accept the risk of discovering that language is not so much a 'medium of expression' as an instrument of inquiry.

To direct students towards competence in writing is a laborious and discouraging task. No wonder most instructors find that they have so much else to do that they have no time for it. Yet there is no substitute for learning to write. Speech will not do as a substitute because it lets us off the hook too easily – both speaker and listener – through the persuasive shorthand of gesture, facial expression, and intonation, and every *bêtise* in public tends to be endearing even if not always pardonable. Hence the great importance traditionally (and correctly) placed in humane education upon writing. There really is no other way of coming to terms seriously with language than by trying to write well. To accept the proposition that writing is outmoded, that society is no longer 'verbal' enough for the skilful conduct of writing to be 'relevant' is to arrest the development of those who – though confident that they can in some sense 'read' – are unaware how easily – by 'reading badly' – they can be made mute victims of cynical manipulation (social, commercial and political), and could become emotional cripples and intellectual dwarfs.

To be not-illiterate is to be able to recognise the unity of the *what*, the *how* and the *why* of anything that is spoken or written. If we cannot recognise by the ring of it that an argument is specious, or that it is no argument at all, being merely a reiteration of emotional catchwords and sophisms; if we cannot tell by the ear the peculiar *timbre* of a third-rate mind fumbling with matters that he neither understands nor respects; if we cannot sniff out the shiftiness of doublespeak, of gross dishonesty and bland self-deception dressed up in jargonish togs of the latest design; if we cannot by ear detect the poverty of dull earnestness or the ponderous tautologies of degenerate abstraction; if we can do none of these things, then we are indeed illiterate, no matter how extensive our vocabulary, no matter how many improving magazines we subscribe to. Illiteracy of that sort thrives, I regret to say, not only among students who might (at their risk) be momentarily pardoned, but also among many who profess to 'teach'.

We must recognise that there are now, and long have been, forces in society that make it their business to induce illiteracy, and that strive to persuade us (often in the name of 'truth', 'objectivity' and the benefits of programmed conformity) that there is no point in listening while we read, or in judging while we listen. It is the duty of schools and universities to keep alive these capacities and to nourish them as fully as may be in every individual who will let us. We can do this by reminding ourselves continuously of something that we know perfectly well and that we live by every hour of the day: that we can tell what people are saying to us and that we can usually judge pretty accurately why they are saying it. To fulfil this duty is of course to be subversive: by seeking to establish the autonomous discrimination of the individual (within reason), we threaten to undermine the programmes of power, authority and abstraction that at present dominate our society. To be subversive in a 'free' society is always sternly punished sooner or later, partly by having a submissive claque called 'the public' organised against us, partly by the betrayal of waverers and opportunists from within. William Tyndale, the first translator of the Bible into English, was exiled from his country and was eventually strangled and burned; there were complex grounds for Henry VIII's displeasure, but treason was not one of them. We no longer burn people in public; we roast them in private – by withholding essential funds, by intrusive legislation, by demanding so much reporting-in-detail that no honest work can be done, by putting about misleading propaganda, in short by cutting off telephones (the approved method of destruction in big business). It is strange that in our society we tenaciously insist upon preserving the authorised conspiracy of trade unions, yet spend much effort in trying quietly to destroy the benign conspiracy of education that we ourselves have authorised by choice.

Human nature being what it is, the direction of wilful human ambition is always degenerate. Yet there is a certain wisdom of the body that can secure our integrity against all the sly tricks from without – and even from the sloth from within that would make us complacent, unwatchful, destitute of delight. Long after the last polar bear has been driven from the last garbage-tip, we shall go on *listening*, unless we destroy our ability to do so. It is of our nature, a habit of growth and preservation, a source of responsive power and refining attention – to listen, not for the sounds of danger only, nor only for the sounds of delight (bird-song, running water, music), but for voices: voices speaking, voices that speak intently to us, one by one, voices that we can recognise and put a name to.[3] This is not a matter of policy, and is therefore unassailable. As instructors, our business is not salvation or programmes for salvation, but simply with helping people to discover their capacities, their intrinsic nature, their selves.

Now for the 'thread' – the bond, that is, between the formal study of 'English' and the quality of 'literacy'. What is the thread we suppose ourselves to be unravelling or following – deliberately or absent-mindedly – and where does it lead us? Let us recognise two things. (1) Our discussion so far has taken the work of school and university as a single continuum, but I have spoken perhaps as though the emphasis fell mostly on the university. As we trace the thread we shall need to pay closer attention to different levels of function, to make some distinctions between the work of primary school, high school and university. (2) In schools, and also (but to a lesser extent) in university, education is not directed exclusively towards the training of experts or the cultivation of highly endowed intelligences. We need to recognise that (for a number of various reasons) a certain number of people are uneducable beyond a very modest level. Nevertheless, we hold as an aim that each individual should ideally be trained to a high level of his own capacity, whatever that may be; and we also wish to arrange the quality of our work in such a way that (as with some artists) the 'picture' in a real sense is complete at every stage; if a person has to stop before reaching the end of a programme (say grade nine or grade thirteen or an honours BA) his education to that point will be coherent and at that level self-consistent. Education is not only for 'experts'; a literate or educated person is *not* an expert, but he does approach in some way the ideal of the 'generally educated person'. Intense and specialised training can assail the integrity of that ideal, and pedantry or the closed mind can destroy it.

If 'English' is to assume from Classics the function of *the* central humane discipline, it must be not only learned but substantial, earthly, physical, subtle and far-ranging. The earthiness, subtlety and range are to be found by concentrating on language. And

'English', though certainly not devoid of 'content', is to be regarded not as a 'subject' but as a discipline in the true sense: a certain way of mind, a habit of mind, a quality of perception – from which all other kinds of study can radiate and in which they can be seen to be rooted. This is an axiom, not an argument. In no other terms could 'English' take on the general educational responsibility that classics traditionally held. Classics had always been a study, not a language and literature only, but of the history, philosophy and social institutions of two complete, highly developed, closely related, and strongly contrasted cultures; a study not only (say) of comparative philosophy and history, but of the origins and growth to civilised stature of philosophy itself, and of historiography; a study not of two foreign languages but of two languages representing two contrasting mentalities, each very different from our own mentality, despite the profound effect both languages have had on our own.

Lacking that complex perspective, and lacking the strong intrinsication or *inward* pull exerted by the study of such flowering-at-the-source, and deprived of the otherness, the sheer strangeness of those two languages and cultures, 'English' has always had to make a deliberate effort not to relapse into a narrow and myopic study of 'English language and literature' as a 'subject'. In my view such a relapse has largely occurred; and I applaud the challenging proposition of my learned colleague Felp Priestley that perhaps English has become an obsolete industry – that is (I take it), that English has become obsolete by being turned into an industry; that 'English' has become a worn-out shorthand omnibus term, an omnibus (to change the image) in which we long ago stopped checking the oil and haven't noticed that rust has afflicted the steering-mechanism.

It is not enough, I suggest, to say that we are going to teach people to read and write and gain a knowledge of literature; nor is it enough to say that literature embraces just about any study you can think of – history, philosophy, politics, psychology, semantics, etc., etc., etc. We need to be continually following a thread that leads us back into the origins of all these special kinds of study – even our own; to be finding in the ways of language, and in literature (as language superlatively realised in any form of expression or in any subject), a continuous discovery and affirmation of the nature of language and of the inventive and integral activities of the whole person that we call 'mind'.

We need to take into account, though, that – as teachers – we are thinking of a continuous process covering usually (without much serious interruption) a span of sixteen to twenty years in the life of a potentially literate person; and also that within such a span, and within the working-span of any single teacher, the vision will be blurred from time to time and that declared purposes will be deflected by waves of irrational fashion, by ignorant intervention, and by crass methodological doctrine. Therefore, in a matter at once complex and elusive, subject to erosion from within by fatigue and languor – or simply by losing the thread – we need some strong and single focus of attention.

We need to recognise that within the field of 'English' there is an almost infinite number of things that we can 'do with' literature, but that not all – or even many – of these have much to do with the central paedagogic value of studying literature. There is a very small nucleus of activity where the going is very hard indeed because what is sought is of the utmost simplicity; and there are a host of peripheral activities that grow up from using literature and language as evidential material for quite other interests. Much of the time and attention of our students is consumed with these peripheral interests. Those interests are legitimate enough in their own way; but, in comparison with what a central educational discipline can be expected to do to us, they offer little more nourishment than lists of irregular verbs or columns of stock-exchange quotations. The nucleus I speak of is not, of course, the exclusive prerogative of 'English'; it is the nucleus of all humane study. But literature and language give a peculiarly direct and penetrating entry to that nucleus, and, although the chances of deflection are abundant and debilitating, it is usually easier in the study of English than in other humane studies to tell (if we are honest with ourselves) whether we are being deflected or not.

I suggest that the nucleus is accessible along a single thread that is composed of two strands – as is the case (I suppose) for all things and states imaginative. These strands are a sense of wonder and a sense of language. Plato said that wonder was the beginning of philosophy – and by 'philosophy' he meant the affectionate pursuit of wisdom. Without a sense of wonder the mind remains closed, or irritably aggressive, or morosely fear-ridden. Wonder is a respectful way of mind, a grace that we seem to be born with; by discipline we can nourish it; it brings with it the exhilarating release, the sheer delight, of discovering living things that are not projections of our selves, and that liberate us by their exuberant vitality, their unaccountable otherness and rightness. By 'a sense of language' I mean a feeling for the physique, the nerves and muscles of words, and for their textures; a feeling for what language is *doing* almost more than what it is saying or 'meaning', for what it is tracing out, acting out, gesturing forth, embodying; a feeling for the *intrinsic* qualities of words, their origins and transformations, their minute particularities as they establish themselves by context, by location, by rhythm; a feeling for their ability to declare, in precise configuration and ordered hierarchy, multiple meanings, often contrary; a feeling for the inner shaping energy that comes to the ear as shapely rhythm, as a tune often so subtle that it might seem to be on the fringes of silence. To follow this thread – a thread that leads *back* into the mind and into the source of our most inventive endowment – is to move toward the centre of articulation and initiative both in ourselves and in what we are studying.

We can pick up the thread at any time, as long as the last vestiges of innocence and candour have not been destroyed, and as long as we are not finally convinced that the mind is a clockword orange constructed on the principles of Newtonian physics; but the earlier we pick it up the better, while the sense of wonder still naturally supervenes upon the fasinating effort of learning to speak. To discover the transfiguration that language is capable of, to come upon the imperishable substance of things-made-in-language that are no more sounds on the air or marks on paper yet are sometimes as deep as life, often as commanding as a presence – this is to experience the synthesis that language flows out of and can bring us to. So to concentrate on dynamics, *dynamis*, energy, the originating and shaping forces that are carried in the bones and nerves of anything well made, is to find a nuclear centre of a minute critical mass. The rest depends upon what, individually, we can do with it.

There is not time, nor is this the occasion, to specify in detail what can be done by picking up this thread and taking the courage to go back into the labyrinth. But I can make a few hints. At the very beginning, writing is making shapes that will evoke sounds; the correlation of sound to shape is seldom very exact, but the letters have shapes interesting in their own right, and they have histories; and, when it comes to spelling, that is a good way of beginning to get a feel for the shapes of words as physical entities. (It is recorded that J. A. Smith, a Wynfleet Professor of Moral and Metaphysical Philosophy at Oxford, came to breakfast after a sleepless night saying what a dreadful thing it would be for a learned Chinese to go blind: some of the ideograms that make Chinese so beautiful when written have no sounds attached to them and can therefore only be read by eye.) The study of grammar, essential I should have thought, but now, I understand, largely neglected in the school as a matter of policy, is to study the intrinsic functions of words, how they 'work', what they have to be to 'work' at all – the static noun that for an adorning or refining touch calls adjectives to itself but won't have more than one at a time (usually) or they will quarrel; the range of functions of the verb from passive and impersonal inaction and neutrality to the vigorous forward thrust in search of an object that imparts such impetus to an utterance that the words have to fall into place because they haven't time to do anything else. Syntax is another matter – the way words actually go together in utterances; and given the terms of identification we can find out by analysis (that is, by unravelling) how in actual cases the words do work together.

Here it is that considerations of 'style', the unique 'thisness' of anything, come to conscious attention, though we had long ago caught the tune of it; under the spell of wonder we may well have taken it for granted. Here we come upon the peculiar nature of language – the fact that we discover our meaning in the wording of it; for it is persons, not words, that mean. In matters of spelling, in identifying parts of speech, and even in classifying figures of speech, we may be able to speak of 'right' and 'wrong' (i.e. correct and incorrect), but as soon as we are dealing with syntax and style we are dealing with the judgement of what 'works', what is 'exactly right', in an actual context. There are many grammatical difficulties that are insoluble except by complete reconstruction; 'rules' are indications, navigational instruments, not immutable imperatives. Here the only test is whether in fact a certain wording 'works', whether it is the best words in the best order – and perhaps nobody can say that for sure except the writer. Hence in 'teaching' writing – if we want to encourage a sense of the dynamics of the language – it is important to reserve 'right' and 'wrong' for the few cases where 'correct' or 'incorrect' can be determined beyond question; elsewhere a scale runs from 'right' to 'not quite right' to 'not right at all' – but neither of the last two is 'wrong' in the sense of 'incorrect'; when we say 'no' to the choice of a word, the position of a phrase, a grammatical construction, we have located a *symptom* that something has gone adrift, slightly or seriously. What has 'gone wrong' has still to be discovered; it is usually in the conceiving of it. What we have to do is not usually to tinker with the words but to reconceive the exact mental action or gesture that we had in mind. I don't know how anybody who does not have a refined sense of language and the patience to weigh minute verbal values in other people's writing can ever hope either to write well or to induce anybody else to write well.[4]

All this places an almost intolerable burden upon the teacher, not least because little of it can be learned by rote. To teach the minutiae of grammar and syntax is a rigorous and exacting matter; yet it is refreshed and reinforced by reading works of literature, to begin with – and perhaps always – for the sheer enjoyment of it, deliberately looking for a spell to fall under; as teachers, explaining as little as possible (because explaining is almost invariably explaining away), and yet encouraging our students as best we can to grasp the multiple activity that goes on in good writing, the many implications that are set in motion and sustained with fine precision. When we are studying literature as a way of finding out how to write well, 'criticism', 'explication' and all the alleged 'tools of research' are to be handled with the utmost delicacy and restraint; if they are really used as 'tools' they will certainly dismember what we seek to grasp whole and intact. And so for all the fascinating details of prosody and versification, the principles by which, in verse, the words have in fact been set in the right order so that they resonate and are transfigured – we need to conceive these principles in dynamic terms, as the disposition of energy in relation to chosen constraints and limits; for a study of prosody can immensely heighten the sense of verbal *drama* – exactly what the words are *doing*, how they are acting (as actors act).

And if, with the advance of self-consciousness, students suspect that the sense of wonder was only a paedagogic trick, it can be restored by examining how poets and artists actually work, how they deal with their need to go to the labour of making things in words, what the relations are between the historic person of the poet and what ends up in his poem. This needs to be handled delicately too, and is probably slippery ground except for those who have practised the art of poetry a bit and are familiar with its forthright and craftsmanlike axioms. A study of artistic making will not *explain* much, but it can restore wonder by clearing away inappropriate assumptions about 'communication' and 'information' and 'messages' and 'media' and 'audience-appeal' and 'the poet's Philosophy' and 'motivation' and 'social commitment'. These drift into the background as too crude to help us, or as totally irrelevant to the poetic matter in hand. There are also questions about 'fact' and 'value', about the alleged 'subjectivity' (unreliability?) of all personal judgements – as though any judgements were anything but personal; about ways of knowing and recognising; about seeing and observing, describing and symbolising and naming; about the enclosed integrity that some poems have and how others are more discursive and open; about the distinction between what is merely actual and what is actually real (the two being concentric); about the relation of feeling to thinking; about the poetic ordonnance that works through metaphor, and how this is different from 'logic', though more intricate, and yet embracing logic (as language must); about the peculiar reality of fictions over against the unreality of descriptions of the actual. Above all we should choose carefully works of such strength and complexity that they force our attention into the symbolic mode and hold it there. Lesser works do not deserve our full attention: they will cheat us by letting us have our own way too easily. Acquaintance is easy enough to arrange, yet the shock of personal discovery must somehow never be destroyed.

This is really a labyrinth, but that's where the thread leads. In such a pass, at the present time, I'm not sure what sort of results we could guarantee – if any; except that we can be reasonably sure that there will always be a few innocents and crackpots to follow Tom Piper's whistle. As instructors we can at least take stock of our individual resources and decide up to what level we can work with confidence, without doing serious (i.e. erosive) damage, making sure that if we are deflecting we are doing so deliberately, and say so. There is of course no one 'answer', in 'technique': the work under inquiry commands the method of inquiry – which is what 'method' means; we need to make that clear too.

Whether it is possible for any one person to achieve what I am talking about I am not sure; but I am confident that, given some vital sense of direction, some sense of the nucleus that will energise whatever we undertake – no matter how minute or even (on the face of it) detached from the nucleus – we can conduct our work at all levels with success, leaving deposits of the solid verbal footing from which a person cannot easily be dislodged. I often wish that there had never been 'the New Criticism', splendid, rich, and penetrating though its best results have been; I wish it were issued with instructions, not on *how*, but on *when* and *how much*; it offers possibilities, it does not provide answers, and it can lead to barren ends. Indeed, in tracing this thread – or even if we are prepared to go no further than to hand on – our concern must be for fruitful questions, not for answers. When literary studies propose only formulated answers, routine 'techniques' and judgements that are expected to be repeated by those who have not discovered and shaped them for themselves, the thread has indeed been lost and the study of letters has come to a dead end.

7   Jane Austen: Poet*

I must confess to a little uneasiness. Except for a long-standing, slow-burning admiration for Jane Austen's writing, for 'the achieve of, the mastery of the thing', I have nothing much to guide me. I have not even written a book on Jane Austen; so who can say where I stand in the critical spectrum, between the ultra-violet Janeites and the infra-red Austenists? There is, I know, a vast ocean of scholarship and criticism, puff-cheeked and sea-monster-haunted, in which Jane's work swims; but I have not studied the 'Sailing-Directions' that could have warned me of the sly currents and deceptive landfalls, and have neglected the 'Notices to Mariners' with their record of the latest wrecks, the unlighted lights, the demolished seamarks, the unswept mine-fields. I feel like one who has been bidden to dine in the Captain's Room at Lloyd's, having no gold ring in the ear. But I recall that Jane had two naval brothers, that she admired both of them very much, and that both became admirals even though they had had less first-hand acquaintance with Pacific Island cannibals than Fanny Burney's midshipman brother had; and pray therefore for the impassivity of Joshua Slocum, who – after his chronometer had gone over the side and his goat had eaten his charts – completed his voyage around the world alone, with no navigational aids beyond an alarm clock and a map torn from a school atlas.

I have, however, tried a little to see whether anybody else thought Jane Austen was a poet; but in vain. I had high hopes of one recent book that had distilled from all known critical approaches a multiplanal technique of analysis that would provide the last word – or almost the last word – on *Mansfield Park*. I peeped inside, but most of what I saw was about Marx and Freud and sociology, which I found unnecessarily distasteful. So I closed

*From *Jane Austen's Achievement*, ed. Juliet McMaster (London: Macmillan, 1976) pp. 106–33.

that book, and turned to Mr Southam's ingenious collection called *The Critical Heritage*. There I found a letter written by George Henry Lewes to Charlotte Brontë in 1848; this seemed a little closer to the mark. Defending Jane Austen as 'one of the greatest artists . . . that ever lived', Lewes went on to say (a little incautiously, as it turned out) that 'Miss Austen is not a poetess, has no "sentiment", . . . no eloquence, none of the ravishing enthusiasm of poetry'. Charlotte replied with proper indignation, 'Can there be a great artist without poetry? What I call . . . a great artist . . . cannot be destitute of the divine gift. But by *poetry*, I am sure, you understand something different to what I do.' It is not easy to see what Lewes meant here by 'poetry'; he says it is what Shakespeare had, and that in place of that we must put Jane Austen's 'daring prose'. But Miss Brontë is not much more lucid: poetry, she says, is passion and rapture, a power so divine that it had elevated George Sand's coarse masculinity and had been able to convert Thackeray's 'corrosive poison into purifying elixir'.[1] Having no acquaintance with corrosive poisons and very little with coarse masculinity, I have had to search my own heart; for Richard Simpson had said emphatically that Jane is no poet, and even Miss Lascelles, in declaring that Jane was no symbolist, may have meant that in her view too Jane was no poet.

Most of what we have of Jane Austen's verse is a sort of polished doggerel, and was not intended to be anything else; even when she came to utter her grief at the untimely death of Anne Lefroy, a niece beloved and almost as gifted as Jane herself, the verse, though noble in sentiment, is flat and rhetorical in execution – in the undesirable sense it is at once too 'poetical' and too 'prosaic'. Perhaps those who have said that Jane was no poet dismissed as of no serious account what (if anything) they knew of her verse, and could find in her novels none of those Icarus-passages of opulent emotive prose that sometimes get printed in italics, nor anything haunted (as Dickens sometimes is) by the submerged run of the blank-verse line or the sonorous rhythms of the Authorised Version of the Bible. Nevertheless, I should still like to suggest that Jane Austen *is* a poet.

Jane Austen is supremely a writer of prose. As Coleridge knew, and Wordsworth echoed, the antithesis of prose is not poetry, but verse; the antithesis of poetry is science. Yeats's tone-deafness steered him away from the contemporary cult of trying to write 'muscial' verse; and brought him to an unmatched sense of the integrity of language – significant words rhythmically disposed, passionate hieratic utterance keyed to the inventive rhythms of the speaking voice. In the same way, Jane Austen's incapacity for composing strong or eloquent verse seems to have endowed her with an incorruptible sense of the integrity of prose, the translucent rhythms of the speaking voice in the other harmony, the peculiar signature of breath and intelligence that identifies a person speaking and the state of mind that from moment to moment informs the voice. Miss Lascelles noticed that in some of Jane Austen's prose there is 'an impression of speed and simplicity not alien from the temper of verse'.[2] Her ear gave her an accurate intuition; I wish she had carried the hint a little further. If we reject the proposition that Jane Austen is a poet, we might be tempted to accept the doctrine that she is some sort of scientist – a microscopically objective recorder of a limited range of human behaviour; a very odd thing to say of a writer whose work is rather like Mozart, without the *Requiem*.

I am impressed by the fact that Jane Austen's characters are autonomous to such a degree that they have in our minds a life of their own, so that we can discuss them with great patience and refinement of perception – and with very little quarrelling – as though they were living persons (which of course they are). That she was able to do that was a marvellous achievement; and that it should be so accounts, I suppose, for the inexhaustible pleasure we find in talking to each other about her people, confident that any obtuseness or lack of a delicate insight on our part will be corrected by the real presence of the persons themselves as we discover and rediscover them in our reading. But I have a suspicion (reinforced by Professor Hardy's theme and by some of the things Professor Litz has said) that her achievement is even more remarkable than that, and feel that we should try to search out the compass of it – difficult though that may be when the achievement is apparently effortless, and the products of it have an impervious seamlessness.

I should like to suggest that Jane Austen is a poet in two senses: (1) in her craftsmanship in language; and (2) in the conduct of the action within each novel. In the first sense, we need to consider fine-grained detail with an ear alert to the dynamics of language; in the second, we are concerned with the disposition of forces within the whole universe of a novel, particularly that mutual definition of plot and character the product of which Aristotle called *drama*, the thing done, or what I may elsewhere – to distinguish it from the 'action' that is sheer motion – also call 'pure action'; the one sense discloses itself on a small scale, the other on a large scale. The evidence for each is of a particular kind, each different from the other. Yet both kinds or functions interact upon each other and can be seen to be poetic because both reside at the heart, or at the roots, of imaginative activity.

I shall not evolve my argument according to the convention that pretends that the conclusion follows necessarily from the evidence. The conclusion of a critical argument is always implicit in the premises, and in the selection and ordering of evidence that the premises direct. So I beg your indulgence to begin (as Aristotle says) 'with first things' – in this case with what I mean by 'poet', 'poetry' and 'imagination'. What I now have to say may be a bit dense, but I'll do the best I can with a topic too simple to be anything but unmanageable. The fact that Jane Austen may not have thought of these things in this way is, I think, neither here nor there.

I take it that imagination is not a 'faculty', but rather an integrated and potent state of the self – a *realising* condition, in which the self and the world are made real. I take it, correspondingly, that the word 'poetry' refers basically to a state of language, a condition qualitatively discernible but not analytically definable – or not yet; a state of language that is noticeably lucid, vivid, nervous, inventive, economical, often translucent, capable of swift movement. Incorrigibly a matter of words (and not dominantly of musical sounds), poetry is informed – or declares itself – by the inventive rhythms of a mind unfolding what cannot be known except in the uttering of it. The rhythms and tone are the indelible marks of energy and of the quality of impulse. To put it another way; poetry is language in the process of symbolising. By 'symbolising' I do not mean so much that poetry typically produces 'symbols' – those distinguishable images that tiresomely invite us to prodigies of allergorical exposition; rather, that 'symbolising' generates (or simply *is*) 'symbolic events', verbal events that are strongly resonant, in which words tend to assume tactual qualities and complex – even contradictory – upper partials of implication. Under the condition of poetry, language becomes 'musicalised'; it discovers – without renouncing the integrity of language – something like the condition of music, showing typically (as language otherwise seldom does) a capacity for swift unprepared change, modulation, variation, transition, and also a capacity for stillness and composure. In this state the logic of thought and grammar is not necessarily dismissed, but language tends to gravitate to a more primitive state, having an active commerce with the senses, and relying upon the intrinsic relations of collision and parataxis (the metaphorical function) and the pure physical interaction of the elements of language as spoken and listened to. 'Symbolising' is the antithesis of 'describing'; 'describing' is language in a scientific mode.

A 'poet', then, may be seen not simply as a manufacturer of verses, or of magniloquent strings of words, but – if we may trust the Greek root of the word – a *maker*, and specifically a maker in words. The art of poetry is a rather physical and forthright business, not devoid of intelligence, but having much to do with craftsmanship and the craftsman's respect for his materials. The gift is a supremely human one, not divine (except as far as some would hold that all our gifts are of divine origin). We are not actually capable of *creating*; we select and arrange what is given to us (though the source may be obscure or totally unknown); a poet allows and encourages promising elements – words and rhythms usually – to assume form, to move in an ordered manner. On the whole, the more intense the poetry, the less mellifluous it is. As David Jones has said, a poet has to use what is around the place, and he can make true poetry only of what he knows and loves. The need to know makes a poet an accurate and patient observer; his love prevents his knowing from stopping short in description. 'Naming' – the affectionate telling-over of things as a liturgy of wonder – is one of the richest subordinate resources of poetry.

A novelist needs a talent for telling a story that a lyrical poet does not need; and his choice of the harmony of prose, and the lengths that prose may drive him to, make demands on him that an epic poet, or perhaps even a writer of formal history, would not encounter. Yet, whatever imaginative universe the novelist may encompass or seek to encompass, the reality and command of it will stand or fall by the quality of his making, and the quality of his wording. The whole thing has to be made in words – not least the characters. The 'better' the wording – that is, the more exactly proper to what in the end proves to have been necessary – the more the novel becomes (like a poem) self-subsistent and self-declarative, depending least upon the person of the novelist even though it must all occur in his mind and will be coloured by it; and probably depending very little upon the author's personal wounds and longings. But language is an unruly servant, especially if roughly handled, being no passive instrument. In the end it will have its way of all imperious masters, will stick out an impish tongue at whatever orotund spaces in the rhetoric it has been forced to set echoing, and at any emotional overindulgence it has been obliged to collude in. Good writing, of whatever kind, seems always to have come into existence as its own utterance, speaking in a conceivable voice, finding its wording as an act of grace. If I think of a novelist as a 'poet', I think of one (certainly) who lives in an imaginative universe that is rooted in life and the ways of human life; but his universe is also haunted by words, shaped by utterances. If these seem large claims, Jane Austen may be allowed her say – even though it comes from an early book and a hilarious setting.

> 'And what are you reading, Miss——?' 'Oh! it is only a novel!' replies the young lady; while she lays down her book with affected indifference, or momentary shame. – 'It is only Cecilia, or Camilla, or Belinda'; or, in short, only some work in which the most thorough knowledge of human nature, the happiest delineation of its varieties, the liveliest effusions of wit and humour are conveyed to the world in the best chosen language. (*NA*, p. 38)

Jane Austen, as far as I know, made no claim for herself as a poet: and I am not trying to show that she was something that she had no idea of being. My concern is simply to allow us to enter into the unique universes of her imagining, and to dwell there if we wish. There would certainly be some danger in expanding the concept of poetry to embrace everything effectively conducted in words (? Newton's *Principia Mathematica*, for example). But the danger of extending 'poetry' some way into the usually acknowledged realm of prose seems to me easier to accept than the distortions that occur when we try to define the novel as though it were absolutely distinct from all other imaginative makings-in-words. Many have called Jane Austen a great artist; I have no quarrel with that. But 'artist' is an elusive term, and 'poet' – if we insist on the word's having an indissoluble connection with language – may serve us better in trying to draw a bounding-line around the specific qualities of Jane Austen's work.

That should provide some sort of setting for the first sense of the word 'poet'. Now, to take a fresh nip and consider the second sense.

Whateley, Macaulay and Lewes, all at an early date, ascribed to Jane Austen an exceptional flair for drawing characters, for discriminating them one from another and presenting them 'dramatically' – that is, in speaking-parts; the 'fools' (or 'noodles', as Lewes liked to call them) they found especially praiseworthy, as though they somehow served a function only loosely connected with the novels in which they found themselves.[3] So impressed were they with Jane Austen's ability in drawing characters that they said it was 'Shakespearean', and Lewes called her a 'Prose Shakespeare'. Richard Simpson, himself a Shakespearean scholar, courteously noticed that it was Heywood who had some time earlier been called the 'Prose Shakespeare', but he agreed that 'Miss Austen much more really deserves the title.' Lewes however had reservations – Jane Austen, he said, sometimes speaks 'through the *personae*', she lacks passion, she has no interest in the picturesque. Simpson had reservations too: 'within her range her characterization is truly Shakespearean; but she has scarcely a spark of poetry'.[4] Having made an important observation, they let the virtue of it slip through their fingers: they seem to have said no more than that at character-drawing she is very good indeed, almost as good as Shakespeare, but of course she really is not so big or grand or poetical as he was – and she did write in prose, you know. If her 'Shakespearean' quality is to be taken as a specific indication, we can give it more point by noticing what Coleridge found impressive about Shakespeare. He rejoiced as much as anybody else in the variety and life-likeness of Shakespeare's characters, and marvelled at the copiousness of his invention. But two things that struck him just as forcibly were these: that none of Shakespeare's characters seemed in any way a projection of Shakespeare himself, and were not drawn naturalistically from the life; and that Shakespeare was never guilty of 'ventriloquism', of speaking deceptively through his characters in his own person. These, I am sure, are also specific qualities in Jane Austen, and we have taken a step forward.

Again, it is a pity to let the just claim for Jane Austen's 'dramatic' power dissolve into no more than a statement that she could call forth a wide variety of lifelike characters and let them talk themselves into existence. Certainly she did that – triumphantly – but what else? Edwin Muir, in his account of the kind of novel he calls 'dramatic', takes us a long step forward, not least because here he is writing about Jane Austen and not about Shakespeare.

> There is in her novels, in the first place, a confinement to one circle, one complex of life, producing naturally an intensification of action; and this intensification is one of the essential attributes of the dramatic novel. In the second place, character is to her no longer a thing merely to delight in . . . . It has consequences. It influences events; it creates difficulties and later, in different circumstances, dissolves them . . . . The balance of all the forces within the novel creates and moulds the plot. There is no external framework, no merely mechanical plot; all is character, and all is at the same time action . . . .
>
> Where this plot [in *Pride and Prejudice*] differs from the plot of a novel of action is in its strict interior causation . . . . The correspondence in a novel of this kind between the action and the characters is so essential that one can hardly find terms to describe it without appearing to exaggerate; one might say that a change in the situation always involves a change in the characters, while every change, dramatic or psychological, external or internal, is either caused or given its form by something in both.[5]

This account of Jane Austen's procedure sounds very much like a direct application of Aristotle's view of tragedy to the conduct of prose fiction. The sources of individual action are internal; a man becomes what he does; the plot is a function of the characters, the characters are continuously changed by the plot but also determine it; the overt plot and the characters – what is done by whom, to whom and why – is not the end (or purpose) of the piece but an aspect of what defines the intricate and finely traced arc of pure action, allows the configuration of action to be traced out in physically discernible and humanly intelligible terms. Aristotle's view of tragedy is dynamic and radical; there is nothing in it to support the weak behaviourist assumption of a 'tragic flaw'; there is no place in it for the arbitrary intervention of the gods of fate; it is inflexibly human; the protagonist is *not* called a 'hero'; least of all does the *Poetics* itself support the notion that Aristotle provided (as the Italians seem to have thought and as many thoughtless instructors continue to suppose) a check-list of the required ingredients for cooking a tragedy. In any case, a cockpit-check tells us whether it is safe to fly; it does not tell us that we are flying, or how well. Aristotle emphatically and repeatedly affirms the indivisible dynamic relation between plot and character. In the fragmentary form in which the *Poetics* has come down to us, he pays much more attention to plot than to character – not because he was thinking of a kind of play different from Shakespeare's or from ours, but because he saw both plot and character as operating as instrumental rather than as an end. His central perception was of an action – a *drama*, a 'pure action' – that plot and character together delineate: the drama traced out by the whole play was what made tragedy specifically tragic. What we had to say about the specific *drama* of comedy is lost to us, but that doesn't bother me much at the moment.

To those of us who are in the habit of thinking of the 'action' in a novel or play or film as the overt (and preferably sensational) things that the people do or have done to them, the internality of Aristotle's view of the nature and sources of tragedy will probably seem a bit esoteric. But Aristotle's view of dramatic action is all of a piece with his ethical view of the sources of human action. And Coleridge, in all his reflections upon moral and dramatic values, also insists upon the internality, the self-originating nature of action; we cannot without damage go behind the statement 'I act'; it is always an 'I' acting, decisively and irreversibly; restraint from action can therefore be an act. He is acutely aware of the bond between action and passion, between doing and being done to, and of the correlation of action and passion in any one person. That actions are literally coloured by what informs them – be it will, desire, impulse or lyrical self-realisation – he is in no doubt; and it is upon these axioms of the nature of human action that his judgement of plays and novels (among many other things) turns; on these grounds he chose Fielding above Richardson, and admired *Tom Jones* as inordinately as anybody ever has. For Coleridge, as I am sure would be the case for Jane Austen if she ever ventured into philosophical discourse, 'moral' and 'aesthetic' are not mutually exclusive terms; he remembered that the root of the word 'aesthetics' is not 'beauty' or 'artistic form', but 'feeling' and 'perception'. If Coleridge sometimes gets into difficulties with the exposition of these intangible home-truths, it is largely because he rejected the whole regressive logic of 'motives', 'drives' and compulsions; like Aristotle he saw 'cause' in the fulfilment of the end. It may take a little effort to adopt a non-behavioural view of character and plot, but I think that we are ill-advised not to try.

As a preliminary propositon, then, I suggest that Jane Austen's novels can fruitfully be regarded as 'poems', in some such sense as I have already unfolded. As long as a novel is considered to be a genuine imaginative construction, the 'fictions' of the novel – whether the doings and happenings, the episodes, places or persons – will be apprehended as 'real' rather than actual, as of universal rather than general import; and we shall expect to see fictional particulars transformed (through the virtue of their particularity) into aspects of universal human values. The test of 'reality' is not whether the episodes and persons represent – or could conceivably represent – actual events and persons, but whether the symbolic transformation into real persons and places and events occurs or not. (Plausibility is a matter of internal judgement, not of sociological generalisation.) Symbolic transformation, I suppose, occurs in the author's mind; but it must occur in physical terms in the body of the book, in the wording and ordonnance of it and not simply in what the words depict. What the actors can be seen to do and suffer is not the end or purpose of the writing, firmly though the actors may command our attention; these are the physical aspects of what allows the arc of pure action, the *drama*, to be traced out in a discernible manner.

Jane Austen was evidently a conscious, perceptive and highly skilled craftsman: in her work, in spite of her exuberance, nothing seems ever to depend upon accident of improvisation; her writing, like her most memorable young ladies, is clear-eyed and of a fine complexion. She said herself, playfully but truly, that 'An artist cannot do anything slovenly' (*Letters*, p. 30). She found her mastery by choosing firm foundations for her style and by writing a great deal from the age of fifteen onward, first of all writing for her family, an audience that shared her sense of fun. From very early on, when she was writing she was listening, judging, refining, attuning, until her pen – which she was incapable of handling clumsily – responded, with the sensitiveness of a gold-leaf electrometer, to that fertile indirection of the mind that (at a loss for terms) we sometimes call 'imagination', and sometimes 'thought', and sometimes 'intention'. Among the six novels that she published there is no performance that can justly be called juvenile or tentative.

The first sense in which Jane Austen's writing can be seen as 'poetic', her verbal craftsmanship or wordsmithery (her particular achievement being of the order of what Coleridge called 'logodaedaly' or 'sleight of words'), falls within the field of what is usually called 'style'. Her style has been examined perceptively by more than one scholar, but not (I think) definitively; and to think of her as a poet is bound to put a sharper and more selective edge than has been customary upon the inquiry into her style.

In saying that Jane Austen is a 'poet' in her handling of words, I do not mean that she writes continuously in a manner that we should agree was noticeably 'poetic'. She has at her disposal the full scope of prose, from plain factual narrative and description to the most refined resources of tone, implication, allusive nuance, pace and emphasis. None of this falls outside the theoretical limits of poetry – if we accept for 'poetry' post-Johnsonian criteria that Jane Austen herself might not have had consciously in mind. Being a poet, she reserves the privilege of making her language 'poetical' only when it needs to be; writing in prose, and not insisting to herself that she is a poet, she has the immense advantage of not feeling all the time on her shoulders the oppressive weight of singing-robes. And yet, even though her language may not be always and recognisably 'musicalised', it seems always to be on the fringes of the musical, capable of moving in and out of the musical state with an effortless rapidity that we associate with the musical state itself. Having established for herself a very small range of rhetorical effects, the slightest variation of tone, pace or activity is immediately noticeable; and we become aware of an undercurrent of verbal possibilities that – breaking the surface and disappearing again – engage us with shocks of delight and recognition. For example, we have the general impression that the staple of Jane Austen's prose is the short, crisp, translucent sentence; but she is no Hemingway. The length and structure of her sentences adapt themselves instantly to local and particular need; whether it is the sinewy suppleness of syntax that can embrace the exact shade of an ironic aside or the lizard-turn of an epigram; or unfold comfortably and at length, as in the long, fervent, almost helter-skelter, self-unfolding sentence in which she measures out the breadth and depth of Fanny Price's love for her sailor brother William (*MP*, pp. 234-5). With her pen, Jane Austen is as dainty as a needle-worker, as purposeful as an axeman.

Let us begin with small things, because Jane Austen, like any poet worth his salt, has a passion for precision. Miss Lascelles notices the force of her 'pregnant abstractions' (of Johnsonian lineage)[6] – Miss Bates's 'desultory good will' (*E*, p. 239; cf. 'ignorant good will' in Yeats's 'Easter 1916'), the basket and big bonnet that constitute for Mrs Elton the 'apparatus of happiness' (*E*, p. 358), and how Sir Walter and his two ladies step forward to greet Lady Dalrymple 'with all the eagerness compatible with anxious elegance' (*P*, p. 184). In such phrases the adjective ceases to act as a mere modifier: like a barber methodically stroking the razor across the palm of his hand, it gives the final honing touch to the edge of humour or irony; multiple implications suddenly build up and hover over the phrase. The pregnant abstraction had its gradations. When Anne walks up to the Lodge 'in a sort of desolate tranquillity', or Mary Musgrove, at the prospect of visiting Kellynch after the Crofts have taken possession of it, is 'in a very animated, comfortable state of imaginary agitation' (*P*, pp. 36, 48), the phrases are not much more than sharply descriptive; when we read of Mrs Allen's 'busy idleness' (*NA*, p. 67), or of 'the business of love-making' that happily relieves the company of Mr Collins's presence (*P&P*, p. 129), or of the 'short parley of compliment' between Henry Crawford and Mr Yates (*MP*, p. 132) something more conspiratorial is afoot. When Mr Collins, in the early morning, bent upon proposing (fruitlessly) to Elizabeth Bennet, escapes from Longbourn House 'with admirable slyness' (*P&P*, p. 121), the phrase resonates; and so it does (but this time with a mocking hint of a cosmic perspective) when Edmund corrects Mary's extravagant estimate of the distance they have walked – 'for he was not yet so much in love as to measure distance, or reckon time, with feminine lawlessness' (*MP*, p. 94). These short phrases, that come suddenly into view and hover for an instant like a dragonfly or a hummingbird and are gone, may stand for irrepressible flashes of humour; but they are also symptoms of strong poetic potential that hums like a fiddle-string below the surface of her apparently decorous prose. The underlying process here is true metaphor: the collision of elements none of which will give up any part of its integrity. The gift for metaphor is peculiarly the poet's gift, and cannot be learned. That it was part of Jane Austen's habit of mind can be seen in her letters, and the effect is not always funny. For example, 'Single Women have a dreadful propensity for being poor – which is one very strong argument in favour of Matrimony' (*Letters*, p. 483); she says of Mrs Cooke, who is perhaps dying of an inflammation of the lungs induced by a chill taken in church, that 'her mind [is] all pious composure, as may be supposed' (p. 245); when her brother is afflicted by the death of his wife, Jane writes to Edward Cooper, hoping that he will not send her brother 'one of his letters of cruel comfort' (p. 222). When she herself is about to venture the journey to Winchester to be treated for her mortal illness, she describes herself as 'a very genteel, portable sort of an Invalid' (p. 494).

In this, we are considering not simply a verbal locution or 'figure of speech' but a commanding process radical to poetry itself – the metaphorical process that secures and enriches the interaction not only of single words, but of elements within sentences, of sentences within paragraphs, and the collisive interaction of elements of much larger scale if they can be constructed with strong-enough identity. Not only do Jane Austen's sentences adapt themselves exquisitely to their syntactical needs, but they also characteristically give the impression of shaping energy contained within deftly chosen limits – which is another indelible mark of poetic practice. On the writer's part this calls up, not simply an alertness to the interactions of the words themselves, but also the sense of musical phrasing. If the metaphorical process gives active substance (as it does at crucial points in Wordsworth's poems) to words that would otherwise be vague abstractions, the sense of phrasing of musical inflection gives body to the most minute movements of mind. Speaking in her own person, she can say of a Mr Wildman who (despite Fanny's advocacy) could see nothing in Jane's novels, 'I particularly respect him for wishing to think well of all young Ladies; it shews an amiable & a delicate Mind' (*Letters*, p. 487).

Jane Austen's impeccable sense of phrasing is a more distinctive mark of her style than her use of the isolable pregnant phrase; and she can impart this to the entirely different voice of one of her characters – for example, Mr Bennet speaking to Elizabeth:

'Next to being married, a girl likes to be crossed in love a little now and then. . . . Now is your time. Here are officers enough at Meryton to disappoint all the young ladies in the country.

> Let Wickman be *your* man. He is a pleasant fellow, and would jilt you creditably.' (*P&P*, pp. 137–8)

She says of Mr Collins that 'The stupidity with which he was favoured by nature, must guard his courtship from any charm that could make a woman wish for its continuance' (p. 122); and of Mrs Allen that she was 'one of that numerous class of females, whose society can raise no other emotion than surprise at there being any men in the world who could like them well enough to marry them' (*NA*, p. 20). In these there is a hovering understatement reinforced by a sequence of double negatives actual or implied – an effect that is scarcely to be discerned in a logical analysis of the wording. When Elinor thinks of Willoughby,

> She felt that his influence over her mind was heightened by circumstances which ought not in reason to have weight; by that person of uncommon attraction, that open, affectionate, and lively manner which it was no merit to possess; and by that still ardent love for Marianne, which it was not even innocent to indulge. (*S&S*, p. 333)

We catch a lighter timbre in the account of Catherine Morland:

> in many other points she came on exceedingly well; for though she could not write sonnets, she brought herself to read them; and though there seemed no chance of her throwing a whole party into raptures by a prelude on the pianoforte, of her own composition, she could listen to other people's performance wth very little fatigue. (*NA*, p. 16)

The representation of Edmund's scrupulous hesitation in confronting his father with what he knows will be a pretty shaky excuse for not stopping the theatrical high jinks that he had himself disapproved of as strongly as he knew his father would – this is managed with superlative allusiveness:

> Edmund's first object the next morning was to see his father alone, and give him a fair statement of the whole acting scheme, defending his own share in it as far only as he could then, in a soberer moment, feel his motives to deserve, and acknowledging with perfect ingenuousness that his concession

had been attended with such partial good as to make his
judgement in it very doubtful. (*MP*, p. 187)

As has often been noticed, a favourite device of Jane Austen's –
learned no doubt from Dr Johnson – is the antithesis. Antithesis
can easily pass over into metaphorical process, and for Jane
Austen often does; and with meditative ease and stylistic assurance
she can extend an antithesis in great variety of shape and range
of complexity to give form to some of her most brilliantly
constructed sentences. For example, the account of John Dash-
wood at the beginning of *Sense and Sensibility*:

> He was not an ill-disposed young man, unless to be rather cold
> hearted, and rather selfish, is to be ill-disposed: but he was, in
> general, well respected; for he conducted himself with propriety
> in the discharge of his ordinary duties. Had he married a more
> amiable woman, he might have been made still more respectable
> than he was: – he might even have been made amiable himself;
> for he was very young when he married, and very fond of his
> wife. But Mrs John Dashwood was a strong caricature of
> himself; – more narrow-minded and selfish. (p. 5)

Sometimes she will extend an antithesis (as perhaps here) to a
third term like an Alexandrine reaching out for its sixth foot; and
with a playful flick at the tip of the tail turn the antithesis into
an outrageous zeugma. For example, in *Mansfield Park*:

> Tom Bertram must have been thought pleasant, indeed, at
> any rate, he was the sort of young man to be generally liked,
> his agreeableness was of the kind to be oftener found agreeable
> than some endowments of a higher stamp, for he had easy
> manners, excellent spirits, a large acquaintance, and a great
> deal to say . . . . (p. 47)

Or in the response to Mrs Churchill's death in *Emma*:

> The great Mrs Churchill was no more.
> It was felt as such things must be felt. Everybody had a
> degree of gravity and sorrow; tenderness towards the departed,
> solicitude for the surviving friends; and, in a reasonable time,
> curiosity to know where she would be buried. (p. 387)

The antithesis may be diffused, as in an aside in *Sense and Sensibility*:

> Lady Middleton was equally pleased with Mrs Dashwood.
> There was a kind of cold hearted selfishness on both sides,
> which mutually attracted them; and they sympathised with
> each other in an insipid propriety of demeanour, and a general
> want of understanding.   (p. 229)

Elsewhere it may be infused with something like the plausible
realism of Mistress Quickly's brainless inconsequence:

> [Mrs Allen's] vacancy of mind and incapacity for thinking
> were such, that as she never talked a great deal, so she could
> never be entirely silent; and, therefore, while she sat at her
> work, if she lost her needle or broke her thread, if she heard a
> carriage in the street, or saw a speck upon her gown, she must
> observe it aloud, whether there were any one at leisure to
> answer her or not.   (*NA*, p. 60)

The model for startling anticlimax can be seen in the juvenile
'Memoirs of Mr Clifford':

> he was a very rich young Man & kept a great many Carriages
> of which I do not recollect half. I can only remember that he
> had a Coach, a Chariot, a Chaise, a Landeau, a Landeaulet,
> a Phaeton, a Gig, a Whisky, an italian Chair, a Buggy, a
> Curricle & a wheelbarrow.   (*MW*, vi, 43)

In its mature development, this figure can have the effect of a
small land-mine, cunningly concealed, with a long-burning fuse.
Of Mrs Palmer:

> The openness and heartiness of her manner, more than atoned
> for that want of recollection and elegance, which made
> her often deficient in the forms of politeness; her kindness,
> recommended by so pretty a face, was engaging; her folly,
> though evident, was not disgusting, because it was not
> conceited; and Elinor could have forgiven every thing but her
> laugh.   (*S&S*, p. 304)

Or of Sir Walter Elliot:

Vanity was the beginning and the end of Sir Walter Elliot's character; vanity of person and of situation. He had been remarkably handsome in his youth; and, at fifty-four, was still a very fine man. Few women could think more of their personal appearance than he did; nor could the valet of any new made lord be more delighted with the place he held in society. He considered the blessing of beauty as inferior only to the blessing of a baronetcy; and the Sir Walter Elliot, who united these gifts, was the constant object of his warmest respect and devotion. (*P*, p. 4)

By a similar process a plain gnomic statement can be suddenly shifted from the world of eternal truisms to the universe of eternal verities, achieving a sort of meditative grandeur.

Seldom, very seldom, does complete truth belong to any human disclosure; seldom can it happen that something is not a little disguised, or a little mistaken; but where, as in this case, though the conduct is mistaken, the feelings are not, it may not be very material. (*E*, p. 431)

There is a salutary reminder for us in what she said to her beloved niece Fanny Knight: 'Wisdom is better than Wit, & in the long run will certainly have the laugh on her side' (*Letters*, p. 410). It may be this recognition that imparts a tinge of elegiac sobriety to the closing paragraph of the last letter we have from Jane Austen's pen – at parting, a little smiling gesture in recognition of her love of life.

You will find Captain — a very respectable, well-meaning man, without much manner, his wife and sister all good humour and obligingness, and I hope (since the fashion allows it) with rather longer petticoats than last year. (*Letters*, p. 498)

We cannot doubt that much of what imparts electrical vitality to Jane Austen's style was her delight in effortless virtuosity, in catching by an impossible fraction of a hair's-breadth the savour of a nuance of implication. I do not wish to venture into the discrimination of minute syntactical categories, and leave to the ingenuity of keener taxonomists than myself the following extracts from her letters.

Mr Heathcote met with a genteel little accident the other day in hunting; he got off to lead his horse over a hedge or a house or a something, & his horse in his haste trod upon his leg, or rather ankle I believe, & it is not certain whether the small bone is not broke.   (p. 85)

I hope it is true that Edward Taylor is to marry his cousin Charlotte. Those beautiful dark Eyes will then adorn another Generation at least in all their purity.   (p. 87)

I give you joy of our new nephew, & hope if he ever comes to be hanged, it will not be till we are too old to care about it.   (p. 272)

[Mr Blackall] was married at Clifton to a Miss Lewis, whose Father had been late of Antigua. I should very much like to know what sort of a Woman she is. He was a piece of Perfection, noisy Perfection himself which I always recollect with regard. . . . I would wish Miss Lewis to be of a silent turn & rather ignorant, but naturally intelligent & wishing to learn; – fond of cold veal pies, green tea in the afternoon, & a green window blind at night.   (p. 317)

Miss H[arding] is an elegant, pleasing, pretty-looking girl, about nineteen, I suppose, or nineteen and a half, or nineteen and a quarter, with flowers in her head and music at her finger ends.   (p. 282)

We plan having a steady Cook, & a young giddy Housemaid, with a sedate, middle aged Man, who is to undertake the double office of Husband to the former & sweetheart to the latter. – No Children of course to be allowed on either side.   (pp. 99–100)

Old Philmore was buried yesterday, & I, by way of saying something to Triggs, observed that it had been a very handsome Funeral, but his manner of reply made me suppose that it was not generally esteemed so. I can only be sure of *one* part being very handsome, Triggs himself, walking behind in his Green Coat.   (pp. 488–9)

A consideration of what looked like a small figure of speech has tendrilled out to embrace most of the nervous web of Jane Austen's prose style – a style so highly charged with energy that the very restraint with which it is commanded makes us aware of a steady (though often submerged) high potential for felicity. Whatever characteristic turn of phrase we may choose, we may find variant examples of it in abundance, but not uniformly distributed either within single novels, or from novel to novel. She can call up these resources whenever occasion demands, with every gradation from plain declaration to high-spirited nonsense, from sharp irony to sombre reflection; or she can refrain from using any of them, so that the alterations from use to restraint become a principle of structure that identifies each of the novels in its own way. Her rendering of individual direct speech (with very few exceptions) is – in identity, tone and pace – flawless. After *Sense and Sensibility* she never again tried to reproduce idiosyncratic phrasing or pronunciation as she did for the pretentious speech of the 'ignorant and illiterate' Lucy Steele; and, if the failure of General Tilney turns upon Jane's failure to find his own voice for him, that too is in an early book. I admire particularly her secure handling of the arcane liturgical usage of naval persons. About her uncanny skill in discovering, without recourse to idiosyncrasy, the precise and recognisable identity of voice for each of her persons, nothing need be said: most of the admirers of Jane Austen's novels are so absorbed in her characters that they could probably, on request, produce the precise inflection of any one of them. As though it were not enough to be able to induce her characters to speak in their own persons, she can make transitions from her own narrative to the indirect speech of her characters, or to the thought of her characters, so effortlessly that it is often difficult to decide in a particular passage whether or not it is her own comment that we are reading. Even when she does speak in her own person, as she often does, that too is usually so deftly 'placed' that it feels less like an intrusion of the omniscient author than a strain in a half-oracular counterpoint of disembodied and wise intelligence.

Another mark of her overarching poetic instinct is to be seen in her handling of detail, economically and vividly, so that actual things at times glow under her eye – a process that I have called 'naming', which, in the perceiving as in the writing, turns upon the vitality of concreteness – what Henry James admirably called 'solidity of specification'. The detail of the contents of Fanny Price's east room in Mansfield Park is an outstanding instance; so too is the detail of Harriet's pathetic little love-trove in *Emma*. Jane recognised the process in actual life when Fanny Knight told her how strangely moved she was, when she went to her lover's room after he had gone away and saw there his 'dirty Shaving Rag' – Jane cried, 'exquisite! – Such a circumstance ought to be in print. Much too good to be lost' (*Letters*, p. 412). For she knew that simple items, told over, almost liturgically, apparently at random, can – in a novel, as in 'life' – be coloured by the consciousness of the person who names them. These items, remaining simply what they are and nothing else, can yet vibrate with an aura of implication in the very act of their being so named, so told over, so noted with solid specification. (There is a heart-rending instance of this process in James Agee's *Let Us Now Praise Famous Men* – in the catalogue of what he found in one room of the share-cropper's house after the family had gone out to work.) This is very different from 'describing' (in any accepted use of that term), as Jane shows when she criticised Anna Austen's novel: 'You describe a sweet place, but your descriptions are often more minute than will be liked. You give too many particulars of right hand & left' (*Letters*, p. 401; cf. p. 78). Describing is a matter of exhaustive delineation; naming is a matter of selective and allusive symbolising: in painting, we see the coincidence of the two perhaps in Canaletto or Vermeer.

But the process of 'naming' applies not only to objects but to the whole sub-symbolic indication of places and of the things contained within them; not simply providing a physical setting in which action can occur, but evoking obliquely from the outset the relations of persons to things, places and other persons, and also establishing the disposition of the persons in physical space and in psychic space. For Jane Austen, the action more often than not unfolds crucially in the enclosedness of a house, a room. We could probably not draw an accurate plan of any of the houses or rooms; yet we feel sure that we could probably move about in them confidently in the dark, as persons familiar and hospitably received. Outstanding instances of the discovery of living figures in a domestic space are to be seen in *Mansfield Park*, where we hear the lovers talking quietly to each other in a room where others are present, a room large enough that they are not overheard, yet intimate enough that at any moment they may be drawn into any of the other rings of conversation that we are aware – as the lovers are – are reverberating at the same time; in the staircase encounter between Fanny and Edmund that Virginia Woolf admired; in the closing scene of *Persuasion*, the evocativeness of which could scarcely have been guessed from the first draft.

I am inclined to think that this same process of 'naming' that evocatively expands from objects to the relation of persons to objects, to a domestic space and the persons related there, applies also to the way Jane Austen draws – and draws forth – her characters: they have, at best, a 'solidity of specification' that allows them to disclose themselves as living, capable of going on surprising us, because they contain within themselves the reason why they are what they are and not otherwise. Like the objects vividly perceived, they have their own peculiar aura of presence. In the same way that we imagine that we could move about in any of Jane Austen's darkened houses, we find in our imagination that the people of her imagining grow in substance, weight and complexity far beyond the particular limits that her economical art has assigned to them in her novels. They have the tactual solidity that can also, in the condition of poetry, be physically imprinted in words.

In *Mansfield Park*, for a time, the sisters Julia and Maria became so sundered from one another that 'there was no outward fellowship between them'; 'They were two solitary sufferers, or connected only by Fanny's consciousness' (*MP*, p. 163). The unifying force in Jane Austen's writing is the unity of her consciousness, subtle, patient, watchful, profound enough to imprint in her memory the most delicate shades of feeling, the most fugitive and ambivalent of emotions. One of Edward's younger daughters recalled how her aunt Jane 'would sit quietly working [i.e. doing needlework] beside the fire in the library, saying nothing for a good while, and then would suddenly burst out laughing, jump up and run across the room to a table where pens and paper were lying, write something down, and then come back to the fire and go on quietly working as before'. On this passage, Miss Lascelles makes this comment:

> She must have developed to a remarkable degree her faculty for living (when she chose) apart in her imagined world – and, further, for keeping the regions of that world distinct in her

imagination. To be engaged at once on *Pride and Prejudice* and *Mansfield Park* – and that while still correcting the proofs of *Sense and Sensibility* – and to preserve entire the peculiar atmosphere of each – this is an achievement which shows that she could project her imagination into one or another of these fragile bubble worlds, and let it dwell here.[7]

Yet the worlds of *Mansfield Park*, *Emma* and *Persuasion* are not bubbles; they are (like Coleridge's nightmares) foot-thick realities, though gossamer-fine. An imagined world, poetically speaking, is a world fully realised. Jane's secretiveness in securing the integrity of her imagined worlds, even from the loving solicitude of her favourite sister Cassandra, is a clear sign of the substance of those worlds: they were vulnerable, but not evanescent; not until they found their final and proper body in words could they stand alone in our world. But the words that could be at once living and impregnable did not come to her easily or quickly. To begin with she had been sheltered by the responsive merriment she was lucky enough to find within her own populous family circle. The early novels – *Northanger Abbey*, *Sense and Sensibility*, *Pride and Prejudice* – though transformed from what they must first have been by the genius that came to her suddenly at Chawton, still rely upon the family convention, but less and less, and least of all in *Pride and Prejudice*. The ease and confidence given her as a writer by her family made her a much more daring writer than any of her contemporaries, especially her female contemporaries: she had discovered how to be lucky in writing, how to give full and risky rein to her exceptional gifts of intelligence, deep feeling and verbal virtuosity. She found how to land on her feet like a cat, and became confident that her verbal reflexes would not betray her daring. She could say to herself, 'You are comfortable because you are under command' (*E*, p. 368).

To insist too much upon Jane Austen as a *comic* writer – even though she is often extremely funny – is to distract attention from the emotional depth and moral scope of her mature work. At times in the early novels she may be tempted into a shrewd nip of sarcastic or satirical comment; but that is not her true bent. Irony – that rarest of all gifts in a writer, a manner that nobody can fabricate – is a habit of her way of seeing, encompassing compassion and grief as well as humour. If irony, in the early novels, is often not much more than a figure of speech, in the mature novels it is the mark of Jane's steady presence behind her pen. *Le style est l'homme.* She is at once a most self-effacing writer, and – as a presence – most pervasive: an unassuming voice, a central reverberating timbre. In this, she is indeed Shakespearean, Chaucerian. For she wrote with the gravity of a born humorist, out of a life that had known its own peculiar sorrows and immedicable desolations.

As for Jane Austen's conduct of overarching drama and the interaction of plot and character, I must be content with a few general observations – because I feel that I may be sickening for a book on Jane Austen. In this there are copious possibilities for disagreement; but Jane never hesitated to take chances, and I think we should honour her instinct. One thing, however, needs to be noted at the outset: the firm singleness of her angle of vision, imparting unquestionable authority to her omniscience; she never resorts to the comfortable convenience of the zoom-lens or the undisciplined confidence-trickery of fluid camera-movement.

In spite of the singleness and rapidity of her progress as a writer, I find in reading the novels that the first three stand in one group – *Northanger Abbey, Sense and Sensibility, Pride and Prejudice* – and *Mansfield Park, Emma* and *Persuasion* in another. *Mansfield Park* is, I think, her great masterpiece: here all the forces are so beautifully disposed, the energy so exquisitely distributed, that even the manifestations of her poetic style (never ornate) scarcely break the surface. I shall therefore in a swift summary try to bring into focus the two poetic senses that I had distinguished at the outset.

Northanger Abbey is informed (to some extent, but not as much as we should like) by that same mode of joyous parody and exuberant burlesque that makes most of the juvenilia in Chapman's volume VI a delight to savour. She may have learned much from the prose style of Dr Johnson and the essayists, and a little from William Cowper; but in this book we meet the gift of a sunny and generous humour that, once fully assimilated into her whole tone of voice and way of seeing, was to become the hallmark of her sanity and penetration. *Northanger Abbey* is a parody of many things, but above all a parody of a certain kind of novel and of the emotional response that was expected to such novels. It is good fun in places, but the high spirits fail to establish their own centre of gravity and become (fatally for this novel) entangled with 'life'; this makes functional demands of General

Tilney that, because of the indistinctness of his nature in the early part of the book, he cannot fulfil – even though he provides one of the most astonishing reversals of expectation in the whole of Jane Austen's writing. At best *Northanger Abbey* is a sort of *Donna Quixote*, without Sancho Panza or Rosinante; and Catherine Morland is silly rather than crazy. Nevertheless, if we are searching out the quality and disposition of Jane Austen's verbal-poietic resources, this book rewards careful attention, for many of the effects lie on the surface.

Sense and Sensibility, although it may have been transformed from an original written in the burlesque manner, is her first attempt at a serious 'novel'. Witty, incisive, at times ironic, at times tender, it makes both play and capital of current expectations about a novel, and particularly about a woman's novel. The resources of a supple and disciplined prose style are here – flexible, epigrammatic if need be, capable of responding to a light touch and of moving with unpredictable swiftness. Her love of parody and a habit of self-mockery have made her a daring, as well as a cunning, navigator; she is finding how to dispose her strongest effects in understatement and obliquity, thereby not only establishing her rhetorical palette for much maturer use, but also drawing the reader from the position of observer to the quiet attentiveness of a confidante. Irony and reticence combine in an undercurrent of active intelligence and emotional precision; everything is on a small scale, the texture exquisite, the tone muted. Yet, for all that can be said in praise of detail and effects, the mastery is not yet assured. There are thin passages, places where inner tension flags and we find ourselves reading – at times (near the end) – out of respect rather than delight. The drawing of Marianne is perhaps tinged more with satire than with irony, the theme is more parabolic than the action can take in its stride, the story an expanded version of antithesis with the elements drawn to life size. She seems to have a point to make, not so much about society as about the relation between art and life. *Sense and Sensibility* is not usually regarded as a defective novel; yet it does, in ways difficult to define, fall short of self-sustaining perfection. It may be a question of her difficulty of combining at one stroke a variety of talents already developed. For all the signs of her genius are present: exhilaration, subtlety of effect, confident delight in the exercise of powers greater than the book calls for, the composure that goes with a knowledge deeper and more comprehensive than is allowed to appear on the surface, a habit of reticence that is much less a figurative device than the ironic exercise of intellectual good manners.

Pride and Prejudice opens *con brio*, with a crackling dramatic *panache* that *Sense and Sensibility* had not prepared us for. Even though the manuscript original of this book is earlier than the original of *Sense and Sensibility*, the book declares, from the very outset, a higher order of accomplishment and assurance. In every way, the advance of *Pride and Prejudice* is impressive, especially in the drawing of the complementary persons of Jane and Elizabeth. If at first Darcy seems, as a gruffer version of that fool Collins, unassimilable to the emotional probabilities of the story, he is in the end satisfactorily transformed into a man worthy to receive Elizabeth's hand; and Jane and Elizabeth are drawn with a depth that prevents the book from settling into the fable-with-a-moral that the title tempts us to expect. The only sign of uncertainty is in her failure to master what practically every novelist that came after her also failed to master – the self-conscious and disturbing awareness that she was writing a *novel*, that certain things were expected of a novel and of its story; even if she were to refrain from doing what was expected, she could not escape that expectation. Rewritten at a single impulse from the version that Cadell had rejected fifteen years earlier, *Pride and Prejudice* is justly esteemed among the small handful of best English novels. Distracted, it may be, by a certain publicity of intent, it is too deceptively effortless to encourage imitation, and is much too adult to be recommended to school-children. If Jane Austen had stopped writing there, she would be seen to have triumphed. But she could do even better than that; and did so, at once, in *Mansfield Park*.

To enjoy *Pride and Prejudice* we accept on trust certain moral conventions with ironic reservation, and with amused detachment observe a microtome slice of the *comédie humaine* so thin that – perhaps because of its very thinness – speaks for a central issue in life, marriage and money; we are allowed to entertain the possibility that the mark of parochial barbarism would be to pretend that the issue of marriage and money is a trivial one. In *Mansfield Park* something rather more compelling happens. Whether or not we accept the conventions, and whether or not we 'identify' with any of the persons in the story, is – as with most fully realised works of art – curiously irrelevant. We are drawn into an action of ineluctable internal power and logic, self-determinate, self-consistent; an action at once simple and complex which, without ever losing its way or checking its momentum, is held in an exquisite balance of composed forces, like the slow movement of a posthumous quartet. A finely articulated universe of feeling and implication grows out of the roots of the life peculiar to it, and reflects back upon life with a strong and penetrating light. There are stylistic and managerial similarities with the novels that came before, and with the two that were to follow; but *Mansfield Park* stands apart as different in kind, ordered from within as none of the others is. The clear identity of each volume gives the book exceptional interior strength and vitality. I have difficulty in reading it as a comedy. How she came upon this universe, constructed it and sustained it, we cannot say; it should not have been possible – or at least no more possible than to trace out the figure of tragedy itself. The book seems to have depended upon a very fragile imaginative poise; when she turned at once to write *Emma* she had lost it.

Jane Austen, like Milton, did not like to repeat herself; after each novel she moved forward to venture something that she had not attempted before. Much of the actual writing of *Emma* is, in detail, apparently more accomplished and of deeper implication than the general run of *Mansfield Park*: she explores, as she had not dared earlier, the intricate and paradoxical inner goings-on of a woman in love; from her love of symmetry, of correspondence and antithesis, of converging and diverging movements, she evolves a pattern almost geometrical in its disposition of internal forces; and with unruffled forthrightness she presents a group of people who from their first utterances give omen of the persons we are to find them to be. Yet the book as a whole is comparatively static, and I do not find Emma's threefold self-imposed ordeal of self-discovery enough of a moral escalation to make the book – as with protective zeal we might have hoped – a sort of *Emma Agonistes*. The luminous integration has gone slightly adrift; not breaking into disorder (for she was incapable of that), but to the subtle undermining of the total dramatic effect that can bring probability and necessity into one identity. Though there is more striking incident in this book than in anything earlier, *Emma* is deficient in commanding action, and feels like a fiction in a way that only *Northanger Abbey* does. Her sheer love of exercising her powers of dramatic invention even leads her at times into slight over-indulgence: some speeches of Miss Bates, though unsurpassed in autonomous vivacity, dislocate the swift apperception of the position Miss Austen has adopted, and interrupt 'the wonderful velocity of thought'. *Emma* is much admired, and rightly so; yet the closing chapter is the one place in all her novels where I feel that she is writing a little perfunctorily, with less respect for her reader than is her use; as though it could be said for the author, rather than for the actors, that all passion is spent.

Persuasion, in its smaller mass, is – like *Emma* – comparatively static, a study rather than a drama. The book was probably intended to be as it is; it is, of its kind, very fine, and is more trenchantly human than *Emma*. A dark emotional tone enfolds the central person (despite her vividness) and spreads through every incident and even into the landscape that Jane Austen is alleged to be insensitive to. The darkness feels as though it sprang from some deep personal source, an acute awareness of how some casual incident or circumstance – that nobody could have recognised as crucial and that could have been rescued only by exceptional vigilance or by grace – can prove to be a sorrowful, even irreversible, turning-point in a life; how in life (Rilke says of art) there are no classes for beginners. Anne's strength and sombre patience is surely Jane's; and, if the reversal of Captain Wentworth's regard seems artificially delayed for the purposes of the plot, and Mrs Smith's privileged information is so complete and accessible as to make her seem a very mundane *dea ex machina*, we can accept all that in gratitude for the disclosure of a heart and mind that we had often caught glimpses of in novels more high-spirited and apparently more superficial. In testing the veracity of our own perception, we may say that for Jane Austen the turning-point in the history of *her* heart came about not through misunderstanding or through accident of occasion, but through death. The darkness may come from life; but the mastery of a pervasive emotional tension flowing (in the novel) from a single experiencing centre, is itself a poetic achievement brought about through command of tonal consistency and the craftsmanship of a spare and finely modulated score. If Jane Austen can be seen as Mozartian, it is in her character that *Persuasion* should be her Clarinet Quintet.

Nothing would be more agreeable than to savour the details of *Mansfield Park*. But I must use despatch and can notice only in general terms some of the poetical features that strike me as essential to the unassuming but masterly conduct of this book. The opening chapter is forthright, abrupt, with an occasional asperity of tone that had not been heard even in *Pride and Prejudice*; it is stylised, urgent, without agreeable obliquity, setting the situation as swiftly and emphatically as possible. The opening is not much less formalised and impatient than the opening of *King Lear*; what is to happen must be seen at once to need to happen according to inner necessity. And, when we come to the end, the book closes with corresponding despatch, yet with something of the elegiac recognition of sheer necessity, not fading back into life but rounding this universe of her imagining to a close without regret. 'I only intreat every body to believe that exactly at the time when it was quite natural that it should be so, and not a week earlier, Edmund did cease to care about Miss Crawford, and became as anxious to marry Fanny, as Fanny herself could desire' (p. 470). Within the boundaries of the abrupt opening and closing of the story, Jane Austen moves with consummate ease so that for the most part we cannot tell the dancer from the dance. All those problems of technique, in securing both the autonomy of characters and the vocal omniscience of the author – problems that seem to have filled the hearts of the other novelists with dismay or turned them at times to grotesque extremes of ingenuity – she manages them all (as Virginia Woolf said with an entirely different import) with 'the swift composure of a fish'. For example, she can, without preparation, begin a monologue which is answered by a second speaker; and gradually we are aware of others present, and of the place, and the disposition of emotional forces at play there, and a whole complex tissue of relations unfolds. This is a feat that I had been led to suppose was Henry James's unique prerogative. Again, the strict constraints that she interposes to shape the energy of invention impart momentous dramatic weight with small effort. When, after the collapse of *Lovers' Vows*, Henry Crawford tells his sister that 'My plan is to make Fanny Price in love with me. . . . I cannot be satisfied without Fanny Price, without making a small hole in Fanny Price's heart' (p. 229), the effect is as shocking as if he were announcing a plan for cold-blooded rape.

I must not multiply examples. I wish to add only that in the poetic conduct of her language in *Mansfield Park*, and in her realising of a stylised plot in probable action, I am reminded of the unconstrained lyrical force of Cézanne's painting, in which naturalistic fidelity, a profound sense of underlying physical structure, and a purely abstract rendering of colour, mass and space combine in the felicity of an axiom. And in *Mansfield Park* I am often reminded too of Bartok's *Music for Strings, Percussion and Celeste*, constructed as it is upon one nerveless little five-note tune: spare, brilliant, inventive, eloquent.

But there is one other suggestion I have to make. It is universally accepted that Jane Austen is a 'comic' writer: she makes us laugh; she traces out (it is said) the foibles, follies and self-deceptions of a society strictly limited in locale and class. The standard scheme for comedy, however, whether on the stage or in a novel, is that it places more or less unchanging figures against a variable and changing social background. And Jane Austen's novels (though they are not all the same) do not match that scheme. In them, the people change within the confines of inflexible social convention, moral prescript and amatory mechanism; they have an acute, almost obsessive, internality; they are enclosed and confined. Edwin Muir (in the chapter from which I have already quoted) said that 'the dramatic novel need not be tragic, and the first novelist who practised it with consummate success in England – Jane Austen – consistently avoided and probably was quite incapable of sounding the tragic note'.[8] I wonder, however, whether we are correct in identifying 'the tragic note' as necessarily dark, disastrous, desolating. Is there no other way of bringing a sense of pity and fear to a state of exaltation – the pleasure peculiar to tragedy? Aristotle tells us that there were tragedies that had a prosperous outcome – by which I take it that he did not mean 'dark' tragedies with a happy ending, because for Aristotle the end is always implicit in the beginning. He evidently knew such tragedies, but none has come to us among the few survivors from the Greek theatre. Aristotle, with his intense concentration on the peculiar configuration of the tragic action and the integrity of it – the single figure the whole play traces – recognised that there were works that traced the specific arc of tragic action under the guidance of stories or plots that were not intrinsically disastrous. It is possible that Jane Austen may have achieved such a feat; not in all her books, to be sure, but in *Mansfield Park*?

I began by declaring my wonder at an achievement in language so marvellous that no term more trifling than 'poetry' could hope to encompass it. I have also hinted that in the dramatic conduct of her novels there may still be depths to be plumbed. Happy the critic of Jane Austen. She has given us plenty to think about, but, with impeccable decorum, she confronts us not with problems nor puzzles, but with marvels; her art is never importunate. If my praise seems excessive, I can reply only with the disclaimer she gave to a man whose coarse pomposity amused and disgusted her: 'I must make use of this opportunity to thank you, dear Sir, for the very high praise you bestow on my . . . novels. I am too vain to wish to convince you that you have praised them beyond their merits' (*Letters*, p. 442). And, if we ask how she did it, the reply seems to be given in *Emma*: 'What did she say? – Just what she ought, of course. A lady always does.'

8 Birthright to the Sea: Some Poems of E. J. Pratt*

You have accorded me a great privilege in inviting me to give the seventh lecture in honour of E. J. Pratt: I admired him as a man and admire his writing, and welcome this opportunity of saying so. I also want to thank you for the generous hospitality you have shown me on this visit, and particularly for the pleasure of spending a few days here after an absence of almost thirty years. To be able to look out to sea across the harbour entrance and go about the country a little and be able to listen to the inflections of Newfoundland speech – all this has called back many memories that I cherish of ships and ship-mates; and I think especially of a ship named *Spikenard*.

This occasion also allows me to acknowledge in his home port an act of hospitable generosity that Ned Pratt did for me and my son some years ago. In the early fall of 1962 Christopher had just turned thirteen; he was a member of the ship's company of the Kingston-built brigantine *St Lawrence II* and already showed himself well able to hand and reef and haul. I gave him a copy of the *Collected Poems* and posted it to Pratt in Toronto asking him to inscribe it, on the pretext that Christopher was also named Gilbert, to honour his descent (on my mother's side of the family) from the Humphrey Gilbert who in September 1583 'was devoured and swallowed up of the sea' in the *Squirrel* of ten tons at night in a tempest off the Azores. After several weeks the book came back inscribed, 'For Christopher Gilbert whose name is in the noble tradition of the sea. E. J. Pratt.' Soon afterwards I heard that Ned Pratt had just died after a long illness.

Pratt knew me only from one or two casual meetings at Queen's University when he taught summer school there. My request based

*E. J. Pratt Memorial Lecture, St John's Newfoundland Memorial University (1978) pp. 3–23.

on affinity with Humphrey Gilbert must have touched in him that resonant order of memory that enfolds this New-Found Land. For 'the noble tradition of the sea' that is ravelled up in this island reaches back to embrace not only the unnamed voyagers and fishermen before Cabot, and Gilbert's first 'plantation' here, and the loneliness of the people left behind for the winter when the summer West countrymen turned homeward; but also – like the track of the cachalot – most of the globe and almost its two poles. For James Cook, who charted with a few hands the whole coast of Newfoundland and part of Labrador too, and wrote *Sailing Directions* that still guide mariners in these waters, after that went by way of the Horn to Tahiti and then to chart the coast of New Zealand and part of Australia. On his second voyage around the world he was sent to search for an ill-surmised Southern Continent; and, finding for certain that no such continent existed, three times crossed the Antarctic Circle trying in ships ill-found for the purpose to penetrate the South Ice in search of the polar continent that he was sure must be there. After their return from that second voyage his principal astronomer, William Wales, was appointed head of the Navigation School at Christ's Hospital in the City of London, and so came to teach mathematics to Charles Lamb and Leigh Hunt and Coleridge, and unwittingly left his mark on 'The Rime of the Ancient Mariner' in the lines

> And ice, mast-high, came floating by,
> As green as emerald.

No doubt Cook, who was much troubled by the need to find names for the many islands and capes and bays and anchorages that he discovered – in the Pacific, on the west coast of America, and on his attempt to make an easterly traverse of the North-West Passage – carried with him many of the sweet names from this island – Quidi Vidi, Come-by-Chance, Heart's Content, Heart's Delight; perhaps some of the names imprinted in Pratt's life too – Twillingate, Bell Island, Portugal Cove; and surely St John's, a mean ironbound slot for a navigator to find in foul weather or in bad visibility, yet a snug haven for so many ships in the long struggle with the dangers of the North Atlantic and 'the violence of the enemy' that 'Newfy-John's' was a name as much to be conjured with as the Murmansk Run or the Rose Garden, but for very different reasons, being a reminder of the hospitality given by the people whose men are recalled by the foreign name Beaumont Hamel, the men to whom this university is a memorial.

It has been said that poetry is made out of poetry. In a sense, I suppose, that is true: all poetry is somehow a transformation – a transfiguration, it may be – of something into words, and a poet is not likely to get the transformation right if he hasn't learned from other poets that it can be done and how it may be done: if he hasn't found out how language – like a ship – once set in motion, has a will of its own and has to be treated with circumspection. But *what* is transformed is not poetry but the feel of life in any of its multitudinous forms, from the visionary exaltation of the mystic to the last incoherence of love inundating the dykes of reason, or grief breaking at the last defences of the heart. 'Experience of life', or something like it, is the source of poetry: not 'experience' in any ordinary sense, for simply to have been there does not make a poet; but harbouring in the mind, in an immediate and sensory manner, the feel of whatever with a certain memorable imprint may have befallen.

I wish to search out a little the specific quality of Pratt's poetry where it is of greatest intensity and of most complex human and emotional implication. What gives definition and force to poems is not simply the subject-matter (which is always recurring in any case); but something intrinsic, with its roots in what has been experienced to the bone, its fibre in the taste of the words and names caught up in the events. For Pratt, that was the sea – or, as a Newfoundlander would say, saltwater.[1]

Ned Pratt lived the first twenty years or more of his life within sight and sound of saltwater, in little communities whose life was the sea, among people for whom the codfish, salmon, lobster, seal, swordfish and whale were creatures of great moment, and the sea a pervasive presence often (like the beating of the heart) below the threshold of awareness: the source of bounty, yet wielding the iron scourge of forces beyond prediction or control, bringing at times the ferocious inexorabilities of storm, ice and fog, and the hallucinations of physical extremity. Here Pratt would see and touch hands scarred and gnarled from setting hooks, hauling lines, splicing rigging, mending nets, handing kutched storm canvas. Here he would be among men who could judge the last mortal moment to shorten sail, by how many cables to risk a leeshore, by how many minutes more the top-burden of ice in the upperworks could be endured before taking the enormous hazard of altering downwind. Young men too, as Cook was a young man on the Newfoundland coast, young at the Barrier Reef, and in the South Ice. Put a seaman in a duffle-coat and woollen cap and by the end of a dirty middle watch you could find it hard to say whether he was eighteen or thirty or sixty. Hence in the speech a slow laconic merriment carrying in its body the exact marks of its inheritance, and a certain look to eyes accustomed to scan the horizon, to evolve from slender evidence the gambits of a storm, or piece together the clues of a deceptive landfall. And the counter-thread of the abrupt transition from the feel of a ship or boat at sea to the feel of her in harbour; the feel of being ashore – another world, domestic, trivial, precious, importunate with its own necessities; secure but for the subliminal recognitions that pluck at a wary instinct at the turn of the tide or a change in the wind's voice. And, like a groundswell lifting unseen in the dark, there was in any village one probability to be lived with: that one night, one dawn, it would be known for certain that some man – husband, son, brother – would never come again to lift the latch of the door; and perhaps, by grace, those who loved him would never see what indignity the sea can work upon the body of a drowned man.

That Pratt wrote some good poems about the sea is acknowledged by all who have written about him. But in what has been written I do not find much firsthand recognition of what Pratt himself so often catches in words: the indifferent beauty and menace of what Dante (no seafarer) called '*il crudele mar*', and the arcane idiom that is as much of the physique of seafaring as the feel of hemp or frozen canvas is, of the lift of the forefoot to a breaking sea. This is the 'unnavigated road' in criticism that I wish to venture – who can say 'By what navigator's sign, / By what vicarious starlight?' I believe it can provide a baseline for triangulating certain distinctive aspects of the whole body of his work.

Pratt had not himself done very much seafaring; he had not ventured as supercargo in a cockleshell to the Azores as John Donne did, was not a fisherman, had not commanded square-rigged ships as Conrad did, or shipped before the mast as Melville and Masefield did. But as a young man he had hauled lines and lobster-pots and had known his moments of anxiety and sheer terror with fog, tide and storm, and knew at first hand much more about salt water than either Coleridge or Gerard Manley Hopkins, both of whom wrote sea-poems that are without peer in the language. He knew what it felt like for the sea to be an inescapable dimension of life; and, whatever his 'actual' experience, it was amplified and given imaginative substance by the speech of the fishermen and the stories they told him in the ancient and arcane idiom peculiar to that way of life. The liturgy of sea-language and the inflections given to ordinary speech by seafaring – a 'laconic speech, close-fitting, clean, / And whittled to the ship's economy' – that too was part of the actual 'experience', supervening upon and giving edge and body to what the records show or what the witnesses can tell to those who were not present. What we are looking for is the *feel* of events, what lies under and beyond the reticent and factual account, what – to use Pratt's own phrase – lies 'behind the log'. That, for a poet, is what – with luck – may claim access to a universal reality.

'Only what is actually loved and known can be seen *sub specie aeternitatis*' – under the figure of eternity. The subject-matter does not usually tell us very clearly what is 'actually loved and known'. Poetry does not move typically from a subject to the tendering of it, but from a complex feeling that seeks a body, that finds for itself, as a 'subject', a physical mode in which the feeling can be articulated in a field of events or discourse proper to it. When we are asleep, physical sensations embody themselves into visual dramas that so command the sleeper's attention that he stays asleep to watch the picture. The same for poetry, a sort of dreamwork; and surely this is the case whether it is Hopkins reading accounts of a shipwreck in the Thames estuary and finding there the body for 'the echo of a new rhythm' that 'I had long had haunting my ear', or Milton pondering for years what substance to give to the impulse that he knew had the scope of epic or tragedy, or Rilke waiting in terror for the last of the *Duino Elegies* to get themselves all made (after the first few) so that the arc of his premonition could be brought to rest. The impulses – the themes – are few, central and importunate; the subjects manifold. We come to the heart of Donne's *Songs and Sonnets* not by studying mediaeval cosmogonies or scholastic angelology, but by reflecting upon the complex and baffling disorder of love human and divine; and the fact that many of his poems were literary exercises in long-established modes enlarges, rather than diminishes, the 'reality' of what he wrote.

Too often we forget the necessary bond between poetry and life – the bond that Aristotle, to our dismay, called *mimesis* – and, supposing that 'life' of the quality that informs durable poetry is easy to come by and that any sort of 'life' will serve, may be surprised to find that the poetry that comes from a 'real life' that is empty, diseased or self-preoccupied may well be trivial, pretentious or merely indulgent. Too often, too, we forget that nobody is likely to be a poet unless he is fascinated with the business of making poems, the logodaedaly, the bold carpentry of song, the fine craft and subtle management of words that depends upon reconciling what is known and wanted with the upwelling of what is at best half-known and beyond bidding, the just correlation of intelligence, habit, concern, will, desire, restraint into a gesture as simple and arrogant as riding a bicycle no-hands (when you know how).

To find the main springs of an author's work we need to look beyond the subject-matter to consider what, in the field of poetry itself, the poet knew and loved and therefore what in-formed his poems. In Pratt's case this is very clear: a taste for a good story well told in the best traditions of the spellbinding storyteller (traditions as old as Homer); a taste for large elemental themes that seldom declare themselves in contemporary events; a boisterous love of words and a taste for the constrained forms of verse that can throw single words into high relief and abrupt interaction; an insatiable taste for technicalities and names – archaeological, electronic – as though these were elements in which could be found the muscle and the detailed articulation of the body of a work by drawing upon a wide range of effects from the hard microscopic precision of the technical term that belongs only in one limited context to the evocative sonority of names of places and mythical persons delivered in liturgical sequence.

In this short list of Pratt's preoccupations the love of technical terms (noticed as a unique and distinguishing mark of his poetic mentality by everybody who has written about him) may seem out of place, even disruptive of what one might expect of high poetic practice; yet not if those terms are inseparable from the field of what he knows and loves. (To my ear the most memorable and lyrical passage in the noble but over-scholarised yarn *Moby Dick* is the detailed account of how you flake down and manage a harpoon-line in an open boat.) Pratt's grasp of some of the technicalities he brings into play is variable; his love of them never is. And there is, I think, a very clear connection between his fascination with technical detail and his sense of certain primordial imperatives as vital and frightening presences in our lives. The imagined forces that compel the prehistoric monster, the giant squid, the sperm whale, the migratory bird – these are refracted and intrinsicated in the named intricacies of the machines and devices that we 'poor forkèd creatures' contrive as extensions to the pathetic range of hands that can reach out only a score or two of inches from our bodies; and the intricacies impose their own menacing imperatives.

When I consider the unfolding of Pratt's work and the scope of it, it seems to me that his 'birthright to the sea' became in his earliest years so deeply a part of his nature that his removal to Toronto, and his life there, were like a long run ashore from which he never returned. The detailed circumstances of the villages and havens and harbours moved farther and farther away from his day-to-day consciousness; he did not run away to sea; service in the war was denied him. Yet always in the darkness of memory, uncalled, the exact feel of salt water kept coming back to haunt him, 'as life returns upon the drowned' – in a sudden stillness perhaps, or in an iron savour under the tongue – and would find for itself a body in verse, even when the verse was about something else. When the 'experience' was closest to him, his mastery of verse was not sure-footed enough always to render with complete certainty the feel of the thing. As the mastery increased and the actual experience receded and other concerns about his craft supervened, he knew that poetry can call forth universal recognitions only through the exact rendering of particulars; he nourished and reinforced the ambience of earlier sensation with a detailed study of ships he has never served in and events which he had not had the privilege of suffering. He had left the salt water and discovered the sea.[2]

The poems that take the sea as their setting fall into three kinds: (1) poems that engage directly the way of life of fishermen and their people, a life divided between salt water and the land, the two parts bound together – mostly in the minds and lives of women – by the foreboding menace of the sea; (2) poems that recount memorable events at sea; (3) fables, in which sea-creatures are depicted and celebrated with enormous zest and admiration, as though they alone were proper to the primordial life-giving ocean – men and ships being trifling intruders, their presence impertinent or obscene and supported by a thread whimsically slender. To the first group many of the early lyrical poems of 1923 belong, and even more memorably a few of the last lyrics. To the second, the early account of a disastrous sealing-expedition – 'The Ice Floes' (1923) – and (in order of publication) 'The *Roosevelt* and the *Antinoe*' (1930), 'The *Titanic*' (1935) and 'Behind the Log' (1947); perhaps 'Dunkirk' (1941) was meant to belong with these. The class of fables, however, proved especially fertile. In 'The Cachalot' (1926) he discovered his individual style; and that undersea epithalamial fantasy 'The Witches' Brew' (1925) laid massive foundations for the Extravaganzas and also provided the procedural armature for the larger narratives. With the fables belong also (for example) 'The Submarine' (1943), and the enfolding theme of 'The *Titanic*', and that potent but unmaritime poem 'The 6000'. 'The Iron Door' (1927), one of the few of his poems to be informed by profound personal grief, stands in a transitional position: published after 'The Cachalot' but presumably composed earlier, it is still dominantly in the early Newfoundland mode, having in it elements of the salt water lyric and of notable events at sea, and it prefigures some of his most powerful devices of allusion, but – perhaps under the pressure of personal emotion – the elements are ill assimilated into the cloudy and portentous rhetoric that may have been part of his inherited understanding of what an 'ode', as a poem of strong feeling, could be expected to be.

If we approach Pratt's poetry looking for the specific and determinate qualities of the man and his work we do well to set about it in the way we infer the character of a ship by studying the configuration of her hull. It's no help to be thinking of Donne, or Hopkins, or Coleridge, or Pound, or Yeats – or even Eliot (who did know a thing or two about offshore sailing). It is no help to claim for his poetry a refined or penetrating intelligence, a subtle insight into the ways of the heart or the textures of society. It is not to his discredit to say that he is no more philosopher than lyrist, the spiritual anguish and the desolations and passion of the saint are outside his compass. His true virtues are other, and (I think) less commonly to be seen in the tradition of our literature. The sea is immensely powerful but it has some limits: the sea did not make a poet of James Cook, or a philosopher of Humphrey Gilbert, or a saint of Sebastian Cabot.

My threefold classification is indicative, not complete. But I am sure that any typology of Pratt's poems needs to take account less of subject-matter and overt theme than of verbal tone and articulation. It seems to me that there are very few of his poems that do not fall within one of these three kinds, or on the functional fringes of one or more of them. His two largest stories – epics, it may be – deal with large-scale episodes in the history of Canada: 'Brébeuf and his Brethren' (1940) on the fate of the Jesuits who sought to bring the Catholic faith into the lives of native Indians; and 'Towards the Last Spike' (1952) on the overmastering of geographical, financial and human improbabilities in order to unite the country with a railroad. Both these historical narratives, like the sea-narratives, serve to evince certain radical human qualities of an exceptional order – heroism and indomitability. In 'Brébeuf' he appreciates the zeal, endurance, appalling suffering of his central figure, but he cannot enter into the obsessive spiritual passion of Brébeuf, has a less secure imaginative understanding of the impulse of martyrdom than (say) Crashaw in his monologue portrait of St Teresa in 'The Flaming Heart'. In the story of the transcontinental railroad (a theme since vulgarised) there are heroes sure enough, but they are the engineers, surveyors and workers; for all his good intentions, Pratt finds it difficult to ascribe grandeur to the politicians and financiers but for whom there would have been no incidental heroism. He assumes a good Ontario admiration for the self-made man, the shrewd politician, the ruthless tycoon, but he has too active a sense of humour to have much enthusiasm for that part of his theme. He is unassimilably a Newfoundlander; and it's my guess that it will be a very long time before Newfoundland merges into the grey and groping materialism that seems to be the fate of Canada between wars.

Those two poems are anomalies in the canon – splendid, confident and impressive, yet drifting away from his home centre. As we trace the development of his work we can see how vulnerable his poetic resources were – as indeed all poetic capacity is, depending for its good health as it always does upon a certain innocence of intent. As time went on – and we see this in the long narrative poems – the subject began to dominate the impulse, the argument began to stand in for the themes that at best had flowed in from the darkness; technical intricacies could become ornament, cadenzas, providing at times – and this had always been a temptation – an opportunity for a dazzling performance. He seeks subjects that will embody large themes, and the authority of events is taken to lie in their factuality, down to the last discoverable detail, rather than in the quality of perceiving them or the way by selection and arrangement they are transfigured. In these conditions, critical judgements based on subject and theme find a specious and deceptive reliability at the cost of neglecting the much less accessible heart of the matter.

The Extravaganzas, however, for all their apparent variety and their restraint from openly serious intent, lie very close to home. In these he sets vibrating a string of peculiar timbre, a sound of distinctive potency. This is the quality most easily recognisable when he deals with ships and their people and the creatures that live in the sea; it always touches upon the nerve of what is most personal in his work, calling forth like a primordial memory the sense of a baffling cosmic order and a noble vision of man.

'The Great Feud' (1926), a palaeological fantasy not innocent of marine and oceanic concerns, is as long as 'The *Titanic*' was to be, but faster paced and written in a shorter breath-length; and 'The Witches' Brew' is, emphatically submarine. But 'The Depression Ends' (1927) and 'The Truant' (1943), though they have nothing maritime about them at all, declare the indomitable dignity of man and the grace of a large generosity that we know Pratt practised and that he regarded as one of the distinctive virtues of the seafaring man. These poems of fancy are gratuitous and guileless outpourings of exuberant language and fertile wit. They are the work of a practised raconteur who can hold an audience spellbound with Rabelais's cumulativeness and Grock's insolence; they have the sheer copiousness of genius. In these poems particularly he discovers a favourite measure in the rhymed tetrameter and achieves his most consistent mastery in it. Once this measure is comfortable to his ear, he can sustain below a sparkling and often comic surface a flickering undercurrent of sharp-edged irony; at times, especially in 'The Depression Ends', it becomes an instrument of pure delight. Here there is nothing nautical except the sheer daring of it: as the wording unfolds it can hover between bathos and meiosis with as complete composure as Blondin frying himself an egg on a tightrope halfway across Niagara Falls.

Very few of Pratt's poems are in any ordinary sense 'personal'; 'The Empty Room' (1937) is, to my ear, a muted exception. There were some things he preferred not to set to verse. Most often, as he approaches (for he seldom embraces) a theme close to his own life – love, wife, children, companionship – the feeling is not bodied forth directly but is refracted into another mode – into fancy, or literary allusion, or figurative conceit. 'The Iron Door' (1927), which we know belonged to an event of personal desolation, is an early instance of this process; elsewhere he draws more confidently upon his untiring love of the extended or fanciful parallel, the broad conspective glance into a sweep of geographical possibilities, or into history, whether literary, geological, anthropological, biological, human, technological. In 'Like Mother, Like Daughter', for example (1937), the literary–classical fantasy that makes up at least half the poem sets the emotional dimension for this most delightful of poems – a little in the manner of Yeats but less trenchant. Here there is nothing confessional and the intimacy of it is in its delicate restraint. 'Come Away, Death' (1943), by contrast, seems to hover on the fringes of some more personal disclosure, but even the intended allusiveness of it is blurred by its elaborately literate opening section. Among the few open declarations of personal feeling – in 'To Angelina, an Old Nurse' (1932) or 'A Reverie on a Dog' (1932) – we find the only touches of sentimentality, the feeling not rendered with definitive accuracy; if there is failure in the wording of it, it must be that out of unguarded open-heartedness he has been less wary than he usually is in securing the distance that self-contained poetry seems always to demand, and both were left out of the second edition of *Collected Poems*.

There are very few *persons* in his poems, but there are many human figures with names; these are often figures of heroic stature of mien, emblems of certain root-like human qualities – the silent dignity of those who suffer and know no comfort, of those who – like ship's captains – live in the solitude of their skilled and mortal destiny. Yet in these poems the emotional light seldom darkens, because of the continuous presence of the man who speaks, the poet himself – variously puckish, ironic, exuberant, of a dionysiac and generous temperament this side of brawling, of a deep compassionate sympathy, yet learned in the high-spirited way of a person who searches the encyclopaedia like a jackdaw. I think Jacquetta Hawkes's *A Land* and David Jones's *Anathemata* could have been favourite books of his.

In poetry every gain in clarity and direction is won at the expense of some preclusive loss. No poet can do everything, and it is often what a poet does not attempt (for whatever reason) that gives distinction to what he does do. Pratt's dominant vision is of man in a heroic mould, enfolded in a lost memory of past happenings and past imperatives that reach back to the beginnings of unrecorded time. His vision tends naturally to hold in single compass all time, all events, all creatures, all circumstances. But how can one embody such a view? Pratt found it, on the whole, not in the condensed economy of lyric, but in the largeness of epic narrative; he would invent a story that disposed the universal elements as he wanted them, or would take an actual story and from that firm centre of fact elaborate the figurative parentheses that often impart the true momentum to his verse and the compelling theme of the story. The origins and voyagings of a whale call up the origins of other creatures and the voyagings of explorers and of those who go about the ocean on their 'lawful occasions'; creatures and geological objects – an iceberg, a headland, a reef, the sea itself – assume human character and even a quasi-human history; and (as is the way of fable) men and women can assume the characteristics of animals (the contemptuous rejection of a challenge is the same for the big dog and the strong man); and ships take on the subtle characters of women and sometimes the tough endurance of men, are their own persons and change the men that serve them to their own character. Machines and great engineering-constructions are for Pratt not *things* of an order different from or contrary to men, but extensions of them, projections of man's capacities and senses, instruments too that affirm, and often betray, the delight or desire or pride of the men who devise them. (Hence the ease with which Pratt introduces machines and technicalities; unlike the pylons that megawatt across the landscape of indignant early Marxist English verse, they are indigenous to the universe of his imagination.) He can see the whale as a marvellous piece of engineering, the submarine as a biological masterpiece, the steam locomotive as an apocalyptic bull its sense of purpose blindly but beautifully disposed, the *Titanic* as a vast organism wired for life – and death. Fishermen and seafaring men bear in their faces and in their eyes the imprint of the swift inexorable decisions that the sea lays upon them, and the marks of the losses that by an unaccountable irony they suffer; and women bear in their faces the imprint of their uttermost desolations. Human suffering can be represented as a geological or glacial event that obliterates a person's features.

Even in most of the Extravaganzas – poems primarily exploring the limits of sustained fancy – Pratt conveys a sense of single events of extreme intensity that open our gaze, if only for a moment, to our fellowship with an order of life that is inevitably shaped by our past on this planet, by things that we were and that happened to us long before we received the definition that could even remotely be called 'human'. 'The Shark', a very early poem, is an imagist poem in motion, the motion being a premonitory gesture unexplained; and it may be that that single vision, standing simply for what it is, is more potent in implication than the later rhetorical identification of a submarine with a shark – an identity that works only for one side in the conflict, when we forget about submariners and their ways on either party. 'Silences' is about hatred; yet the most memorable image of that memorable poem is the closing glimpse of the undersea:

For only such culture could grow in a climate of silence, –
Away back before the emergence of fur or feather, back to the unvocal
    sea and down deep where the darkness spills its wash on the threshold
    of light, where the lids never close upon the eyes, where the inhabitants
slay in silence and are as silently slain.

And the sea is the commanding presence in Pratt's poetry and in his mind, symbolising life and death, standing for an inscrutable primordial value, like the salt carried ashore in the blood long before the evolution of primates and still persisting, a fact of life that leaves indelible marks if we embrace it, and brings us to betrayal if we renounce it.

The figure that haunts the earliest collection, *Newfoundland Verse* (1923), is the drowned man. In 'Lantern Light',

> I could not paint, nor could I draw
>   The look that searched the night;
> The bleak refinement of the face I saw
>   In lantern light.
>
> A cunning hand might seize the crag,
>   Or stay the flight of a gull,
> Or the rocket's flash; or more – the lightning jag
>   That lit the hull.
>
> But as a man born blind must steal
>   His colours from the night
> By hand, I had to touch that face to feel
>   It marble white.

The point of the poem is the horrifying tactile sense of the fact of death; the point would perhaps have been made more forcefully – certainly more laconically and with no loss of directness – by omitting the second stanza. But the allusiveness is an aspect of reticence, a direct function of the strength of feeling, the intolerable shock of stunned incredulity. In 'The Drag Irons', on the indignity of death by drowning, he was to make the same point by a different sort of obliquity – through sardonic wit, epigrammatic detachment, a touch of racy dialect.

> He who had learned for thirty years to ride
> The seas and storms in punt and skiff and brig,
> Would hardly scorn to take before he died
> His final lap in Neptune's whirligig.
>
> But with his Captain's blood he did resent,
> With livid silence and with glassy look,
> This fishy treatment when his years were spent –
> To come up dead upon a grapnel hook.

In the same volume, *Many Moods* (1932), he crystallised in final form a theme that he had several times ventured before and that he would never leave: the wound that sudden death at sea inflicts upon the person most intimately connected with him. The final image – the face as rock suddenly stricken with a geological process that should be infinitesimally slow – appears and reappears in many other settings; it is the sort of change that only human beings can suffer; the iceberg that sank the *Titanic* is too brutal to suffer such a change.

> EROSION
> It took the sea a thousand years,
> A thousand years to trace
> The granite features of this cliff,
> In crag and scarp and base.
>
> It took the sea an hour one night,
> An hour of storm to place
> The sculpture of these granite seams
> Upon a woman's face.

In a very early poem we see the same instant recognition of

disaster from within: that from this moment, nothing – not the wind, not even the hand of God – can 'lift a door-latch up / That a lad may enter in' ('Great Tides'). Underneath the brutality of fact is a hint of the mockery of sunlight and quiet water when the murderous storm has died down. The truth is inscrutable; it cannot be *seen*; perhaps it can be grasped in the way a blind man knows.

> I wondered by what navigator's sign,
> By what vicarious starlight, you could trace
> Horizons which were never yours nor mine,
> Until your wistful fingers sought my face.
>
> ('Blind')

In 'The *Titanic*' and 'Behind the Log' a dense accumulation of actual detail is an essential element in the construction. There are, I feel, defects of judgement in the disposition of the episodic masses in both these poems, and in 'Behind the Log' the naval detail is not fully enough assimilated to consort justly with the precision and eloquence of naval dialect; in both poems – as more noticeably in 'Dunkirk' – there are a few dismaying touches of the journalist's superficial rhetoric, in the choice of personal names and in the idiom of class-inflected dialogue; this may be from expecting too amiable or impressionable an audience. Nevertheless, both poems have passages remarkable for their precise rendering of the way of the sea – remarkable, that is, not simply for descriptive accuracy but for their symbolic embodying of the feel of the thing. This quality was present in some of the earliest poems. Consider the fog in the poem of that name in *Newfoundland Verse*, already ingenious and grimly playful:

> It stole in on us like a foot-pad,
> Somewhere out of the sea and air,
> Heavy with rifling Polaris
> And the Seven Stars.
> It left our eyes untouched,
> But took our sight,
> And then,
> Silently,
> It drew the song from our throats,
> And the supple bend from our ash-blades;

For the bandit,
With occult fingering,
Had tangled up
The four threads of the compass,
And fouled the snarl around our dory.

In a much later poem – 'The Radio in the Ivory Tower' (1943) – the sea and fog are a single pervasive presence in the lighthouse.

But only ferrets of sound
Came out of the fog
To worm themselves through the cracks in the cobbles.
The waters leaped at the splayed bastions –
The might of the waters
Against the strength of the steel –
But only the dull reverberation of their paws
Disturbed the insulation of the tower;
Only the faintest echoes seeped through the copper roof
As the gulls screamed around the weather vane.

In 'Behind the Log' three Irish hands in a merchantman would, he says, have plenty to say about the action of the doomed convoy when their ship made port –

but somehow
The water and the salt got in their throats
The moment when the *Stargard* took them under.

In 'The *Titanic*', Pratt's words at times have the clarity of an obsessive nightmare – as when the sea is inexorably invading the vitals of the huge ship and the indolent water laps in darkness up the long sloping foredeck.

The fo'c'sle had gone under the creep
Of the water. Though without a wind, a lop
Was forming on the wells now fathoms deep.
The seventy feet – the boat deck's normal drop –
Was down to ten. Rising, falling, and waiting,
Rising again, the swell that edged and curled.
Around the second bridge, over the top

Of the air-shafts, backed, resurged and whirled
Into the stokehold through the fiddley grating.

At the end of that poem, the ominous precision that has embraced
the stricken ship and her people in their long passion drifts with
no sense of transition outward to the occasion of the disaster –
the iceberg, as brutal as the sea itself, being of the sea's nature,
without history, brainless, inscrutable, inert, powerful beyond
imagining.

And out there in the starlight, with no trace
Upon it of its deed but the last wave
From the *Titanic* fretting at its base,
Silent, composed, ringed by its icy broods,
The grey shape with the paleolithic face
Was still the master of the longitudes.

In 'The *Titanic*', however, Pratt may have ventured too daringly
in trying to combine the overt moral of 'the ancient *hybris* in the
dreams of men' with the copious records of circumstantial detail
that had survived. Perhaps he had moved a little too far
from the looms of the ash-blades to a theme oceanic, social,
cosmopolitan. For in this poem the sea – the omen to which his
pulse always stirs, as Vaughan Williams's did to the tune of *Dives
and Lazarus* – the sea has lost definitive control and other
concerns have supervened: not least his fascination with technical
minutiae – in which, paradoxically, his strength lies – and with
his sheer astonishment at some of the things that actually
happened and are of record.

If much of the strength of his poetry lies in a certain disarming
naïveté, both intellectual and technical, so also there is a source
of weakness in his failure at times to master the dramatic order
of language and its disposition in psychic space as distinct from
the dramatic order of events. For example, in the impressive early
narrative poem *The Ice Floes* – in many respects a unique piece
of 'polar' writing, set to a tune so compelling that it can even
submerge the nagging demands of dactylic verse – he devotes
nineteen lines to an account of the 'bobbing-holes' of the seals –
that is, almost as much as to the killing of the seals, and a quarter
as much as the final disastrous dénouement of the blizzard. What
does a poet *do* with what he knows? How can he make special

knowledge as familiar and accessible to the novice as to the old hand? Poets are by nature not detached and uninformed spectators, but 'insiders'; in the end, in the poem, everything must be 'inside', known to the marrow and so below the threshold of recognition. In the matter of the bobbing-holes, Pratt's passionate curiosity overrides the cognitive inwardness that elsewhere marks the poem, and tempts him into digressive elaboration. So it is in the fantasy of the wireless waves in 'The *Roosevelt* and the *Antinoe*' and in the shorthand history of acoustics that supports the Asdic set in 'Behind the Log'. I think of Masefield's 'Dauber', a marvel of nautical precision, the whole naming and working of a four-masted barque coming to his call as simple as a breath, as direct as an oath, and none of it explained. Once there is any loss of precision an infective rhetoric may enter. In 'The *Titanic*' a 'knot' sometimes becomes a measure of distance, not of speed; in 'The Submarine' the search is carried out and the attack conducted in a manner that would surely bring the submariners home with their torpedoes unexpended; in 'The Cachalot' (in which a touch of exaggeration may be venial) there is a whaling-ship that crosses royals and sky-sails, and she sets studding-sails to sail ten miles in pursuit of a whale. Minor flaws, no doubt; yet true poetry is nothing if not an instrument of verniered and infinitesimal precision.

The outstanding sea-poem, to my mind, is 'The *Roosevelt* and the *Antinoe*'. As in 'The *Titanic*' there may be a little awkwardness in setting the action in motion; since there is no need, as in 'The *Titanic*', to dispose resources for 'a study in irony – the web of Fate,' a swifter entrance would have helped. But, once the elements of the story are set, the whole thing moves with an ineluctable and compelling fascination to give an account of the sea at its most merciless, and of what is demanded of men who 'go down to the sea in ships'. Especially, he calls forth his dominant figure of man as coming to his full stature (master or man) in the face of death, matching himself with physical courage and endurance to what is inevitable by drawing upon that 'unexplored residuum', 'the bone-and-marrow judgment of a sailor'.

> The final manner native to the breed
> Of men forging decision into deed –
> Of getting down again into the sea,

> And testing rowlocks in an open boat,
> Of grappling with the storm-king bodily,
> And placing Northern fingers on his throat.

The Roosevelt, hearing the *Antinoe's* interrupted call of distress in the hurricane, finds her, against all odds and reason,

> With Jack reversed, the freighter like a lone
> Sea-mallard with a broken wing was seen
> Ahead, lee-rail awash, taking it green
> At the bow.

With judgement and resolution beyond human limits, and at mortal risk, the *Roosevelt* maintains contact with the *Antinoe*; for, when life is at issue, the sea recognises no limit to the call of duty. After four days of struggle, in which the *Roosevelt* loses some of her own men, all the *Antinoe's* people are finally taken aboard and the sinking ship abandoned. The survivors find themselves

> Where men are shepherded in the old way
> Of the sea, where drowned men come to life, they say,
> Under such calls to breathe as never come
> To those that roam the uplands of this earth.

If it can be difficult to begin a poem, it can be just as difficult to end it. This one ends with a brief cadence that restores the rhythm of life and sanity. The survivors are put ashore at the nearest harbour, and the *Roosevelt*

> Swung out the Sound, with her day's work well done,
> And in an hour was on the Channel sea.[3]

The mind arches back, through the recovery of the *Antinoe's* people to the figure of the drowned man, and another poem lamenting the loss of a proud ship and her people – Gerard Manley Hopkins's '*Eurydice*'.

> O his nimble finger, his gnarled grip!
> Leagues, leagues of seamanship

> Slumber in these forsaken
> Bones, this sinew, and will not waken.

The theme of nautical virtue, undemonstrative in its recognition of a shared nature and a shared fate, Pratt embodied in 'The *Roosevelt* and the *Antinoe*'. He was to utter it again but in a different mode, in one of the last poems he wrote, a poem in which he celebrates the masters of that virtue, the Newfoundland seamen.

> This is their culture, this – their master passion
> Of giving shelter and of sharing bread,
> Of answering rocket signals in the fashion
> Of losing life to save it; in the spread
> Of time – the Gilbert–Grenfell–Bartlett span –
> The headlines cannot dim their daily story,
> Nor calls like London! Gander! Teheran!
> Outplay the drama of the sled and dory.
>
> The wonders fade. There overhead a mile,
> Planes bank like gulls: like curlews scream the jets.
> The caravans move on in radar file
> Scarce noticed by the sailors at their nets,
> Bracing their bodies to their tasks, as when,
> Centuries before Argentina's smoking funnels,
> That small ancestral band of Devon men
> Red-boned their knuckles on the *Squirrel* gunwales.
>
> As old as it is new, as new as old,
> Enduring as a cape, as fresh as dulse,
> This is the Terra Nova record told
> Of uncontractual blood behind the pulse
> On sea or land . . . .

Pratt's *Collected Poems* were published in 1946, and again in an extended and rearranged edition in 1958; he had a considerable reputation in Canada and the United States. The last of his larger poems had been published at a time when other concerns were afoot in Canadian poetry – endeavours rather more self-conscious than his, more deliberately cosmopolitan, at times determined to spin poetry out of poetry and to entwine learned allusion with a contemporary realism in a way that might suggest cosmic irony. Pratt was not dismayed or deflected by any of that, even though a mounting wave of Canadian self-preoccupation was soon to canonise other masters claiming a higher degree of sophistication and was also soon to bring to bear upon the writing of some minor practitioners a detailed critical scrutiny that it can ill withstand. If Pratt, as a poet in the public eye, had consistently sought safety in irony or had been more fastidious (as Yeats was) in deciding how best to arrange each of his collections, his work might have established itself more securely than it has and with readers other than Canadian. But to have done so – and it was not his way – could only have accentuated the enormous energy that informs his work; and energy has a very long rhythm of survival. When the next edition of his *Collected Poems* is prepared, Pratt's virtues as a poet would be more clearly seen if the general arrangement of 1958 collection-by-collection were followed, but collecting the Extravaganzas together, as they were in 1946, and the narrative poems as (with two intrusions) they were in 1958. Each of Pratt's smaller collections (except 1937) closed with a narrative poem or an Extravaganza because there was no place else to put a poem of such extent; but that accident of arrangement need not be canonised. It is well to read the Extravaganzas together, and it would be well to take back 'The Fable of the Goats': though that is now as improbable a fable for our times as it was when Pratt wrote it, let us hope that it is not inconceivable that some day the lamb will be able to lie down by the lion, and the goat with the goat. And the Narrative Poems should open with 'The Ice Floes'.

Some Canadian poetry may now have achieved a scope and subtlety – a stature and intelligence, even – that Pratt could hardly have forseen. Yet much of it – even much that is widely acclaimed – is attenuated in a way that the muscles and thews of Pratt's verse put to shame. If some later poetry is daintier, it is not necessarily more profound; and, if some of it is aggressively hirsute in manner, very little of it is masculine in the way Pratt's verse is. For he wrote with open-handed enjoyment, for friends, for those who knew how to listen companionably. What he has bequeathed is strength and sanity.

Near the end of his life, Pratt was intrigued by the thought of bouncing radar-waves off the moon. He did not live to see (at a remove) the landings on the moon, or hear the grotesque banalities of speech with which that remarkable event was celebrated. In his own lifetime he knew by touch the bond between a man and a ship, between the hunter and the hunted, between action and suffering, between the act of anonymous self-sacrifice and the fruits of that act. I wonder whether he would now feel that that bond has been dissolved: that there is little connection between a computer and the mind, between a Mach 2 fighter and a ship, between a homing missile and the art of naval gunnery. Once machines cease to be extensions of man, they can become pitiless instruments that take on the deceitful appearance of man's purpose while they lapse into the stupor of a sinister autonomy, swift, immoral, brainless, drawing us down (if we allow it) into their own nature, as cruelty can make a shark of a man. Against that betrayal, Pratt's affirmation, charged with his sense of wonder, stands in the memorable patterns of his words.

For to be masculine in the character that he disclosed to us is not only to be courageous, enduring, strong and skilful, but also to be compassionate, patient, self-sacrificing, unassuming, hospitable, reticent, knowing that we share at times delight and accomplishment, and certainly that we share suffering and loss. Whenever he wrote, whether with a light heart and with outrageous panache, or with a premonitory sense of dread, he prepared himself meticulously for the task; and in carrying it out declared his own virtues and the virtues of the people he had grown up among. From them he learned to keep a weather ear lifting for the subtle inflections of speech; and from them came that deep imprint upon his character and upon the dark places of his memory that his poetry so often sprang from – his 'birthright to the sea'.

9 Literature: An Instrument of Inquiry*

I know only what I know how to handle.

As early as the eighteenth century – and probably much earlier than that – the custom was established that on taking up his chair, the professor would declare in an inaugural lecture what his policies would be and what he intended to do. In those days professorships were for life; a man could afford to be leisurely. Thomas Gray, on being appointed to the chair of History and Modern Languages at Cambridge began to prepare his inaugural address – in an elegant style of Latin – but lost the thread and never got round to delivering it. The important thing was that he had the chair; he had desired it for a long time, and when it was providentially offered to him (through the good offices of a friend) he accepted the offer with as much alacrity as he had declined the poet laureateship a little earlier. He died three years later, leaving no inaugural, and no record that he had ever given a lecture on history, or tutored a single undergraduate. Yet he is still a man of renown, well remembered for his elegy on the death by drowning of Horace Walpole's cat.

The choice of illustration is not entirely casual. I have three years to go before I walk the academic plank; and since I was, I believe, the first James A. Cappon Professor almost fifteen years ago (and therefore feel a little like one who follows a silent *Doppelgänger* towards a hypothetical destination) I regard this launching with considerable interest. Dr Samuel Johnson tells us that to inaugurate is 'to begin with good omen'. Better to do it

*The James A. Cappon Inaugural Lecture, Queen's University, 28 November 1977; published in *Humanities Association Review*, vol. 29 (1978) pp. 243–59.

197

with divination from the flight of birds than by the gruesome examination of entrails. And, if a launching, perhaps a ship, even though we know from the evidence of King Canute that a chair is not a very good device for stemming tides. Yet spice islands and continents and whole new worlds have been discovered in vessels not much more rationally designed for seafaring nor much more secure. So I am happy to set forth by saying, not what I shall do, but what I see.

The programme that I should like to see confirmed is conceived from the inside outward: working from a central educational purpose to the detailed realising of that purpose in the hands of instructors variously gifted, accomplished, experienced. It would be a study in the ways of languages and the ways of the mind, to harmonise with the principal purpose of the whole Faculty and of the University at large: to develop the capacities of each individual student to a level of mastery in his chosen field, and to clarify the process of self-discovery and self-realisation – which I take to be the ultimate end of higher education.

I should like to see our work disposed in appropriate patterns and phases in order to fulfil such an educational function in recognisable stages of progress for the various kinds of students who work with us to satisfy the various purposes they may individually have in mind. By tradition, the centre of our attention has been directed to train as best we can those who wish to become teachers and instructors of language and literature in schools and universities, and those who aspire to become literary scholars (we have always been a little wary of literary critics). The desire to produce 'professionals' is proper – as long as we refrain from insisting that 'professionals' must be in our own image; but to produce 'professional academics' has never been our exclusive aim. The study of English we have always supposed was for all comers; and, although we have never persuaded anybody that it would sink many ships or thicken many pockets, we have had, over the years, some success (I think) in leaving an unexpected and lasting impression on some who have worked with us.

I suggest, therefore, that we do well to set course according to the value of our 'unprofessional' work, all of which has to be a matter of playing for keeps. I believe that it is of paramount importance that every student who works with us – especially those who, for whatever reason, take only one course with us –

should never fully recover from that association. I should want them to have discovered indelibly something about their ability to read and to listen, and if not to write in a masterly way at least to learn respect for language as an instrument to inquire with; to enjoy things that they know have no ulterior use, to respect what they cannot hope to understand, to value those things that are strangely unlike themselves or remote from their (often unexamined) view of life. For it is salutary to find in works that we could not conceivably have made ourselves the substance of our own nature, and to find in such commanding presences an exhilarating liberation – if only momentary – from the oppressive circularity of our own personal limitations, the squalor of our desires, the stifling self-preoccupation that we are often told is the necessary condition of modern man. Literature has this effect because by its very nature it is the opposite of an escape: imagination is a realising-process, making the world real, making us real; in this way, poetry is – as Collingwood has said – not an enchantment but a disenchantment.

So I should wish our students, when they leave us, to go on developing each in his own way, in his own time, according to his own initiative, and vision, having caught at least a glimpse here – in this accelerated process of self-discovery – of what they most care about; and that they will have some confidence that they can sustain that vision through the habits of patient discrimination and refined perception that they will have tested and made subtle in coming to terms with works of literature.

Just about everybody who can get hold of a microphone these days or a typewriter or a soap-box, tells us that we must all become political and economic animals. I believe that it is much more important that we be *human* animals. Animals of a sort we certainly are, though marked by a development of the roofbrain that some consider excessive, and by a capacity for greed and cynicism that is not to be discerned even in (what Valéry calls) 'the shrewd implacable physiognomy of cats'. But one attainment we have that is peculiar to man – the gift of language; and, although language suffers monstrous distortion and sad erosion in careless hands, it is at its best the vehicle of an inexhaustible and fruitful inventiveness. It may be that it is through language as much as anything else that we discover integrity of purpose and integrity of action, recognising that by taking irreversible acts of judgement and decision we change and make ourselves from inside (for better, for worse), being by nature something other than the simple products of those causes of which we have little knowledge and over which we have no control. For to refrain from acting is itself a positive act, and to listen is the positive counterpart to speech – as space is a positive element of design whether in a printed page or a musical score. And from language we find – not so much from what it says as from the way it works – that if we are gifted to think, perceive, speak, we are also responsible – to ourselves if to nobody else – for the quality of our thinking, perceiving and speaking. For we leave in our speech and writing, as in our actions, not simply the ghost of a meaning, but rather the physical and permanent imprint of what we are, and what we care for, disclosing beyond question, and by means neither conventional nor cryptographic, what we have in mind.

For which reasons a university department of language and literature – especially a department that is dedicated to the language and literature of our own tongue – is empowered to discharge a momentous and delicate responsibility. Some might, with qualification, call it a 'civilising' function; I prefer to call it a 'realising' function. This responsibility gives access to radical sources of influence that we know – especially from recent history – can be turned to furtive and cynical ends. (We shall be careful not to abuse our privilege by offering instruction in sophistry and deliberate misrepresentation.) Certainly the study of literature has implications and possibilities not usually accorded to a 'subject'. The study of literature is, I suppose, one of the very few formal studies that can properly be called a discipline; for, if successful, it shows us how to dispose our minds to matters impalpable and of profound personal importance; it also shows us how to come to terms with the world and with ourselves through a reconciliatory quietness, through modes of heuristic reflection that are perhaps as far as we can get from tautology. Our 'discipline' is indeed a *disciplina* – a way of tempering the mind to a task made almost impossible by its simplicity.

I do not say that the study of English language and literature is the only line along which these ends can be realised. I merely say that this study provides an exceptional opportunity and privilege – in being able to concentrate attention on the language we speak and use, upon the literature made in our language, and upon the educational resources that these disclose to us. To encounter literature for what it is and on its own terms is an art not easily mastered, once one has crossed the watershed of self-consciousness; but that attempt can most readily be made through our own language, provided we allow for the way familiarity can blunt the senses. I am confident that English is a tough-enough language to hold our attention, being eloquent and infinitely subtle; and, given the 'monuments of its own magnificence' drawn from a span of some ten centuries, we need never feel that we are provided with inadequate equipment or that the country we seek to explore is poverty-stricken or of parochial extent.

These propositions probably sound 'unrealistic', 'out of touch with the modern temper', useless in an 'age of computer technology'. Nevertheless, I believe that it is our duty to see our responsibilities as clearly as we can and to carry them out. It is not, I think, the business of a university to mirror modern circumstances, but rather to secure the habit of looking at those circumstances narrowly and critically – if need be with mockery, even self-mockery. The simple law of economy would in any case keep us out of a field already overcrowded with the purveyors of 'an easy blend of news, reviews, and interviews'.

To keep steadily in view the large responsibility we are given, and the exceptional resources at our disposal, takes constant vigilance and a devotion to principles that are virtually impossible to formulate. What matters in the end is not so much the design of courses, and programmes – essential though that is – as the living presentation by instructors of the principles and qualities that we espouse. Each finds this in his own way, according to temperament, way of mind, passion, and not least by the intense concentration of his imaginative and intellectual powers in his own scholarship. If this is a time for stock-taking, so is every year and every day of the week. And, if this might seem a time for stock-taking because we have suffered rejection, diminution of resources, and the reversal of golden expectations, that would be much too limited a view of the matter. The issue goes farther back, and the symptoms of malaise in the 'civilisation industry' that were a nagging worry ten or fifteen years ago have now become a crucial issue – the survival of a literate civilisation. This is very much our concern, and a little history may help to clarify our present context and the directions in which we should be well-advised to be looking.

In the first quarter of this century the central educational functions that had been traditionally served by the study of the classics shifted – or slithered, for it seemed almost by accident – to the study of English language and literature. This got away to a rather shaky start, even though the shakiness was for a time concealed by the pure ebullience of the warriors who came home to the universities after 1945. The staple of classical studies had been the study of language and literature, of philosophy, of history and of social institutions. Much of its force turned upon the comparatively limited and enclosed scope of the primary materials; it could be managed – conceivably, though not easily – with an air of finality, with a sense almost of artistic unity. The shift to English suddenly opened a field of inquiry that in some respects was much wider and more various; but it also involved an abrupt narrowing of attention: from three languages (Greek, Latin and English) to one (English), from literature, philosophy, history and social institutions to literature alone, in a sense that has become increasingly limited and specialised. Furthermore the literature of the English language is still living and growing; and the language itself, not caught like a bee in amber, is also living and growing; and both our literature and our language are always prone to degenerate and lose vitality. To lose the perspective of distant time, to lose the picture of closed societies and a completed history, and to lose the strangeness of languages that embodied two radically different ways of mind, two temperaments different from our own, two languages that have influenced our own language in profound and contradictory ways – to lose these was to lose the cutting-edge of stylisation indispensable in education (as in art) as a means of penetrating the bland surfaces of the familiar, the commonplace, the naturalistic, the banal.

The position of English literature has been further weakened, not only by trying to narrow the 'field of knowledge', not only by submitting in very recent years to much 'ignorant good-will' and sentimental egalitarianism, but by an attitude among those who profess it which is at once complacent and defensive. We have too readily endorsed the remarkable proposition that literature is easily accessible because we can all read and we all know the language; we declare that literature is noble stuff, and that it is good for you; we assert that English is as respectable as any other 'subject', that it is as difficult to 'learn' as any other subject, and if those claims seem a little old-fashioned we muster a considerable armoury of 'scientific methodology'. From time to time we think wistfully about these things, because like everybody else we are authorities on education. But we have not been of one mind; and we have not considered carefully enough how the study of our literature is to serve its primary civilising and educational function. Fortunately, in this university, by scholarly habit, we have insisted upon the need for a thorough and omnivorous study of literature; we have insisted on high standards of scholarship; we have been able to maintain (on the whole) the principle that it is more profitable to study the works of giants than of dwarfs. Few universities have been able so to insist, but we have; and as the old instinct brings back the old names any departures from so conservative and rigorous a position have been greeted within our own walls with comfortable irony. The effect has on the whole been salutary under the sheer momentum of our habitual assumptions about this discipline: you have to read Milton even if it means swallowing some intractable theology, for without the theology you can't read him. That high-minded and uncritical momentum, I think, is beginning to be retarded by a formidable deterioration in the potential for literary studies of high quality.

A clear sign of faltering momentum is when people think of themselves as 'teaching literature'. There was a time in this university when no self-respecting professor of literature would allow it to be thought that he *taught* anything. He would say that it was his agreeable duty to transmit from the past the treasures of intellect and imagination, and to draw attention to anything of the sort that seemed to be coming into existence in the present. He would also say that without an intimate acquaintance with those treasures the serious study of literature could scarcely begin. But he would regard all that as axiomatic and leave it unsaid. He would probably also leave unsaid his conviction – he would expect you to know this too – that he was engaged in an enterprise less aggressive and more artful than teaching, simply because what he was seeking to achieve can – sometimes, by grace and good fortune – be educed but cannot be taught.

The failure to articulate the educational virtues of a classical education – that it seeks not simply to give us more knowledge but to make us more knowing – was probably one of the reasons the classics ceased to be the central humanist discipline. Another reason was the rapid spread of a universal literacy that has proved to be a universal illiteracy – a monolithic burden that is already threatening the good health of English studies. Because we find it difficult to engage the subtle processes to which literature gives superior access, we try to force the issue (usually represented as the intransigence or ignorance of our students) by *teaching* literature, by placing the emphasis on content, interpretation, social and historical context, and by using the works of literature as occasions for digression into history, politics, sociology, amateur philosophy and uncontrolled self-indulgence. We do this, in desperation, I suppose, guilelessly presenting effects and expecting that causes will naturally flow from them; maintaining that our students have little or no acquaintance with the literary tradition, that they do not know their own language or any other, and that therefore we must teach them these things before we can get down to serious work. I maintain, to the contrary, that all our students have powers of perception, of responsive sensibility, and an understanding of language-in-action that allows them to engage at once the peculiar educational resources of the study of language and literature; and that, although it is certainly an immeasurable advantage to have some previous and vital acquaintance with literature, it is neither necessary – nor even advisable – to expect a student to be learned in literature *before* the virtues of literary study can be engaged. The first requirement for a student of literature is to be a good reader. It is salutary to remind ourselves that not all good readers are scholars, and not all scholars are good readers.

The social and political upheavals of the sixties and seventies nudged us into accepting, under the name of 'flexibility' and 'freedom of choice', and for reasons that had little to do with education, some indiscipline, a little superficiality and mediocrity, and we have submitted a little to the claim that the contemporary matters most. It is no longer enough to say that Chaucer, Shakespeare, Milton, Wordsworth (and the rest) are 'great' poets and should therefore be studied; we have to be able to say why they should be studied. And, when we can say that, we also have to be able to say with some conviction which writers do not merit formal *study*, even though almost anything may – some time, to somebody – be worth reading.

These are matters that need to be examined, not simply in terms of social and political trends, but primarily on educational grounds. Once we shift our attention in that way our line is very clear. The potency of our work is best released by insisting that students be confronted with the realities of great literature – not so much so that they can *learn* the literature, but so that it will begin to initiate the processes of self-education and the widening and clarifying of their awareness. This is clearly not what most students expect; it is not what their previous experience leads them to expect; it is not what 'society' shows any signs of wanting them to expect. And many will run for cover when it becomes clear that the undertaking is neither self-indulgent nor reducible to formula, and that the placid absorptive qualities of a sponge will not quite serve the purpose.

It seems to me unlikely that any instructor in this department does not in some way work to these axioms; and I am sure that if asked what the purpose of their instruction was they would reply bluntly, 'To teach people to read and write.' Furthermore I am sure that each instructor has his own particular way of introducing what after all must be the passion of our lives – whether through the minutiae of an author in whose work he is 'expert beyond experience', or by turning every text into a pretext to explore and expose the primary purpose that lies at the roots of our work.

Yet we are faced by the increasing inertia of those students who (before coming to university) have attempted little or no writing, of students who have read very little and have little taste for reading, who know no other language, and who expect to be 'taught' in such a way that those deficiencies will not prove fatal. What in conscience can we do, beginning so late? Below a certain level of literary sensibility, nothing happens; and there are no elementary short-cuts or easy alternatives. At some time we have to be able to assume that our students can and do read and to insist that it is a waste of our educational privilege to use any course in literature simply to acquaint students with the contents of certain texts. Time is short and precious, and needs to be directed as far as possible to the delicate and prolonged business of showing how to read better and better, how to come to terms with a writer of substance; how to 'qualify' to enter into another mind – if only momentarily – and to find one's quality of perception altered thereby for good and all; how to develop confidence in the accuracy of the perceptual powers we are all endowed with; how to be guided by the flickering sense of value, exact and precisely located, that is typical of the experience of a good reader. Yet all this is within the reach of those who can find out how to subdue a blinding sophistication and an aggressive 'rationality'.

The word 'literature' is clumsy – and unlovely when pronounced without a neat articulation of the 't's; so I shall now use the word 'poetry' instead of 'literature', and shall refer to a work of literature as a 'poem': that is, any shapely and self-contained piece of writing noticeably above the level of discursive competence. I cannot in short compass say what I take poetry to be. For a start we should be on firm ground if we believe – as I do, and as Coleridge said – that 'all men are poets', even though 'unfortunately most of them are damned bad ones'. Poetry is a human business, not divine; and I hold with St Augustine and others that 'creation' and 'creativity' are not properly within human compass. What poets do is to select and arrange, and by various means intensify and find significance in what they find or what is given to them, and what at a certain level of energy haunts the dark places of the mind – and so to make poems out of words. That is no trifling achievement, and the achievement is supremely human: for 'The idea of *making* is the first and most human of ideas.'

Theoretically poetry can encompass anything whatsoever, with the single proviso that it be encompassed by a poet; and the ruthless limitation on his activity is that he can work only from what he knows and loves (as David Jones has memorably said) [in the Preface to *The Anathemeta*]; and he cannot escape from the fact that the quality of his knowing and loving will be indelibly imprinted in what he has written – not as a thumb-print of personal expression (a device that no serious artist is interested in) but establishing the status and stature of the thing-written. For 'making a work is not thinking thoughts but accomplishing an actual journey'; when the journey has crystallised into a substantial and stable form, the poem moves away from the maker of it, assumes its own life, begins its own history; to the poet it will become increasingly strange, inscrutable, an existence to which – even though he brought it into being – he has no special privilege of entry or explanation. There are multitudes of poems, and they can be seen to fall into different kinds more or less distinct, some in verse, some in prose; yet each one is in a just sense unique, and its uniqueness dominates consideration of likeness to other poems – even other poems made by the same poet. So how do we get to know them? And, if we could, what good would that be?

I come to my paradoxical title: 'Literature: An Instrument of Inquiry'. These days I find it assumed that there is only one way to knowing and that we all have easy access to it as an act of will. If you want to know anything you 'study' it, you bring your mind to bear on it, you force its meaning out of it, you analyse it, master it, control it. It is assumed that there is only one way of getting 'knowledge' and that we all know how this is done. But in what sense can it be said that we 'know' a poem? My proposal is that, if we hold sensitive and forthright commerce with poems, the poems themselves become instruments of inquiry, they tell us how to get to know, and we can direct the instrument both towards the poem and towards ourselves. This is what Bacon and Coleridge both meant by 'method' – not technique, or working to preformulated scheme, but a 'way through', a way of doing what is to be done (in this case getting to know the poem). If we approach in the technical manner we always find exactly what the technique was designed to find and usually not much more, and the heuristic impulse, the sheer desire and longing to 'know', the 'intellecturition', is frustrated by a nauseating tautology. It is like looking in a mirror and never seeing anything but your own face. If we do not find our instruments of inquiry in the poem, somehow self-fashioned and placed by the grace of quietness in our own hands, our efforts at literary inquiry will have a curious progeny – logically consistent, even plausible, but parodies none the less; speculations that look impressive and intelligent but have become fantasies from losing touch with what they are about – grave discourses on the obvious, the solemn unfolding of straightforward matters for which we need neither the stimulus nor the authority of poetry; demonstrations that prove almost anything except that we are on a right course or that our thinking has taken a fertile turn.

As philosophy begins in wonder, so poetry begins in delight. The primary end of poetry is pleasure; the ultimate end is truth. If we could hold poetry in the field of delight, as children do, we could be knowing in a very profound and fruitful way. But our minds nag at us: we worry about 'meaning'; we want to 'understand', to 'know more'. And here everything can go wrong, because the means of inquiry can determine the nature of the poem by altering the subject to suit the technique. Our concern is first of all, and properly, to make sure that we do not *mis*understand. A search for meaning and understanding, if not conducted sensitively and with respect for the integrity of the original, converts the poem into a piece of more or less logical discourse, treated as a 'phenomenon', shorn of those elements of sound, rhythm and patterned dynamics that are both its body and much of its reason for having come into existence. For a poem is not an alternative or approximate record; it is the only way that what is to be said could have been said. And, since its integrity grows from the fact that every part is indispensable and every part is an intimation of the whole, it cannot even be 'taken apart' without becoming something else.

If it is the poem we want to know, we must know it for what it is and for what it does (for what it acts out). It is in the inquiry into poetry that we discover just how difficult – how almost impossible – it is to keep the eyes (and ears) firmly on the object, to be sure that we are paying close attention to what is actually being said, what is actually going on, what sounds and rhythms are actually audible and to be heard. For a poem, stable and plain enough on the page, is not a thing, but a complex mental event articulated in the uttering of it. As a verbal statement it will say something very clearly, and that is the very least we need to get from it accurately; but it will not disclose its whole presence to verbal analysis – partly because you never know where to begin the analysis or what emphasis to give to the various elements isolated in analysis, and the central matters may completely elude the analytical procedure we happen to be using. Although the substance of a poem eludes all the usual tests of 'fact', it has elements of reliable certainty that one can grasp as moments of cognitive affirmation, and these are usually of an order of certainty and worth superior to what is commonly called 'fact'. We come to see that the reliability of what in a poem is perceived as important depends not upon the common tests of fact, but upon the quality of the reader's perception. In the same way that the quality of an idea depends upon the quality of the mind that generates or transmits it, so a reader 'qualifies' – not by mastering certain theories and procedures but by achieving the quality of mind required by the work he wishes to read, and by discovering 'analysis' as the patient and respectful unravelling of the complex presence the poem confronts us with. It is precisely that 'quality of mind', subtle and infinitely responsive, that we wish to secure –

in ourselves, and in others. The 'problems' do not reside in the poems, but in ourselves.

'In art, as in life, there are no classes for beginners.' As readers we should have no difficulty in grasping works of an imaginative order, simply because they are 'entities of direct appeal' and because they are in resonance with our own radical ways of knowing, recalling, making, remaking. But right at the beginning we are landed with the whole baffling complex, and there is no way of dealing with it bit by bit, or of formulating an adequate preparation. We can find, nevertheless, that the poem itself becomes an instrument of inquiry by directing our attention to whatever depth of thought or refinement of perception it demands; most of all the poem holds us firmly in the universe of language. It is one thing to regard language as our most specifically human gift, our stake of pure inventiveness and lyrical improvisation in the face of all attempts to treat us as little machines constructed out of 'motives' and 'causes'; it is quite another to have a highly cultivated sense of language, and without a reader cannot seriously expect to keep pace with poets, their universe being a verbal universe, their preoccupation making, their substantial material language and all the ways of language. And, with all this, we need to approach with a quiet mind, subduing our prejudices, presuppositions and formulated responses, even our approximate expectations.

The beauty of this process is that we can always tell whether it is working or not. If there is not emotional and cognitive engagement with the poem – if the poem does not begin to assume a self-declarative life of its own – the poem has slipped away and nothing is there; as a poem, the poem does not exist; there is nothing to be known, except in a trivial and adventitious sense. If we are honest with ourselves we can always tell whether this initial requirement is being met; if it isn't, the position cannot be forced by an act of analytical will. And you can always test the appropriateness and reliability of your thinking about the poem by referring it back to the poem – as part now of your own mental furniture – and see whether the poem will have it or not. In this way our sense of the poem crystallises, not along a single line of inquiry or according to any single theory of interpretation, but by alterations between analysis and synthesis, synthesis being a mental process entirely different from analysis. Analysis divides into conceptual parts, and in doing so loses the bond between the parts as integral to the whole; synthesis encompasses the poem as an integral whole of which each part is an intimation. These are not procedures but ways of mind – dynamic dispositions of the self which we evoke according to the direction and quality of our intention. Neither the one nor the other can effect everything; only in just consort do we get to know – and it matters very much how we approach.

So a respectable critic needs to be more than a little learned; and a respectable scholar needs to be a bit of a poet – to which the earliest great Alexandrian textual scholars give splendid witness for their sensibility rather than merely for their industry. Reflection over literary texts refracts into a great number of different special activities and procedures: some are more or less descriptive and empirical, others technical and even scientific; some are largely speculative and imaginative. In any comprehensive treatment of literary texts they tend to interlock and interact; but the closer we get to the imaginative reconstruction of a poem – the good-reading of it, the realising of it – the less we find we can rely on these special procedures alone. So the hope of something like an overarching 'scientific' procedure vanishes. The reason is obvious: the premisses which make sustained historical or scientific thinking possible are very different from the premisses that assist the making of a poem or the remaking of a poem in the reader's mind. These sets of premisses – even though we need both of them, even within the field of literary inquiry – are mutually exclusive: in particular, one is a system of value, the other is not. For which reason we cannot remake a poem if we regard it as a phenomenon; it has to be regarded as something like a living entity, a dynamic event that unfolds according to its own internal principles – a little like a person who has to be approached with respect, almost courted.

For the making of a poem, even when the poem is (as is often the case) carefully thought out, intelligently disposed and of fine craftsmanship, is itself a process of discovery guided primarily by an exquisite sense of what is 'right' for the poem coming into existence. The test is neither logical coherence (though that may well be required), nor a plausible similarity to a world generally known, nor the poet's deliberate intention or expectation (if known or knowable), but simply and pitilessly what belongs – and will be found to belong – to the unique universe that is coming into existence. A good reader develops a corresponding sense of 'rightness' to guide his analysis, to discern the pattern and disposition of forces, to realise the drama that declares itself. Much literary criticism has, in this last half-century, put on airs, presuming to be superior to the literature it studies, seeking to control literature by formulating ingenious categories and *schē mata* and by invoking ghostly primary elements so accommodating and indistinct that we can, with little difficulty, find them wherever we look for them. I claim for criticism a humble and ancillary duty: to seek fidelity, to heighten awareness, to disclose the literature intact and well lighted.

But how do we provide the appropriate kinds of learning, the disciplined habits that are at once exacting enough and delicate enough? How do we develop the sense that language is really something other than a conventional discursive notation: that for language to assume the state that we call 'poetic' is a matter not of vocabulary or even of theme, but of a musical capacity for swift unprepared change, for timbre, resonance, manifold implication, simultaneous meanings disposed above each other – even contraries – yet not in conflict? For without that sense of language only a limited amount can be achieved.

So the question of 'literacy' rises, returning to us quite predictably like a very familiar ghost from the past but with sharper teeth. For this I have no panacea. It's fashionable these days to regard anything that can be called a 'rule' as oppressive and anti-democratic. A cooler intelligence might point out that as far as grammar and syntax are concerned, the 'rules' can be seen as formulations of the commonest symptoms of incoherence and of defiance of the nature of language itself. Wilfully to ignore the 'rules' of grammar or to be ignorant of them and to make no effort to discover what they describe is like insisting upon reinventing the wheel when you don't even want to build a wagon. Yet it is not well, I think, to suppose that the problem of 'illiteracy' (to use an inflammatory term) can be solved by 'teaching writing skills'. There is no skill that can be separated out from the act and process of writing or speaking; for skilful writing and speaking grow out of a very complex integrative state of mind. But we can teach principles of logical coherence; we can teach a descriptive vocabulary for the elements of language and we can teach a way of using those definitions and categories to analyse the coherence and structure of actual pieces of wording; we can teach the primitive system of punctuation by which, conventionally, we score written language to show where the breath-pauses come and how long they are to be, and in complicated sentences to mark out the elements – logical or rhetorical – of the structure. All this is essential, but none of it is within shouting distance of finding out how to reach the deceptively elementary aim of 'clear, simple statement'.

When it comes to verse, some rudiments of versification and metrics can be taught by counting lines, examining rhyme-schemes, and the finger-counting of feet or accents in a line. But, as we know well, few have a fine enough ear to carry this beyond crude mechanics into that area of exact discrimination in which the values of the actual sounds, patterns, emphases and dynamics of the internal energy – that is, the whole drama of energy interacting upon deftly chosen formative limits – declare themselves as significant; a setting in which (incidentally) onomatopoeia is often the least interesting or remarkable feature in an infinite range of auditory possibilities. The ear *can* be trained – both the ear of the student and the ear of the teacher – and it has to be trained to the music of language – which is not the same as the music of music; but that can no more be *taught* than a violinist can be taught flawless intonation or a comedian the sense of timing; and none of these things can be learned unless a person has a passionate and scrupulous desire to learn them. Like recognising and naming type-faces at a glance, or identifying the work of a composer by the inflection of his melodic phrasing or the timbre of his orchestration, this level of discrimination is probably not within everybody's capacity; and, unless a teacher cares passionately about these things, he is unlikely to be able to generate a love for them. Listen to the opening lines of *Paradise Lost* or 'Kubla Khan' or 'The Wreck of the *Deutschland*'. You cannot be a musician without a refined capacity for listening; the same for a poet; the same for an informed reader of literature.

The depth and scope of the 'problem of illiteracy' is to be seen in the pervasiveness of it. Not to be able to spell, or punctuate, or job together a coherent sentence is not a hopeless state of affairs; and most young people speak well enough to be able to find some sort of foundation for the much more artificial business of writing. The frightening question is what to do about poverty of mental landscape. Where do we begin with a student who mistakes 'wandering bark' for the bark of a dog when in the context it obviously refers to a ship; or for another who supposes that 'jesting Pilate' refers, not to a Roman governor involved in some questionable decisions at a turning-point in history, but to a navigator?

I would ask that for a start students be taught simply to listen; that they should read verse rather than prose, and that the verse be strong, tough and demanding, so there will be some encounter with language in a poetic mode. I would ask too that students be made to hear what they are reading, otherwise they will not be able to engage the rhythms that are the physical traces of vitality. I would ask further that popular, topical and allegedly sensational books be avoided for teaching-purposes: you can easily get a 'response' from these, but you also get a great deal of deflection and very little effective educational mileage. For the point of studying literature is first to enjoy it, then to find in it the figures of a life and intelligence and imagination that is clearly not our own. The only way to populate the mind with reverberant materials (which is not quite the same as 'knowledge') is by caring for, or being fascinated by, what we know or are learning. No doubt every mind is provided with its own reverberant materials, but they may be very limited in extent and inappropriate for literary purposes. Whether a young person has a well-stocked mind is no doubt an accident of circumstances and temperament; but it's never too late to begin. Many have to begin in the university; and it is encouraging to find what spectacular advances some make in this in only three or four years. Given a little diligence and a capacity for delight, the accumulative process once started will go on, without effort, the better for not being systematic.

I make these points almost in desperation because I don't know how the situation is to be effectively reversed. What I do know is that, unless it is attempted soon, our literate culture is in serious danger of disappearing, leaving only a few idiosyncratic bookworms to tend the guttering candles in the next Dark Age. Yet a dead tradition, like a dead metaphor, is never absolutely dead; it is dead only in the mind of the person who finds it dead. The life is there to revive at the first breath of considerate attention, at the first attempt at humble access.

I have chosen to speak about poems, about the highest manifestations in the range of literature, because I wanted to make clear that the poetic way of mind is part of our heritage and essential to our health and wholeness as individuals and as

a society. I think we recognise the poetic habit of mind well
enough when we come across it; it is penetrating, disrespectful,
subversive; affirming a profound law of our own nature, accusing
the rules of logic of emptiness and tautology, questioning the
underpinnings of abstraction; stern guardian and courageous
ring-master of words. Yet it is all done for a song, and, as a song,
gratuitously, innocently, for the sheer delight of it; that is, very
seriously, but not earnestly. If we wish to come to that universe
of value, intensely human and beautifully organised, we follow
the process sketched out by Coleridge as an apparent definition
of Dramatic Illusion: we achieve 'that willing suspension of
disbelief-for-the-moment that constitutes poetic faith'. We decide
not to say no; we reject indulgent fantasy; we cross the threshold
into a country that is at once strange and familiar; we behave,
not like marauding hooligans or philistine tourists, but like guests,
according to ancient custom, because this is our own country. By
coming here we come to ourselves. Coleridge has caught this
perfectly in his prose gloss to the account of the journeying moon
in 'The Rime of the Ancient Mariner'.

> In his loneliness and fixedness he yearneth towards the journey-
> ing Moon, and the stars that still sojourn, yet still move
> onward; and every where the blue sky belongs to them, and is
> their appointed rest, and their native country and their own
> natural homes, which they enter unannounced, as lords that
> are certainly expected and yet there is a silent joy at their
> arrival.

10   Teaching Poetry*

I hope nobody supposed from this title that I would begin by handing round copies of poems, and would then proceed to demonstrate in detail how best to 'teach' those poems; or that I would survey all known approaches, techniques of analysis, forms of explication, tricks of haruspication, systems of classification, and proposals for achieving scientific objectivity in the examination of poems, and then say which I recommend. My purpose is more modest than that. I simply wish to ask what could conceivably be meant by the shorthand phrase 'teaching poetry', and why such an undertaking could be considered to be of more than common importance in education. I shall say a little about knowing and thinking. I may be a little theoretical at times. I ask you to be patient.

'To teach' has a disagreeably aggressive sound to it, but I let that pass. Do we teach poetry, or do we teach students? It seems safe to suggest that 'to teach' is either 'to cause somebody to know something' or 'to cause somebody to know how to do something'. I conclude from the prevalence of such phrases as 'to acquire knowledge', 'to contribute to the fund of knowledge', 'to work at the fringes of knowledge', etc., that we are inclined to think of 'knowing' as the gathering of reliable pieces of 'information' – largely perhaps because we tend to think of 'knowing' on the analogy of seeing. If we are provided with suitable visual equipment (the supposition seems to go), we can see what is visible. There is a seeing subject and a visible object; the relation between the two is (so to speak) instrumental. Good results depend upon good visual equipment and clear conditions for observation; results improve as the instrumental errors are adjusted and the lighting approaches the optimum. Both these conditions, it follows from the analogy, can to some extent be prepared ahead of time. Again, we commonly think (analogically) of seeing-with-the-mind's-eye; sometimes we call it 'intuition' (in which we perceive clearly at a glance), sometimes we call it 'understanding'

* *The Compass*, no. 5 (1979) pp. 1–15.

(in which we see through something complex and grasp the scheme of its inner relations and workings). The usual preface to a statement arising from, or affirming, either kind of knowing is 'I know that . . .', even though sometimes the statement may prove to be incorrect. Some philosophers have even stated that, if we cannot say distinctly *what* is known, there is no knowing. But I'm not so sure.

When the object known begins to lose clear definition as an entity, the verb 'to know' loses its affirmative clarity and changes its meaning. When I say, 'I know that person', I am most likely to mean, 'I've seen that person before' or 'I know that person's name.' If I say, 'I know that poem', I probably mean, 'I can tell you its title and who wrote it.' In both cases I am then dealing in items of verifiable information, in themselves more or less trivial. If the intent is more profound, the inflection changes: 'I *know* that person' (meaning 'I know him through and through; he has no secrets from me'), or 'I *know* that poem' (meaning 'I am thoroughly acquainted with the poem – or with that piece of music or the work of the writer'). I have then moved into an area in which the object cannot be fully accounted for by any number of statements in the form 'I know that . . .'; not only does verification of points of detail become difficult, but the unity of conception tends to dissolve in a multiplicity of descriptive detail. Yet, as the word 'intuition' implies, I *can* mean something genuine – and something different in quality and extent from an accumulation of verifiable detail – when I say, 'I know that person' or 'I know that poem.'

This is a very crude way of saying that there are different orders of knowing; and that what is knowable or to be known is the exponent of the quality of knowing required to encompass it – that is, that the nature and status of the knowable not only invokes the process of mind required to know it, but also that it leaves in the product of the knowing the marks of that nature and status. At the level of veridical information this involves no difficulty. But when the object-to-be-known passes out of the range of sensory or logical verification, we find that our minds can easily short-circuit the difficulty by assigning to what-is-to-be-known a nature and status that makes it readily knowable: that is, we work from the answer to the question instead of from the question to the answer.

I suggest that because poetry lies at a profound meeting-point of two extremely complex variables – life and the mind – poetry may well tax our cognitive ingenuity rather severely.

The distinctive marks of poetry are – in part, at least: precision, economy, multivalency, the condition of music. Poetry is a necessary and inevitable mode of utterance. Like all works of imagination, poems are entities of direct appeal. Given our natural capacity for the integrative and energetic state called 'imagination', and granted our gift of language – our most specifically human endowment – it would be surprising if reading and listening to poetry would not be the most natural thing in the world. I suggest, therefore, that, if we are using literature as an educational instrument, we should always begin with poetry; for poetry is not a sub-species of literature (as prose fiction is, or drama) but the prototype of whatever in language we call 'imaginative' or 'symbolic'.

'In art as in life there are no classes for beginners' – and with poetry there don't have to be any classes for beginners. Nor can there be, because there is no such thing as elementary or rudimentary poetry – there is only poetry more or less clearly defined. In order to establish the peculiar 'feel' of poetry, we must always begin with highly developed and complex examples of art. That at least will accustom the ear to the tune and shapeliness of the thing. There are other advantages. We can also establish confidence that even 'difficult' poetry is directly accessible (even though not immediately intelligible) to an untrained reader – as music is accessible to listeners untrained in the art of music. We can also establish the fact that we can *experience* poetry without fully understanding the poem. Until a poem is in some sense experienced, it does not exist in the mind; nothing relevant to the poem can be done with it. An elaborate expository or analytical reconstruction of the 'meaning' of the poem cannot substitute for direct perceptual experience at the outset; and it is unlikely to serve well as an introduction for a responsive activity that best arises from innocence of intent and is free from anxiety about 'meaning'.

Poetry seems to have a double nature: as a substantial thing to be grasped primarily by the senses; and as a complex mental event. Whether or not a poem records a mental event that 'actually' occurred in the poet who made it, it certainly is itself a complex mental event standing on its own feet, and capable of regenerating in a reader (or listener) a mental event corresponding in some way to itself in quality, power and configuration. As an 'event' a poem presents itself to us directly, and invites us to enter into it and partake of its activity; there's nothing else we can *do* with it. The *substance* of a poem, on the other hand, the fact that it can present itself to us as a solid presence (like Coleridge's nightmares, 'a foot-thick reality') arises not so much from the physical circumstance that it is printed on a page or uttered on the air; it arises rather from the fact that is made in language, that it presents itself as having certain formal and temporal limits and patterns accessible only to the ear and (by synaesthetic transfer) to the sense of touch; through these perceptual relations it induces refined and subtle patterns of 'feeling' (or psychic energy). By 'experiencing' a poem I mean paying attention to it as though it were not primarily a mental abstraction, but as though it were designed to be grasped directly by the senses, inviting us to 'function in the perceptual mode'. Poetry can and does make its primary engagement through the senses as much when a poem demands strenuous conceptual activity as when it is as purely musical as the specific music of language will allow.

Poems have *substance* – that is, they have the qualities that make them not presences only, but *physical* presences – in virtue of being made of words, of language organised dominantly according to metaphorical or symbolic relations. Our bond with language is primarily through the sense of *hearing*, a radical sense that – like touch, but unlike sight – does not readily evoke the conceptual processes of abstraction and generalisation. For educational purposes it is essential that poems be actually heard and listened to, whether as actually spoken aloud or as literally heard when reading in silence. The proper and discreet speaking of poetry provides a double physical bond: we not only hear, but also feel – in the musculature of tongue, lips, throat and face – the physical articulation of the words, the shape, mass, movement, impulse of the thing. In my own experience, most students looking at poetry need deliberately to subdue their cerebral anxiety. The first lesson is to engage the senses; not as an agreeable adjunct to other more intellectual delights, but as the necessary means to hold the mind in the perceptual mode, to keep the habits of abstraction and generalisation in their place. Once the senses are engaged all sorts of reflective activities are possible. If that has *not* happened we cannot expect much beyond a feeble pastiche of what is thought to be scholarly behaviour.

That such an elementary point should be worth making draws attention to some curious (but tacit) assumptions we seem commonly to make about the stuff we are working with. We seem to assume that, if we can postulate an external cause for an event, we can understand and interpret that event. But sometimes we assign ridiculous 'causes' – self-expression, the desire to communicate, a hunger to declare the position of man in a hostile world, and so on. In fact, the central preoccupation of a poet is to *make* poems, to construct stable and patterned word-things. These things-made arise from life, certainly, and reflect back upon life, but they are not '*about* life'. They are incorrigibly made in words, the words becoming unaccountably solid and tactual under the fingers of the mind. Paul Valéry has some very penetrating things to say about how and why poems get made. A poet, he says, is distinguished by the ease with which he enters the poetic state – 'a mysterious apparatus of life that has as its function to compose all differences, to make what no longer exists act on what does exist, to make what is absent present to us, to produce great effects by insignificant means'. A poet is 'an individual in whom the agility, subtlety, ubiquity, and fecundity of this all-powerful economy are found in the highest degree'. And a poem: 'a kind of machine for producing the poetic state of mind by means of words'. Again, the universe of poetry is a harmonic universe: in it 'resonance triumphs over causality'. The cause is intrinsic to the poem and can be discerned only within the poem. And 'If I am asked what I "wanted to say" in a certain poem, I reply I did not *want to say* but *wanted to make*, and that it was the intention of *making* which *wanted* what I *said*.' (In support of this last, I think of Hopkins's 'Wreck of the *Deutschland*', or Valéry's 'Le Cimitière Marin', or of those four lines of a Wyatt sonnet that were important in shaping Auden's rhythms.)

If the end of our endeavour is to know poems – not simply to know about them – then the beginning and end of our work, the essence of it, will be to induce that quality of knowing appropriate to the psychic events that we call 'poems'. But it is clear to me that if we actually attempt to '*teach* poetry' we shall end up in one or several of the plausible evasions that are the hazard of our profession: either teaching how to 'interpret' poems, by extracting the 'meaning' as though it could be separated out from the physical body of the poem, as though 'interpretation', like many other analytic procedures, were an end rather than a means; treating the poem as a puzzle to be solved; teaching how to classify a poem so that the awkward uniqueness of the individual poem can be dissolved into generalised discourse upon the category to which the poem is alleged to belong; teaching analytical 'approaches' and 'techniques', providing check-lists of symptoms to watch for (vowel-sounds, irony, ambiguity, meta-phor, paradox, etc., etc., etc.); and so on. Admittedly all these – and many more – will at some time be essential to the student of literature, but not at the beginning, and not indiscriminately. All of them are pretty blunt-edged tools, and can easily encourage presumptions and habits of mind not altogether appropriate to a delicate and heuristic enterprise.

Now I must speak for myself – not expecting that my views are either exclusively my own, or of any great originality. I can only hope that those who share them will take pleasure in hearing them repeated. What we must *teach* from the outset is the discipline (*disciplina*) of 'heuristic reading'; the end is the cultivation of heightened and informed awareness. Everybody has to do his own knowing; the best we can do is to train our students in how to get to know. Beyond that we shall want to show them (as best we can) how to sustain reflection upon a poem, how to develop confidence in their own perceptions, and what to do if reflection becomes blocked in tautology or in some gross disproportion between the tone and mass of the poem and the tone and depth of our cognitive response to it.

For some years children have been taught in school to read rapidly by eye. The first thing, then, is to make sure that a student can actually *hear* what he is reading; for if he cannot hear, he will not be aware of the rhythmic declaration of the energy and intricacy of the poem – the life, that is: nor will he be able to enter into the harmonic universe of the poem and be able to sense the dynamics or discern the *drama*, the trajectory of pure action traced out by the whole poem. Then – and always – anything that helps to cultivate a rich and subtle sense of language is of value; not only the multiple meanings of words, but their sounds and histories, and the way – in that activity in which the senses reverberate with each other – words can assume a physical and tactual quality, having configuration, mass, texture, trans-lucence, intrinsic energy, active function; and how in a poem words typically assume manifold, even conflicting, simultaneous meanings. The sense of language, and the cultivation of sensibility, the ability to hold cognitive activity in the perceptual mode as the root of the operation, with looped excursions into the conceptual (abstractive and generalising) processes always return-ing to the physical actuality and presence of the poem itself – these can all develop together, and are probably best drawn from a serious and minute study of poems of high quality, rather than from theoretical or generalised descriptions examined in the absence of actual poems. (In the study of poetry the integrity of the particular is paramount. The illuminating function of trying to categorise a poem is to be able to see in what precise respect the poem does *not* match the assumed category).

Once a student stops looking only for 'meaning', and engages the ear in the activity of the poem, the poem will begin to present a contoured shape rather than a plane surface of uniform emphasis; it will present itself as a patterned activity, shapely and self-consistent, with nodes of force that initiate and guide complex mental activity. (These patterns of force are often at variance with the surface 'meaning' and logical progress of the matter.) Altogether this encourages confidence in 'the gift of seeing more than one knows'. This phase of the work is largely carried out in the state called 'contemplative', the mind gazing. This 'synthesis' is the way of finding out what is what in a poem.

I can see three advantages in separating this phase out, deliberately and markedly, by strong imperatives *against* 'interpretation' and against 'thinking *about*' the poem. (Indeed it may be useful to advise students to sublimate their habit of thinking-about by telling them not to expect a poem to *mean* anything more specific than we expect of a piece of music; this throws the emphasis upon listening.) The three advantages are as follows. (1) The student becomes increasingly aware of a changing quality of relation between himself and the poem; his presumption that he is a knowing *subject* and the poem a knowable *object* has changed into a cognitive *relation*, dominantly perceptual, in which the initiative begins to shift from himself as knower to the poem as capable of directing the process of getting to know – a process (as I suggested) that is very much like getting to know a person. (2) Instead of the reader dominating and commanding the poem, the poem begins to command the reader's attention and to establish a hierarchy of relevance – the sense of a centre and a periphery. Instead of telling the poem to 'get known', he finds that the poem is somehow vicariously making him over into its own shape and dynamics. (3) As the obsession with 'meaning' dwindles, the reader becomes aware of the poem as a harmonic system in which many kinds of resonance begin to be discernible, that these resonances are by no means all auditory, that to a great extent they actually constitute the substance of the poem.

All this can come about without any prior knowledge about poetry or about forms of verse, metrics, philology, or theories of analytical procedure. The poetry comes in through the porches of the ear. Inasmuch as most of this, as far as possible, is conducted in the perceptual mode, the experience of the poem is largely in terms of 'feeling' (psychic energy as distinct from 'emotion'). Clearly *this* is not what the kids used unprettily to call a 'gut response'; for the feeling is not only generated by the poem, but it is also controlled – with increasing fineness – by the poem itself (the substance of the poem being defined largely in terms of feeling). So the 'sense of fact' and the 'sense of relevance' begin to develop. The *facts* of a poem are the substantial centres of attention as presented to us – things that certainly happen, and that happen at a perceived level of quality and energy. The sense of relevance is simply a matter of being able to discern what goes with what, what is more important than what; it is associated with a sense of proportion, relation, fittingness – the same sense of 'rightness' that 'unaccountably) guides the poet in his making.

The first engagement is by Tom Piper's whistle: the poem calls out to us, arrests and holds our attention. This is also the way an object in the outside world – something seen or heard – will command a poet's attention and, usually by being named or found a physical body in words, will become the germ around which a symbolic event grows. At first, by quietness and submission, a reader will seem to merge with the poem, and so can treat the poem as a 'self-unravelling clue' (which is what Coleridge says 'method' is); but the sign of a maturing cognitive process is the way the poem separates itself from the reader, becomes a 'thing out there', unchanged by inquiry, distinct and separate, with a life of its own – certainly not a projection of ourselves. As the poem moves away from us, we are aware that we are no longer merely 'experiencing' the poem; we are getting to *know* it as it becomes less and less like ourselves. What seemed at first little more than an intriguing encounter with a dark stranger becomes cause for a careful and faithful tracing out of the nature of the poem's existence, the universe it represents – or simply what it is and how it lives. The perceived contouring of the poem, its pattern of forces, allows us to separate out our own 'errors and ignorances' from the real issues and questions raised by the poem itself. We can then venture a little analysis.

This is the crucial phase in reflective inquiry. In order to remove the element of accident or the merely personal, to confirm and consolidate the cognitive experience, we shall seek to analyse complex impressions, loosen them into their elements so that we can see them more clearly. But, unless our analysis is guided by a firm perceptual grasp of the whole complex, the poem itself somehow accepting and adjusting whatever we offer to it, we shall probably find ourselves constructing a surrogate poem as a plausible substitute for the true poem. Unfortunately it is towards the construction of such fantasy poems that much of our formal school and university training prepares us. The result can be, for the thinker, very satisfactory: it is a way of dispensing with the unmanageable uniqueness and strangeness of the poem by converting it into something differently constituted, and because we have made it ourselves (a littly slyly) it will be utterly familiar.

Coming back to the beginning again – we are very much inclined not to recognise how profoundly the quality of our thinking is affected by the state of mind we bring to the thinking. If we imagine that we are not changed by what we know, if we imagine that we are knowing-machines that are not modified by their own knowing, our attempts to get to know can become aggressive and can destroy what we thought we wanted to know. The adjustment of the mind to a complex and delicate task is not primarily the selection of certain procedures or techniques, but rather the assumption of *discipline* – the quiet and submissive preparation of the mind for its task. Not only the temper of the mind needs to be adjusted, but also the 'colour'. Hence the immense importance of delight, wonder, affection, respect – opening the mind, making it alert, sensitive, receptive, hesitant to impose itself. The more intimate one's sense of what language is doing and can do in a poem, the more exact our appreciation of the complex and fugitive activities of mind involved in the making of a poem, the more inclined we are to feel delight, wonder, respect. This is an instance of the way that what we know can extend our ability to know further; the first knowing is not directed as a technical weapon towards the poem – it has imparted the tone and clarity that allows the mind to function appropriately in a task that cannot be forecast and for which therefore we cannot make specific and deliberate preparation. Yet the attitudes of mind that I suggest are fruitful (and a matter of virtue to attain to) are the very qualities that 'technical analysis' tends to dismiss as interfering with 'objectivity' and 'rigour'.

The only name I can think of for the process I have been describing – a phrase introduced by Alex Corry some years ago – is 'reflective inquiry'; and the theory of such an activity could be called 'heuristics' – the business of searching out something that is at once familiar and unknown, according to rules of search that are determined largely by the quarry, not by the hunter; and, as the quarry is uncatchable (though knowable), the process will establish an intimate bond between the hunter and the hunted until it is not certain which is the quarry and which the hunter. This reversal of apparent causal sequence is not uncommon in human affairs; even psychologists have noticed it. If all goes well, you get something like a reverse Pavlov effect: the dog eats its dinner and the doctor rings the bell.

Suppose we have (by 'teaching') trained a person to be a 'good reader'. He would have a fine ear, a rich and subtle sense of language, a copious store of learning gathered so affectionately and so promiscuously that it had all become like housemates, cherished but half-forgotten, reverberant to the lightest touch of association. He would be capable of clearing the line of vision by getting his own ignorances, preferences and fantasies out of the light so that (by grace or luck) it is the poem and not himself he's looking at, and so would be capable of sustained reflection over the poem, not seriously troubled by the fact that there can be no end to his reflection (unless he has chosen a poem so trifling that it will not support much reflection). Then what? What can he *do* with these marvellous capacities?

It may be that it is precisely at this point we fail to see that we have – as far as direct commerce with poems is concerned – fulfilled our task. What comes next is either not our business as teachers, or else it is almost entirely beyond our influence; for the next phase – if separable – is what we *do* with our knowing. We are all very inclined (as teachers) to try to make over our students into our image; as most of us are primarily scholars (rather than poets), we try to make our students over into scholars. No reflection over poems can proceed far without sound and comprehensive scholarship; but scholarship by itself will never produce the qualities of a fine reader – even though scholarship cannot get very far unless it is informed by an alert sense of what is going on in the body of its chosen material. The crux, from a paedagogic point of view, is in the body of literature itself, the stuff it is made in – language, words. At some point thinking must achieve body

and articulation by being worded – another clue must be paid
out for unravelling – not simply in order to 'record' what has
happened in the thinking, but as a means of defining, of sustaining
and illuminating our own inquiry, the sustaining of our thinking.
As the making of a poem is always a process of discovery, so the
wording-out of reflection becomes itself a process of discovery;
and this goes well or ill according to the precision and fertility of
the wording itself. Hence the immense importance of teaching
precision in choosing and applying special terms – not merely for
purposes of accurate definition, but in order to keep the line of
vision clear, to keep the mind in sharp focus so that the glimpse
of a fruitful possibility can be traced analytically to its most
remote consequences. Hence the need to be wary of inflated,
honorific and vogue terms, of catch-phrases that make the head
nod slowly in impassive approval like certain Chinese figures
without ruffling the surface of the brain-pan. Where better can
one learn the functional virtues of a fine precision in words than
in poetry itself? Or where better study the crucial implications of
that precision as the condition under which alone symbolic
activity can occur – not least in the 'other harmony' of prose? If,
like myself, you can see the end of good reading (?criticism) to
be heightened and informed awareness, the question for written
or spoken 'reflective inquiry' is not simply whether a record of
that awareness will be a 'contribution to knowledge', but whether
it will make somebody else more aware, with a refreshed capacity
for knowing, the perceptions purified, the object of inquiry placed
intact in the mind of the reader as matter for further inquiry and
further delight. In this way, literature itself becomes an *instrument*
of inquiry, showing us how far a question can be pursued, to
what self-revealing end a glimpse of a possibility can lead.

   To expect all our students to engage in such an activity is
probably an unreal – and unreasonable – hope. For a great many
students the best that can be hoped for is that they will have
become better – that is, more perceptive – readers, that through
their contact with us they will (as Frost says of a good poem)
have suffered an immortal wound and will never get over it. That
would be no trivial accomplishment. A few certainly will take up
the clue, the scent, the pursuit; and of those a smaller few will
succeed beyond any reasonable expectation. But we need to be
clear, in setting exercises and encouraging certain ways of speaking
and writing, what the exercise is meant to achieve. If we are

inviting students to venture into an area of discourse unfamiliar to them, we need to be sure that there are excellent examples of the art available for study (that is, for listening to); otherwise we get imitations of allegedly learned articles that are themselves too often, alas, no better than lifeless parodies of both genuine scholarship and genuine reflective inquiry. The limits of behaviourism are obvious and sombre.

One of the great advantages of working at literature is that it engenders something of the devil-may-care, jackdaw mentality that makes poets objects of our scholarly envy and indignation. We learn from literature to develop a sense of humour, to feel an instinctive disrespect for grave formulations that purport to provide a fulcrum to move the whole universe of literature. We find that some of the more fruitful (though limited) methods of analytical inquiry need little or no theoretical or philosophical underpinning; they are clever paedagogic devices that sometimes and in some cases put us on a right track, and work well if we don't press them beyond their limits. (And yet where would the calculus be without the clever deceit of dx/dy?) We find that certain theories, catch-phrases, axioms, thoughtless epigrams thrown out by artists themselves – the tune of this man's way of thinking, or the translucence of that man's prose – are of value (is it disreputable to admit this?) not as dogmas or as technical directions, but as talismans which quieten and dispose our minds; objects the contemplation of which clear our vision, relax our nerves, tempt us to dangerous enterprises. If we take any of these devices too earnestly we endanger the delicate heuristic poise of our minds.

For the mind is (in one sense) a symmetrical integrative energy-system, complete in itself and constantly completing itself. Like any energy-system, the mind seeks equilibrium and repose by the swiftest means available. Take the example of what Gabriel Marcel calls 'reflection'. To be looking for something you care about induces a specific state of mind, characterised by certain dynamics that cannot be induced otherwise. The essential functional element is 'concern'. If I am looking for some *thing* that I care about and already know – something lost (say) that I care about – I am not looking for the thing but for the whereness of the thing. The urgency of my search, the induced activity of mind, is a direct function not of the intrinsic value of the thing but of my concern for it. When I have discovered the whereness, the activity of the mind relapses into composure. Correspondingly, if I seek to know a poem (or to know it better), and approach it through a formula for finding it or a formula for recognising it, my mind is oriented by the formula, and achieves penetrating power by being concentrated in that way. But, if it is the fulfilment or matching of the formula I am looking for, that is certainly where the search will end – in the tautology of what I started with, not in a fresh discovery of what, not-knowing, I set out to get to know. If, however, our intent is set upon knowing the poem, and we are prepared to use for what it is worth any promising device, means, formula or incantation, then we stand some reasonable chance of finding what we are looking for. Beforehand we can never be certain that any preconceived method will 'work': the poem has to decide that.

We have to be a little quizzical and light-hearted about ourselves too; because we are well aware that the fact that we knew something once does not mean that we know it for good and all – not because we can forget and do forget, but because we may not be lucky enough to pick up the clue again. The authentic value lies not in the *product* of the knowing, but in the act and process of knowing, and in how we handle that knowing. Usually, I think, we cannot remember the act of knowing itself; what we remember is that that act occurred and what it felt like; and we may be more or less confident that we can recover the act, or that we can regenerate an even more valuable act of knowing in the presence of the same objects of our reflection. By grace, through patience, and through a curious combination of passive attention and alert response, we are certain that we can enter into the universes of poems, and that these are new worlds that for all their strangeness are recognisably our worlds; that, if we can read perceptively and are learned enough and innocent enough to respond deeply and richly to something conceived in a mind more copious, daring and agile than our own, then our relation with poems will surely sustain and nourish reflection, and may now and then bring us, through the necessary articulation that alone sustains thinking, to see something worth seeing and to say something that may be worth remembering – if only as a talisman. Most valuable, if the integrity of the poem is of primary concern, is the way this kind of reflection reverses (as it were) that habitual reconciliatory movement of the mind from the particular to the general, from the less to the more, which is a spontaneous resolution to equilibrium (so that there's no more work to be done). Reflective inquiry shows us how to think from the more to the less, from the generalised to the particular; and this, when luminous, evokes the otherwise unattainable recognition of the universal. In this too we re-enter the universe of the poet – our birthright if we have a clue to it. It would be disingenuous, however, not to repeat a remark of Valéry's on the 'marvellous economy needed for the beginnings of Poetry'.

> If one knew a little more about it, one could hope in consequence to form a fairly clear idea of the poetic essence. . . . A little metaphysics, a little mysticism, and much mythology will for a long time yet be all we have to take the place of positive knowledge in this kind of question.

The same goes for reflective inquiry, for sustained thinking.

I have been speaking of a propaedeutic, not a system nor a whole programme. I would do or say nothing to diminish the importance of profound learning, of skill in analysis guided to remote consequences, of the capacity for sustained – even ruthless – logical sequence, for that elegance in exposition that is the crown both of mathematics and of music. I would however encourage a little self-mockery in supposing ourselves capable of undertaking work of such alarming educational possibilities and of such subtle privacy. Because poetry is the heart and prototype of all literature, we must be prepared at all stages to lose the thread.

As far as the teaching of poetry is concerned, probably the best we can do – each in his own way – is to find out how to bring our students into the presence of poems. We must also find ways of preventing them from aborting their acquaintance by short-circuiting their mental activity into thinking about something else, and so bringing their minds to rest. The most valuable thing we can do, I think, is to allow students to *witness* the heuristic processes I have been speaking about and the quality of sustained reflection; to encourage them to gain confidence in the accuracy of their own perceptions and their own judgements; to encourage them to engage all their faculties, especially at the level of perception, and so to advance towards a disciplined – that is, submissive – adjustment of themselves to the inexhaustible business of getting to know; to encourage in them, by example, confidence that their own perceptions and judgements can be tested against the consistency of the poem; to demonstrate that the quality of an idea depends upon the quality of the mind that holds it, that the quality of an inquiry depends not so much upon technical skill as upon fineness of discrimination and quality of intelligence. We need also to make clear the hazard that our desire to understand and to unify brings us into; how the phase of analysis is always in danger of losing us by attaching us to a plausible will-o'-the-wisp; and how, if we are to move out of the area of mere accident, we must take that risk over and over again – with the confidence of a person walking a tightrope with no net under him.

Above all, in an age bemused by the specious beguilements and expectations of parascientism, by attempts to represent all human action – no matter how lyrical or inventive – as the products of Newtonian machines of no great sophistication, it is the business of poetry – and our professional business – to affirm and enjoin a way of mind that is specifically human, inventive and daring, a way of mind that can include everything the mind can encompass and every way the mind has of working; and to spread that infection with all the subversive and light-hearted zest that poetry makes us heir to.

11 The Humanities in the World at Large*

Through the last half-century – a very short time – the humanities have come to be held in lower and lower esteem in the eyes of the public and of the official representatives of the people; as though the humanities can now be seen to be ineffectual, obsolescent, of slight relevance to modern circumstances. Since by tradition the humanities are the heart of a university, the universities have also come to be regarded with quizzical contempt, except as far as they provide training for 'practical' or lucrative professions. The respect – the almost superstitious veneration – for the humanities that propelled me as a child into classical studies, even at a time when Greek had vanished from the schools and Latin was rapidly disappearing – that regard has turned into an attitude of condescension, the mild compassion we feel for a dying species. The earlier respect was generated by persons of incorruptible conviction; often people of some cultivation, but by no means all of them. If the history of education in the early development of this country tells us anything, it is that a desire for education, to be able to realise the self to its full capacity, was a powerful and disinterested groundswell among people of all sorts and conditions; education was not seen as a desirable ornament jealously preserved by a privileged few. The history of the foundation of Canadian universities confirms this; so does the biography of most of the Canadians who are remembered for their lasting contribution to the quality of life in this country.

In talking about the humanities we are talking about education: the *nisus formativus*, the formative impulse, of social man. For several centuries, and until quite recently, the humanities – or humane studies, as I should prefer to say – were acknowledged

**Queen's Quarterly*, vol. 86 (1978) pp. 1–15.

as the foundation, source and propaedeutic, not only for school-teachers, scholars and professors, but for those who (whether or not they intended to do so) came to play an active part in the life of society, and particularly in those ways of life in which clear thinking, versatility, articulate speech and writing, and accuracy of judgement were essential – in public service, in government, the Church, the law, and other once-learned professions; not least in that most 'practical' art of preserving the vitality of education itself, fostering and transmitting the learning without which knowledge has little substance and no cutting-edge, without which humane studies fail to heighten the quality of perception and the capacity for sustained reflection. In two world wars, humanists from many walks of life have demonstrated their skill in worldly matters, their adaptability, their courage, clear vision, firm judgement; have left the academy to become leaders and have often chosen to return to the academy, considering that to be a responsibility worth having fought for. Persons educated in the humanities have for a long time been sought out for their intellectual and moral qualities – as administrators and leaders in government and university, as directors in industry and finance, and in highly technical fields. It would be very strange (and wasteful) if that were not so.

How pervasive the rejection of the humanities may be is difficult to assess; that the rejection *is* pervasive is an observed fact. It is also an observed fact that our governments show little inclination or concern to reverse that trend. Perhaps that is understandable at a time when government is consumed with a desire to control and predict; for governments seem to have redirected their efforts from 'the art of the possible' to 'the technique of the manipulable'. Anybody who 'refuses to obey any injunction the basis of which cannot be verified' is an enemy of order, an anarchist; and anybody who insists upon being human – that is, upon exercising the energy and inventiveness of his mind – is by definition unpredictable. Teachers and humanists tend to be of that nature – disturbing, potentially subversive. Such people can be expected to have a rough time in a computer-controlled society. No doubt changes in social expectations and certain generalised considerations of 'social justice' have placed upon our educational system a confusing burden unprecedented. I have no doubt at all that teachers, from their very nature, can deal with that burden if they are allowed to do so; for their resilience and ingenuity, and their devotion to values other than mere 'usefulness', are indomitable.

If we examine carefully the way the wave of neglect of the humanities has mounted in recent years, and as a response to what forces and influences, we may be able to decide whether the humanities are indeed an archaic convention that should now be allowed to pass quietly out of existence; or whether (as I suppose) society has lost the thread – or has been induced to lose the thread – and is in danger of doing itself a serious mischief if it does not pick it up again pretty quickly. That would not be merely a matter of formulating policies, but of finding and affirming as a basis for any conceivable policy an image of man, and believing in it. I think we can infer pretty accurately from current policies, trends of fashion, market forces and other implied affiliations of interest what the dominant images of man are at present. On the whole, they seem to me less than admirable. I prefer the humanist's image, the image necessarily in his mind's eye throughout his reflections – not a generalised view but, in the artist's way, a particular image – in the way Bronowski, for example, thinks of 'the kind of man I honour: dexterous, observant, thoughtful, passionate, able to manipulate in the mind the symbols of language and mathematics both, and also the visions of art and geometry and poetry and science'.

The spectacular series of discoveries in atomic physics in the early years of this century, following hard on the dislocation of beliefs in the later nineteenth century by 'scientific' theories of the evolution of man, established an unprecedented esteem for pure science. Evolutionary theories of the origins of man need not have had an adverse effect upon religion, but they did; the theory of relativity and the theory of quantum mechanics should theoretically have strengthened the position of the humanities, but they haven't. As the power of pure science declared itself, and the cleverness of technology swam in its wake, it seemed that science was a conquering idea that would presently encompass the whole field of knowledge. The fact that pure science and the humanities are interdependent and complementary did not interfere with the common view that they were so distinct as to be contrary – that, as the one advanced, the other must retreat; and a common definition of the humanities became 'all those studies that are clearly distinguished in content and method from the physical and biological sciences'.

To show that such a view is not only irrational but damaging to both is a subtle matter requiring a little patience to unravel. But it can be shown briefly through the history of the two words 'humanities' and 'science', and by considering a little the dynamic constitution of the human mind – that the two embody not two mutually exclusive activities, but two complementary ways of mind that we all partake of.

The term 'humanity' or 'humanities' came into English in the fifteenth and sixteenth centuries by way of French and Italian to represent the Latin word *humanitas* in the sense used by Aulus Gellius, Cicero and others: 'mental cultivation befitting a man, liberal education'. For Cicero this involved the study of literature, effective utterance, and the cultivation of the qualities and inclinations proper to mankind – good manners, consideration, compassion – a backward glance at Plato's Guardians and a foretaste of the qualities ascribed by Thomas Arnold to the 'gentleman'. In the early Middle Ages seven 'liberal arts' had been recognised: four of them mathematical and three to do with grammar, rhetoric and logic. (Mathematics as an essential component in a liberal education is a view still held at Cambridge.) This form of study represented intellectual cultivation, the training that produced it, and the refinement of the instruments proper to that training. By the sixteenth century the central university studies were directed to grammar, rhetoric, poetry and especially the received classics in Latin and Greek. By 1535 'Lectures in humanity, that is, in the classical literature, were established in all colleges' at Oxford, and the School of *literae humaniores* ('Greats') 'made its way under the well-deserved name of Humanity to the head of the Faculty of Arts'. The singular word 'humanity' is still used in Scotland, but referring only to Latin studies. (There is some seamy history in the background of all this, but to keep the picture clear let's pretend there wasn't: it didn't in the end make much difference.)

The plural form 'humanities' seems in some sense to have been accidental, though reinforced in recent years by the tendency for fields of knowledge to diffract into lesser fields, and by the tendency of each of these fragments to call itself a 'discipline' (although there are probably no more than four or five definable disciplines – i.e. ways of adjusting the mind methodically – to deal with the whole field of knowledge). The word 'humanities' may seem to refer to a number of subject-areas – e.g. philosophy, literature, history, language, social institutions – together making up the whole field of humane studies; but these are rather facets of a broad and intimately unified field of inquiry, the identifiable 'subjects' representing not divisions of the field, but reconciliatory adjustments to variations in the field and to the typical intent of the inquirer.

The word 'science' is the English form of Latin *scientia*, meaning simply 'knowledge'. In the Middle Ages the seven liberal arts were indifferently called the seven liberal sciences, and much later the word 'science' was used to refer to that part of 'Greats' that dealt with philosophy, logic and associated matters. Not until the end of the eighteenth century, largely on the success of Newton and Laplace, did 'natural philosophy' presume to the status of 'science' – that is, came to be recognised as a genuine and reliable form of *scientia*, knowledge. It took about a century for the word 'science' to be disengaged unambiguously into the sense we now exclusively assign to it: observed facts systematically classified and more or less bound together by being brought under general laws, including trustworthy methods for discovering new truths within its own domain.

In his *Advancement of Learning* (1605) Francis Bacon (considered by some as the father of modern science) recognised 'three knowledges, Divine Philosophy, Natural Philosophy, and Humane Philosophy, or Humanities'. For Bacon, the central term was 'philosophy', embracing all knowledge – as it had been in the capacious and systematising minds of Plato and Aristotle, and later, up to the middle of the nineteenth century, in the minds of the great heuristic virtuosi and polymaths – Leonardo, Dante, Erasmus, Vico, Bently, Goethe, Coleridge (to mention only a few). It appears, then, that 'the sciences', which now seem to be counter to, even in aggressive conflict with, the humanities, evolved from the same single (ill-defined) focus of systematic reflection as the humanities. We can also see that the apparent split between humane studies and sciences represents not a dividing-up of the field of knowledge, but the application, to an increasing range of that field, of the 'scientific method' that had triumphed in astronomy and physics, and that helped, with increasing momentum, to refine and concentrate the practical applications of physical laws and processes.

Both represent the increasing power of our abstractive capacities, and the specialisation of each of the two phases or modes that all our minds exhibit, two ways of mind: the contemplative and the practical, the central process of one being 'synthesis' and of the other 'analysis'. Both ways of mind are the properties of all our minds; without the analytical mode the humanist could not refine and give substance to his reflection; without the synthesising mode the physicist would not be able to make the imaginative leap that seizes the visionary possibilities of his glimpse of a luminous relation, a conceivable hypothesis, a possible law. For it is clear that in no mind can mere facts or data generate the laws that order them.

In the interaction of the two modes we see the identity of intellect and imagination. And the complementarity of the two modes is shown in the way poetry strives towards the condition of music, and science strives towards the condition of mathematics. Yet music and mathematics, though apparently inseparable in the mind of Pythagoras, are not the same; and there are specific differences between humane studies and science because they proceed through different orders of abstraction – the one moving in one such order of abstraction towards something like 'pure intellect', the other more towards the physical specificity of perception. That specific difference is a large one. For the one (the scientist) is preoccupied with the world of nature; the other (the humanist) is preoccupied with the world of man. All we know is that the two are bonded together in the nature of mind itself.

I should like to unfold that difference a little, by placing the emphasis on what I know best – the world of the humanist. One of the distinctive marks of the humanist is his insistence upon handling everything 'philosophically' in order to secure the integrity of the matter under inquiry, his central 'facts' being not phenomena but 'facts of mind'. Through facts of mind and the reconstruction of facts of mind, he seeks to disclose and affirm the unifying vision that is the distinctive function of the mind. In the face of the explosive disintegration of 'knowledge' as 'things known', and the apparent disintegration of the whole field of what is knowable into an infinity of mere facts of observation, his central reality is that remarkable integrative power for which we reserve the word 'imagination', seeing it as our principal means of making ourselves real, and of holding to the conviction that though knowledge is manifold, truth is one.

Let me illustrate the quality of mind that seems to me to

represent well the humanist. Listen to Paul Valéry, poet, man of action, as much a polymath as Goethe, a man of refined scientific instinct – reflecting upon the Greek genius for pure intellectual discovery:

> Greece founded geometry. It was a mad undertaking: we are still arguing about the *possibility* of such a folly.
>
> What did it take to bring out that fantastic creation? Consider that neither the Egyptians nor the Chinese nor the Chaldeans nor the Hindus managed it. Consider what a fascinating adventure it was, a conquest a thousand times richer and actually far more poetic than that of the Golden Fleece. No sheepskin is worth the golden thigh of Pythagoras.
>
> This was an enterprise requiring gifts that, when found together, are usually the most incompatible. It required argonauts of the mind, tough pilots who refused to be either lost in their thoughts or distracted by their impressions. Neither the fraility of the premises that supported them, nor the infinite number and subtlety of the inferences they explored could dismay them . . . . They accomplished the extremely delicate and improbable feat of adapting common speech to precise reasoning; they analysed the most complex combinations of motor and visual functions, and found that these corresponded to certain linguistic and grammatical properties; they trusted in words to lead them through space like far-seeing blind men. And space itself became, from century to century, a richer and more surprising creation, as thought gained possession of itself, and had more confidence in the marvellous system of reason and in the original intuition which had endowed it with such incomparable instruments and definitions, axioms, lemmas, theorems, problems, porisms.

Valéry, who at the age of twenty-two wrote an essay 'On the Method of Leonardo da Vinci' that still makes the hair bristle to read, also wrote a memorable record of his reflections upon a seashell. In this he says something startling about ignorance, the matrix, the mothering confines of our knowing: that

> Ignorance is a treasure of infinite price that most men squander, when they should cherish its least fragments; some ruin it by educating themselves, others, unable so much as to conceive

of making use of it, let it waste away. Quite on the contrary, we should search for it assiduously in what we think we know best. In the matter of snails, I did my best to define my ignorance, to organise it, and above all to preserve it.

He meditates upon a seashell. He knows that, although he has no reason to question the foot-thick substance of the physical world, it is not actually the *world* he is getting to know, but his mind trying to look at the world, and his mind trying to look at his mind trying to look at the world. That is the sort of thing Kant had been saying systematically, in his own way, starting with 'Pure Reason'; and that is what Werner Heisenberg, the constructor of quantum mechanics, tells us is forced upon our recognition by modern atomic physics. One is not surprised to find that Valéry was a friend of Einstein (who was also a class II violinist) – the man who (as Bronowski put it) changed Newton's God's-eye-view of the universe to the relativist's man's-eye-view of the universe. Here again we encounter, in the physicist's laws of probability and complementarity, the translucent impenetrability of the human mind as a marvellous instrument of knowing – for a long time a truism to the humanist.

Let me take a fresh nip and see whether, against the background of what looks like sweet reason, we can trace the way humane studies have fallen into contempt, overshadowed by 'science' in public esteem. Here we intersect with an easily recognisable world, in which special interests and politicians are at work, and in which the fallibility of human judgement is not far to seek.

A while ago, when the Russians put up the first sputnik, a notable wave of panic swept through the non-Russian world: everybody must be trained in 'science', and all national resources must (as far as possible) be redirected to that end. This drastic, though no doubt politically plausible, piece of sail-trimming had a secondary effect that was probably never intended or foreseen in the corridors of power: the public dutifully lined up behind the latest policy, neglecting (as usual) everything but the punch-line: and the humanities were thrown into the shade.

One of the most interesting peripheral manifestations in that era was the appearance in a not-very-widely-circulated English paper of a journalistic article: it was called 'The Two Cultures'. In no time at all it was a topic of earnest and tedious debate all around the world. The interesting thing is that the author, whose prestige as a scientist was not of a particularly high order, set the cat amongst the pigeons by seeming to exalt the virtues of 'scientists' above the virtues of the 'humanists', when he was in fact saying something quite different. He made no serious attempt to examine or discuss the fundamental differences between science and the humanities as modes of inquiry or ways of mind; nor did he examine – in terms, say, of cognitive theory and human experience – the relations that might obtain between them. What he was actually doing was launching, on a wave of sentimental rhetoric, a class-action on behalf of 'scientists' (honest and harmless moujiks he represented them as being, innocent of intent though wearing ragged clothes) against the alleged arrogance and obfuscation of a complacent and privileged upper class – the 'humanists'.

The transmission of ideas has its own dynamics and its own laws, which, though empirical, seem to be absolute in contemporary society. The First Law is, 'If what is said is bad enough it must be true.' According to this law, Snow's tirade – 'One up for Science' – was bound to stick like a burr, especially when it was reinforced by the Second Law: 'Indecent exposure is better than no exposure at all.' For a time, the Third Law was operative: 'If anything is repeated often enough it will certainly be taken for truth.' After a while the Fourth Law (also known as the Nixon Parallax) supervened. 'If something is repeated often enough it will nauseate the hearer.'

The phrase 'The Two Cultures' passed out of currency (as all vogues happily do), and now has something of the melancholy savour of a shameful overindulgence; but in its brief heyday it did a good deal of damage, some of it probably irreparable. What was in fact a social and class issue was generally received as though it had metaphysical or epistemological substance. An extremely subtle, profound and important *distinction* (between science and the humanities) was taken for a black-and-white *division* that implied that a chasm lay across the whole field of learning, marking one kind (or class) of person from another; technology – the great anti-humanist reaction – came to be confused with 'science' and even to be called by the name 'science' (although it is well known that a pure scientist or a mathematician is a person a humanist will dance a farandole with any day of the week). In the universities all 'disciplines' (i.e. distinguishable areas of study) were considered to be of equal educational value, and all claimed the right to equal exposure in the academic supermarket; and the word went round that the humanities were obsolete, a relic from a Dark Age, and could no longer survive in the dry light of the modern age. All these dangerous confusions, singly or in combination, are now pretty firmly established by the Third Law – truth by reiteration – even though the academic supermarket seems to be trying to change itself back into a village general store again, pot-bellied stove and all.

I venture to formulate yet another law – a Fifth Law: 'The quality of an idea depends upon the quality of the mind that holds or transmits it.' *Corollary*: a banal mind will reduce everything it touches to banality. *Conclusion*: we are in danger, as a society, of feeling most comfortable in a *Reader's Digest* world in which nothing is fit to be received into the field of attention until it has been predigested to that level of banality at which it can be readily absorbed, without effort, by a person of very modest intelligence. The clear symptoms of the operation of this law are to be seen in the exaltation of journalism, and in the notion that the prime ingredients in modern intellectual activity are 'information' and 'entertainment'.

A second panic has now set in – this one financial and economic. Everything must now be turned to commerce, industry, finance, anything that will 'attract investment' and 'create jobs'. A little cash may be spared for the fine arts because they produce objects and spectacles that can be put on display; otherwise all available funds must be withdrawn from any activity that can be classed as 'unproductive'. By definition, the humanities can expect no mercy, because it is not their business to make things that can be put on display. (Would you like to watch a professor reading a book? Or listen to him giving a lecture? On national television?) It is their duty to teach people to think – whether through teaching or writing – and to help individuals to discover themselves and to realise the extent of their capacities; but all that is too imprecise and subversive a 'goal' to merit a productivity-rating.

In the first panic – the Snow-job – the humanist, though endangered, was still regarded with whimsical affection, as an endangered species, a duck-billed platypus or a whooping crane. In the second panic, except for a few atavists who mutter about the importance of 'basic education', the humanities are thought to be utterly irrelevant. This attitude is more ruthless and far more dangerous to society than the first. As university enrolments drop, and the chances of graduates getting any sort of job diminish, the brighter kids are moving away from the humanities into medicine, law, commerce, economics. I would not suggest that there is anything particularly brutish about training in any of those professions; and it is the case that you can't escape into law or medicine without at least a smattering of the humane studies. But I do suggest that there are some very important matters that fall outside the field of any of those professions, that need to be very carefully thought about if we are to avoid a descent into barbarism. One question is whether economic determinism is the best net to get caught in if it's swimming or flying we're interested in.

In the crude mechanics of the 'practical world', where almost everything has to be done at the wrong time and without cool consideration, and fineness of intent is obliterated by the coarse-grained and rough-hewn results that usually accrue, the apparent outmanoeuvring of the humanities – cock of the walk for several centuries – looks like a pretty heady advance for modernism. What it actually shows is the now well-known process of 'politicis-ation' – the confusion of terms in the rhetoric of expediency. As Philip Guedalla once observed, 'You can take any stigma to beat a dogma' – a variant on my First Law. As long as any activity can be represented, or misrepresented, in the current jargon of politics, no matter of what colour – Liberal, Conservative, Socialist, Marxist – it can be quickly shown to be either on the side of the angels, or ready for the outer darkness of neglect. You can tell: when they take away your telephone, you know it's time to take up bird-watching.

What I'm trying to do is to sketch out the process by which the public has come to its present attitude of neglect and apathy towards what has traditionally been the rock on which our education was built. It's hard not to be seeing enemies, even though the *real* enemy is the idle and uncritical mind. It may sound as though I am establishing three categories: humanities (good); pure sciences (different from humanities, but good – though of little direct human import); and between them technology (the worst of both worlds). Let me modulate that scheme a little.

None of those three terms is entirely stable; nor are the bounding-lines between them distinct – especially when we consider that all can be, and not infrequently are, encompassed by a single mind. As I see it, the source of impatient misunderstanding is in the middle zone, only one aspect of which is properly speaking 'technology'. Technology at best provides instruments, tools and toys that are of neutral value until we begin to use them; at worst it provides devices and concoctions of such destructiveness or futility that, although they may be readily marketable, it is unwise even to contemplate using them at all. Pure science, art, humane studies – those are all gratuitous, non-utile; technology is nothing if not useful. But there is a curious inversion to the logic of technology: the logic that constructs usable variations on the principles of pure science automatically precludes the inferences that might secure their beneficent use, or the inferences that might determine the limits of their beneficent application. In its designedness becoming almost a parody of pure science, technology seems to me rather like a monstrously ingenious idiot playing successfully with a very complex Meccano set. (I happen to love complex machines, delicate instruments, triumphs of engineering.) The sheer brilliance of some of the physical and chemical contrivances beguiles us into thinking that their uses are as benign as their ingenuity is elegant: it would not take much effort to call up examples – but I refrain.

A more serious aspect of the 'middle zone' is represented by the parasciences – those activities in which an attempt is made to apply scientific and statistical method to areas of inquiry into human matters that humanists have traditionally considered in a qualitative manner: psychology, certain kinds of history, politics and economics; linguistics; that curious hybrid sociology; anthropology; and some others. I have already suggested that these attempts do not constitute an invasion of territory or a take-over from the humanities. Yet there are no grounds that I know of for considering that 'scientific' inquiry into our 'inner goings-on' or into the state of society is so clearly superior to a philosophic approach that everybody but 'scientists' must withdraw from those fields. Much of this work is still at a rudimentary level, working from limited, even bizarre, hypotheses; but there is no reason why they should not have a contribution to make; and indeed valuable contributions have been made, and continue to be made. But scientific method – with its exclusion of value judgements, its attempt at 'objectivity' (i.e. the theoretical exclusion of a human observer), and its limited assumptions about fact and causality – does not look like the most promising instrument for exploring the complexities of perceiving, knowing, feeling, recognising, interpreting, judging.

Be that as it may, what concerns me most of all is the way the philosophical nature of humane studies has suffered attrition from within its own ranks, presumably under the pressure of the success of 'science'; with the implicit assumption (seldom if ever uttered) that the study of literature (for example) should become 'scientific' so that its results will be 'cumulative'. I can think of no other reason for the narrowing of the field of inquiry as I see it in the study of literature: with the exaltation of the 'specialist', the suspicion of the generalist, the retreat from inquiries that necessarily intersect in the study of literature – philosophy, pyschology, epistemology, ethics. If it is the case that the true humanist is free from the absolutes equally of the philosopher, the scientist and the artist, then a drift of humanists towards a parascientific specialisation is a disturbing manifestation. Certainly it produces some very unlovely writing, and presents to the world an uncouth image of the humanist.

Another troublesome symptom is the way the Canadian Broadcasting Corporation has been forced from its founding intention to a steady diet of 'news, reviews, and interviews'; and the way the Canada Council has been divided up with a shift of directive authority that suggests a shift of intent from disinterested to interested. I refrain from comment on the CBC because I have always admired its best work. And I pass by the splintering of the Canada Council in silence – except to object to the subordination of the humanities to the social sciences, and to the use of the word 'research' as an inadequate term for the humanist's reflective activity. My worry again is over 'politicisation' – by which I do not mean the intrusion of politicians into areas where there omniscience might be ill at ease; but the use of a fallacy so old that Aristotle had a name for it: 'metabasis eis allo genos' ('the clandestine passing over from one kind into another kind'). In both cases the command is to give society what they want, and to be economically productive. It seems to me that, within the current jargon of conflict, competition and compromise, the notions of 'productivity' and of the wishes of 'society' are both equally meaningless when we direct them towards the institutions in question, the CBC and Social Sciences and Humanities Research Council of Canada: for the humanities are an educative discipline, that is not designed for making *things* (except for the overflow of their reflection into scholarly and reflective writing – which is something society has never to my knowledge asked for); and the CBC is an institution educative and instructive that was never conceived as fulfilling its destiny by competing in the manufacture of a neutral (if 'entertaining') carrier-wave for advertising. Both moves are ostensibly in the name of 'sound economic principle' – to which the reply may be that an economy is not a society.

If it is complained that humane studies are outmoded because they are not sciences, I can only reply that (for reasons already given) it is the business of the humanities to be *un*like the sciences, being complementary to them; as it is the business of the humanities to see that that difference, essential to a sane society, is not obliterated.

In such a context the word 'culture' usually swims to the surface. Is it not the case (it will be said) that government 'backs culture': buys Canadian paintings, sends poets hurtling from Inuvik to Litovsk to read their verse; provides subventions for publishers; supports symphonies, ballet-companies and theatrical groups; commissions compositions, dispenses awards? That is well. If it goes on for long enough, 'culture' in that sense might become as much a part of our lives as breathing is. The humanities, however, are a 'culture' in the biological sense – the surround that supports and nourishes life. Nothing will grow except in a suitable culture.

From the humanist's point of view, certain things must be made accessible to us, especially in education; the possibility can be enjoined, but not the outcome; the desired end must in some way be implicit at the beginning, the various phases of the process bearing to each other the same prophetic relation that the parts of a work of art bear to the whole work. The way of sustaining such a process is called 'method' – not technique, and not a progress according to formula towards a predefined end. Coleridge has written eloquently and incisively about method, likening the growth of the intellect to the growth of a child.

> We are aware, that it is with our cognitions [i.e. the growth of our ways of getting to know] as with our children. There is a period in which the method of nature is working for them; a period of aimless activity and unregulated accumulation, during which it is enough if we can preserve them in health

and *out of harm's way*. Again, there is a period of orderliness, or circumspection, of discipline, in which we purify, separate, define, select, arrange, and settle the nomenclature of communication. There is also a period of dawning and twilight, a period of anticipation, affording trials of strength. And all these, both in the growth of the sciences and in the mind of a rightly-educated individual, will precede the attainment of a scientific METHOD. But, notwithstanding this, unless the importance of the latter [i.e. method] be felt and acknowledged, unless its attainment be looked forward to and from the very beginning prepared for, there is little hope and small chance that any education will be conducted aright; or will ever prove in reality worth the name .... Alas! how many examples are now present to our memory, of young men the most anxiously and expensively be-schoolmastered, be-tutored, be-lectured, any thing but *educated*; who have received arms and ammunition, instead of skill, strength and courage; varnished rather than polished; perilously over-civilised, and most pitiably uncultivated! And all from inattention to the method dictated by nature herself to the simple truth, that as the forms in all organized existence, so must all true and living knowledge proceed from within; that it may be trained, supported, fed, excited, but can never be infused or impressed.

After more than thirty years of what is oddly called 'teaching' I find that this statement strikes straight to the heart of the matter – it is (in the Homeric phrase) a 'winged word', at once both arrow and bull's-eye. As humanists we train, support, feed, excite; we try to teach people how to *read*, so that they can enter directly into the activity of the most powerful and penetrating minds that we have record of, and so to find how miraculously complex, integrative and inventive the human mind is, and language too; and so to discover themselves by losing themselves. We try to teach people how to *write*, so that their states of feeling, their sense of value, the quality and accuracy of their perception become clear and ordered, their awareness of all things heightened, their capacity for sustained reflection strengthened – recognising that everybody has in the end to do his own work, has to work out his own integrity and destiny in solitude. In the course of this we come to recognise how intermittent and excruciating our grasp of reality is, how hard-won and hard-sustained our integrity, how fugitive any profound occasion of knowing, how almost impossible it is to convey it to somebody else. Hence the starting-point of this endeavour is delight, wonder, respect, quietness – and the sustaining of it calls for strong nerves, the rejection of short-cuts, the refusal to relax our tenuous grasp upon what matters most of all to us.

No wonder that in a university the results are unpredictable, even at short range, and even when candidates are carefully selected. All are not equally endowed to succeed *professionally* in an enterprise that is about as complex as a five-dimensional chess-game and as delicate as handling gold-leaf with the bare fingers. Yet because the work of the humanities touches constantly upon the central nervous system of the self, in the disciplining of language, intelligence and feeling, the success of the enterprise is not to be measured simply by the number who become school-teachers, or scholars, or professors, or writers widely read or of wide influence. Robert Frost once said that 'When a good reader meets a good poem he suffers an immortal wound and knows that he will never recover from it.' If it were not so, the humanities would have no just claim to stand at the heart of education. (And Robert Frost also said, on receiving honorary degrees from Oxford, Cambridge and Edinburgh, 'It is better to receive a degree from a university than an education.') To accumulate knowledge and to be able to repeat it is not the primary educational end for the humanities; rather, the purpose (which is scarcely definable) is fulfilled upon the whole person, in the secret places of the mind and memory, and is to be seen in the integrity of perception, judgement, recognition; and in a quality of action that is recognisable, but neither definable nor predictable. This process, though accelerated (if it can occur at all) in a university, can prosper anywhere; yet such is the fugitiveness of intent needed to sustain that possibility that some people devote their whole lives to it – living the values and relations that we seek to disclose, turning them over constantly in the mind, in the writing, in the critical devotion to the 'monuments of its own magnificence'.

There are many other things that I should like to have discussed, but I am prevented. Let me then venture to say what I take to be the business of humane studies; at the centre of it always the human mind with its exquisite system of responses and its flair for initiative.

To secure and disclose to sustained and continuous reflection those forms and makings in which the image of man and of his remarkable capacities are embodied; at the same time encompassing with wonder and respect the images of the world and its creatures (for we too are voracious observers and watchers). To remind us of the fragility and transience of intellectual achievement, how delicately achieved, how easily and brutally disrupted (how we forget, and lose the thread, and have to start again, and how each one of us – as individual person or as poet or artist – has in some sense to start all over again from the beginning to discover how to see, how to think, how to make, how to discover our integrity and preserve it). Further, it is the humanist's business to remind us how nothing of value can be transmitted from one person to another without the receiver attaining the quality of mind in which the original was conceived; how in life, as in art, there are no classes for beginners – that we have to do all the most difficult things at the beginning; how we need to have before our mind's eye, as the Chinese calligrapher does, almost as talismans, 'excellent examples of the art' – the art of making, of speaking, of living; how not everything can be understood or explained under a single figure or analogy and that we corrupt our inquiry (and ourselves) when we suppose that they can; and how it is better to be determined not to misunderstand, than to be determined to understand (for the hypothesis or analogue or – in the modern jargon, the 'model' – most convenient for purposes of measurement, prediction and control will probably not be the figure that pays most faithful attention to the reality of that complex). It is also the humanist's business to show how the premises from which an argument is to be evolved are already shaped by the ghost of the conclusion that we desire the argument to arrive at; how 'objectivity' is a conventional assumption that holds only at a level that in human terms doesn't much matter, and how the now-despised 'subjectivity', which we have always insisted was essential to our arts, is in fact the 'relativity' that physics has been telling us about for more than seventy years – seeing the real world not as a pattern of *things*, but as relations, in a qualitative mode; how nothing is achieved in poetry or in action without the loss of something that might otherwise conceivably have been included. And, finally, how at the roots of all this we find language, and the ways of language, and our ways of using language not simply as an instrument of communication for sending messages, but as an inseparable component of our nature, indispensable to our individual development as human beings, and acting reciprocally upon us and our minds and feelings according to the reconciliaton we can effect with it, the aim being fidelity to the object, and the integrity of the subject.

I affirm that I do not see in the modern world anything as humane or as daring as the philosophical virtues we have inherited from Plato and Aristotle through the long rich humanist tradition of Europe, seeking a grasp of mind that is at once enormous and minute; seeking illumination, and illuminating; trusting what we see with the armed vision and what we handle with the fingers of the mind; seeking in wonder (which is the beginning of philosophy) incandescent moments of knowing. Whatever improvement there may have been – in methods of inquiry, in understanding the ways of language, and in interpreting the condition and capacities of man – we welcome these; but I cannot see that the constantly exploding universe of imaginative and intellectual materials alters in any way the nature or function of the humanist's enterprise (though it may put some strain on him). A mind 'habituated to the *Vast*' is what Coleridge as a child knew was his sort of mind; and it is the childlike quality of mind that astonishes us about Newton and Einstein as it does about every artist worth his salt. To reject the beguilements of a universe of 'knowledge' made up of 'little things', and to seek a certain quality of 'knowing' – this is the habit of mind of the generation of humanists of which I am a survivor; and, because I believe it to be a vision as pertinent today as ever it was, I declare it to you here because we have come together to seek a new coalition.

No doubt we shall be asking for money – everybody asks for money these days, deflect our eyes though we may from the carnal impulses of this wicked world. The humanities are blissfully and unrepentantly counter to the present mood of society and to the present aspirations of government as we see them. To us the position of the humanities is perfectly clear; its educational function is, for a civilised society, indispensable. I hope it does not seem arrogant to suggest that the question for society is not 'Why the humanities?' but 'Why not?'

I don't know what will do the trick. Money in itself won't; and turning the knobs on the promotional machines won't – unless there are some strong and beguiling voices to be heard over the equipment. Certainly the answer is not to be found in pretending that the humanities are a form of 'science' and that its practitioners are a species of specialist technician.

In one of the last poems he wrote before his death, David Jones – painter, poet, calligrapher – made a prayer against the imperative of the 'rootless uniformities':

> When they sit in *Consilium*
> to liquidate the holy diversities
>> mother of particular perfections
>> queen of otherness
>> mistress of asymmetry
> patroness of things counter, parti, pied, several
> protectress of things known and handled
> help of things familiar and small
>> wardress of the secret crevices
>> of things wrapped and hidden . . .
> empress of the labyrinth
>> receive our prayers . . . .
> When the technicians manipulate the dead limbs of our culture as though it yet had life, have mercy on us.

'The empress of the labyrinth', 'wardress of the secret crevices'. Humane studies, at their obscure and subversive best – in the distant past and at this time – are a disease of sanity. It is essential that we nourish and prize the culture in which that infection grows. I cannot see how our society can be healthy unless we are deeply infected with the disease of wonder and respect.

I therefore ask you to listen, to be patient, to be subtle, to take care.

Notes

CHAPTER ONE: THE MARINER AND THE ALBATROSS

1. *Letters of Charles and Mary Lamb*, ed. E. V. Lucas (London, 1935) I, 240.
2. Ibid., I, 185.
3. Ibid., II, 191.
4. *Collected Letters of Samuel Taylor Coleridge* [hereafter referred to as CL], ed. E. L. Griggs (Oxford, 1956–71) IV, 975 (? Nov 1819). Coleridge may be thinking of his 'Allegoric Vision' – *The Complete Poetical Works of Samuel Taylor Coleridge*, ed. E. H. Coleridge (Oxford, 1912) II, 1091–6. This prose allegory, written August 1795, was successively used for an attack on the Church of England, for an attack on the Church of Rome, and in the introduction to *A Lay Sermon: Addressed to the Higher and Middle Classes*. In the 'Allegoric Vision' Coleridge does not in any sense allegorise himself.
5. For a consideration of the place of opium as inducing Coleridge's 'Bad most shocking Dreams', as an element in the composition of 'The Ancient Mariner', and specifically as a factor in the image of Life-in-Death, see R. C. Bald, 'Coleridge and "The Ancient Mariner"', in *Nineteenth-Century Studies*, ed. H. Davis, W. C. De Vane and R. C. Bald (Ithaca, NY, 1940).
6. 'The Nightingale: A Conversation Poem' (Apr 1798).
7. *CL*, IV, 974–5. This passage immediately precedes the passage quoted above (n. 4).
8. 1798 version. Unless otherwise indicated, quotations from the poem follow the 1834 version.
9. See *CL*, VI, 963; cf. 970, 973, and *Poetical Works*, I, 492.
10. Cf. 1798 version: 'And Christ would take no pity on'.
11. For Coleridge on birds, see n. 46 below.
12. Emphasis added.
13. Too little is known of the date of composition of the gloss, and of the process of revision. For the date of important revisions to 'The Ancient Mariner', see J. L. Lowes, *The Road to Xanadu*, rev. edn (Boston, Mass., and New York, 1930) pp. 475–6. For successive changes in the 'Courts of the Sun' gloss, see ibid., pp. 164ff.
14. Cf. Edmund Blunden in *Coleridge: Studies by Several Hands on the Hundredth Anniversary of His Death*, ed. E. Blunden and E. L. Griggs (London, 1934) p. 66: 'I sometimes wonder whether, germinally, the "Ancient Mariner"

249

altogether is not one of his Christ's Hospital poems. I mean . . . that he had to travel through a long period of haunted solitariness.'

15. *CL*, I, 178–9 (29 Jan 1796).
16. 'To the Rev. George Coleridge' (26 May 1797).
17. *CL*, I, 369 (6 Jan 1798). Cf. *The Notebooks of Samuel Taylor Coleridge* [hereafter referred to as *CN*], ed. Kathleen Coburn (New York and London, 1957–72) III, 3324: 'when I am in company with Mr Sharp [*et al.*] . . . I feel like a Child – nay, rather like an Inhabitant of another Planet – their very faces all act upon me, sometimes, as if they were Ghosts, but more often as if I were a Ghost among them – at all times, as if we were not *consubstantial*'.
18. 'Dejection: An Ode' (4 April 1802). Emphasis added.
19. Cf. *CL*, II, 959 (1 Aug 1803). Emphasis added. He speaks of himself as 'an involuntary Impostor'. The whole letter is of importance for the statements which lead to the conclusion: 'This on my honor is as fair a statement of my habitual Haunting, as I could give before the Tribunal of Heaven / How it arose in me, I have but lately discovered.'
20. *CN*, III, 4040. Emphasis added.
21. *CN*, I, 1554.
22. *CN*, I, 263. *CN*, II, shows that the voyage to Malta, Coleridge's loneliness there and the establishment of the opium addiction, and also the circumstances of his return to England, provide again fulfilment of the prophecy of 'The Ancient Mariner'.
23. 'Work without Hope' (21 Feb 1825).
24. Lamb's critical comment is again of interest: 'The Ancient Mariner undergoes such Trials, as overwhelm and bury all individuality or memory of what he was, like the state of man in a Bad dream, one terrible peculiarity of which is: that all consciousness of personality is gone' (*Letters of Charles and Mary Lamb*, I, 240). Cf. *CN*, I, 1834.
25. 'Christ's Hospital Five and Thirty Years Ago'.
26. *CN*, I, 1622, 1624, 1625, 1627, 1628, 1635, 1648, 1649, 1650.
27. *CN*, II, 2139.
28. Cf. an amusing parallel in *CL*, I, 658. 'In truth, my Glass being opposite to the Window, I seldom shave without cutting myself. Some Mountain or Peak is rising out of the Mist, or some slanting Column of misty Sunlight is sailing across me / so that I offer up soap & blood daily, as an Eye-servant of the Goddess Nature.'
29. Cf. *CL*, II, 1202: '55 days of literal Horror [at sea], almost daily expecting and wishing to die'; and IV, 673: 'I longed for Death with an intensity that I have never seen expressed but in the Book of Job'.
30. See the dream epitaph in *CL*, II, 992:

> Here sleeps at length poor Col. & without Screaming,
> Who died, as he did always liv'd, a dreaming:
> Shot dead, while sleeping, by the Gout within,
> Alone, and all unknown, at E'nbro' in an Inn.

31. *CL*, II, 991. Emphasis added. Many other of his letters voice the same theme.

32. Opium is certainly responsible for the horror of these dreams. Coleridge's interest in the nature of his nightmares and reveries, and the acuteness of his introspective analysis of dream phenomena, are to be seen in *CL*, II, *passim* and elsewhere in his writing. Bald, in *Nineteenth-Century Studies*, pp. 29–35, examines closely the responsibility for opium in Coleridge's dreams of horror; and at pp. 40–3 he considers Coleridge's distinction between dream, reverie and nightmare.

33. *CL*, II, 714 (to Godwin, 25 Mar 1801). Cf. p. 831 (July 1802): 'All my poetic Genius . . . is gone . . . .'

34. The manuscript of *Sibylline Leaves*, including 'The Ancient Mariner', seems to have gone to the printer in August or September 1815.

35. This conclusion would be less tenable if the poet were almost anybody except Coleridge. In this respect 'The Ancient Mariner' stands in sharp contrast to 'Christabel'. 'Christabel' was left in a fragmentary state even though Coleridge 'had the whole present to my mind, with the wholeness, no less than the liveliness of a vision'. The passage on broken friendship is almost the only clear personal trace of Coleridge in 'Christabel'. 'Christabel' was far more 'a work of pure imagination' than 'The Ancient Mariner': it had so little personal significance for him that he was unable to overcome the practical difficulties of completing it.

36. *CL*, I, 272. (This refers to a suggestion that Coleridge might move from Stowey to 'cursed Acton'.)

37. 'To a Young Friend'.

38. *CL*, I, 320.

39. 'To the Rev. George Coleridge'.

40. The earliest reference to the use of opium, *CL*, I, 188 (1791), implies earlier medicinal use; cf. p. 186 (12 Mar 1796).

41. See Bald, in *Nineteenth-Century Studies*, pp. 33ff.

42. Lowes, *The Road to Xanadu*, p. 221.

43. Cf. ibid., p. 303. Lowes emphasises the *triviality* of the deed and suggests that Coleridge required a trivial deed to set the punishment in motion.

44. Cf. T. S. Eliot, *The Use of Poetry and the Use of Criticism* (London, 1933) p. 69, where the eagle is used as the symbol of the creative imagination. Coleridge also seems to be using the symbol in an epigram of 1807 in reply to Poole's encouragement: 'Let Eagle bid the Tortoise sunward rise – / As vainly Strength speaks to a broken mind' (*Poetical Works*, II, 1001). Cf. Shelley's description of Coleridge as 'a hooded eagle among blinking owls.'

45. *The Poetical Works of William Wordsworth*, ed. E. de Selincourt and Helen Darbishire (Oxford, 1940–9) I, 360–1.

46. Coleridge's keen interest in birds is shown by his footnote to 'This Lime-Tree Bower', and by a manuscript note in a copy of Gilbert White's *Works*: 'I have myself made & collected a better table of characters of Flight and Motion [of birds].' See also *CN*, II, 3182, 3184; III, 3314, 3359.

47. The giant albatross probably would occur to Coleridge's mind. Notice Wordsworth's mention of 'wingspan of 12 or 13 feet'. But see Lowes, *The Road to Xanadu*, pp. 266–7 and 529, for the 'feasible' species; and *CN*, II, 1957: 'Saw a . . . Boy running up to the Main top with a large Leg of Mutton swung, Albatross-fashion about his neck.'

48. *Biographia Literaria*, ch. 9.

49. *CN*, II, 2546 (14 Apr 1805). See also III, 3762: 'words are not mere symbols of things & thoughts, but themselves things – and . . . any harmony in the things symbolised will perforce be presented to us more easily as well as with additional beauty by a correspondent harmony of the Symbols with each other.'

50. *CN*, I, 2372.

51. *CN*, II, 3136. This parallel is offered with caution.

52. But see n. 44 above for an example in Coleridge's writing. *CN*, II, 3182 is also of interest: 'The moulting Peacock, with only two of his long tail-feathers remaining, & those sadly in tatters, yet proudly as ever spreads out his ruined fan in the Sun & Breeze.' This may be a direct observation; but it is also one of several instances of Coleridge using a bird as a self-image.

53. *Table Talk*, 31 May 1830. Henry Nelson Coleridge, in his review of the *Poetical Works* 1834, observed; 'It was a sad mistake in the able artist – Mr Scott, we believe – who in his engravings has made the ancient mariner an old decrepit man. That is not the true image; no! he should have been a growthless, decayless being, impassive to time or season, a silent cloud – the wandering Jew.' The remark is made on the authority of an unpublished entry in the manuscript of *Table Talk*.

54. *CL*, V, 125–6.

55. Bald (pp. 39ff.), in interpreting this passage, is concerned to explain the *amoral* attitude as a characteristic of opium reverie. Lamb notes the same quality in the Mariner without reference to opium.

56. *CL*, V, 478. E. H. Coleridge noted the first appearance of this recurrent stock sentence in the *Morning Post* of 2 Jan 1800 – *Essays on his Own Times*, I, 197–8.

57. 'The Pains of Sleep'. Emphasis added.

58. *CL*, III, 476: Coleridge, here replying to Joseph Cottle's harsh accusations, is thinking specifically of the opium habit, but he recognised it as a symptom and did not regard it as the 'sin' itself.

59. *CL*, III, 73–4 (17 Feb 1808).

60. *Biographia Literaria*, ch. 1. See also *CL*, V, 125–6.

61. 'Dejection', ll. 82–93. 'Dejection' is echoed in 'To William Wordsworth' (1807).

62. Thomas Carlyle, *The Life of John Sterling*, in *Complete Works of Thomas Carlyle* (New York, 1853) xx, 60.

63. *CL*, III, 337 (12 Oct 1811).

64. *CL*, III, 476 (26 Apr 1814).

65. *CL*, VI, 770–1 (9 Nov 1828).

CHAPTER THREE: ON TRANSLATING ARISTOTLE'S POETICS

1. If we ignore Theodore Coulston (1623), who made a Latin version of Castelvetro, and Thomas Rymer (1674), who translated René Rapin, and two anonymous versions (1705, 1775 – the first from André Dacier), and Pye (1788), who graciously conceded the palm to Twining, the first English

translation of the *Poetics* was by Thomas Twining (1789). It reigned until Butcher's translation of 1895. But Bywater followed Butcher in 1905, and thereafter there have been a number of English translations, none of which has succeeded in dislodging Butcher from the university anthologies.

2. S. H. Butcher, *Aristotle's Theory of Poetry and Fine Art with a Critical Text and Translation of 'The Poetics'* (1st edn 1895; 4th edn 1907; rev. posthumously 1911 and repr. several times; the translation repr. frequently in collections of critical texts, including Saintsbury and Ross; reissued in paperback in 1951 from plates of the 4th edn). The 1951 reissue has a note at the end of the bibliography suggesting that 'critics are likely to agree with the opinion of Professor W. K. Wimsatt, Jr . . . that the revisions of the text, derived from the Arabic version and MS Riccardianus 49 [*sic*] "are not as a matter of fact important enough to have worked any substantial damage to the theoretical part of Butcher's labor".' This statement, if written after 1965, would seem to be ill informed or disingenuous.

3. Werner Jaeger, *Aristotle: Fundamentals of the History of his Development*, trs. Richard Robinson (Oxford, 1948) p. 7.

4. Ingram Bywater, *Aristotle on the Art of Poetry* (Oxford, 1909) p. ix.

5. Lane Cooper and Alfred Gudeman, *A Bibliography of the Poetics of Aristotle*, Cornell Studies in English, vol. XI (1928). Listed 1583 items. Marvin T. Herrick provided a supplement in 1931, and in 1954–5 Gerald Else published 'A Survey of Work on Aristotle's *Poetics*, 1940–1954'.

6. Jaeger, *Aristotle*, p. 24.

7. D. W. Lucas, *Aristotle's Poetics: Introduction, Commentary and Appendixes* (Oxford, 1968) p. ix. My summary here is based in part on Lucas's Introduction.

8. *Aristotelis de arte poetica liber recognovit brevique adnotatione critica instruxit Rudolphus Kassel* (Oxford, 1965; repr. with corrections 1966); printed as Greek text to Lucas's 'Introduction, Commentary, and Appendixes', *Aristotle: Poetics*, pp. 3–52. Gerald Else based his massive *Aristotle's 'Poetics': The Argument* (Cambridge, Mass., 1957) on Rostagni's 2nd edn (1945); but in his *Translation* (Ann Arbor, 1967) he used Kassel's text, remarking that it 'makes all previous editions obsolete, being the only one that provides anything like full and accurate reports from all four text witnesses'. Lucas perhaps had this comment in mind when he wrote that Bywater's 'great edition . . . remains after half a century far from obsolete'.

9. Jaeger, *Aristotle*, pp. 3–5. The original ed, *Aristoteles, Grundlegung einer Geschichte seiner Entwicklung*, was first published in Berlin in 1923. For the 1st English ed, see n. 3 above.

10. Jaeger, *Aristotle*, pp. 6, 13. Only the first is indexed.

11. Ibid., p. 3.

12. Marjorie Grene, in assailing the view encouraged by Jaeger that Aristotle started as a Platonist, puts this point neatly: 'Plato was a Platonist to the last, and Aristotle an Aristotelian from the first, or very near it' – *A Portrait of Aristotle* (London, 1963) p. 256.

13. F. Solmsen, in an impressive article, 'The Origin and Methods of Aristotle's *Poetics*', *Classical Quarterly*, 29 (1935) 192–201, recognises an 'original train of thought and . . . later additions', but does not venture a more exact consideration of the span of possible dates. The only recognisable piece of

internal evidence for some part of the *Poetics* having been written in Athens (i.e. before 348 BC or after 335 BC) is 1448^a 31 – a passage that Solmsen considers to be 'late'.

14. The first hint that this might be possible came to me from the working version Gerald Else uses in his *Argument*, though he says that it is 'not meant to be read by itself, as a "translation" of the *Poetics*'. It is 'rigidly literal', preserves the length and structure of Aristotle's sentences, yet allows some flexibility in extending words and phrases by 'translating out' for clarity, and avoids rigidity in applying key terms. See *Argument*, p. xvi.

15. One promising resource has come to us indirectly from Greek in the nouns (now often neologisms) ending in '-ism', but we have never made careful use of them. If these words were thought of as coming directly from Greek processive verbs ending in *-zein*, they would imply process. Unfortunately they have been deflected through German into the collective abstraction of static nouns standing for 'ideas', and even the '-ism' words that do not come to us from German now have this character. In critical discussion, for example, it is useful to insist that 'realism' refers to a method, not a quality; but some people are hard to persuade. And I like to think of 'criticism' as a process of getting-to-discern.

16. The alleged inferiority of Aristotle's 'style' to Plato's has historically encouraged the view of Aristotle's work as static and monolithic, and has tempted some to try to make his writings into 'readable handbooks' (see Jaeger, *Aristotle*, p. 6). See also ibid., p. 30, n. 2: 'The only mark of good style laid down by previous rhetoricians that A. recognizes is lucidity . . . A. thinks of knowledge as a force that must alter everything, language included.'

17. Valuable detailed proposals have been made in recent years by Solmsen, Rostagni, de Montmollin and Else. The prevailing attitude at present towards 'systematic attempts . . . to remove incoherencies and inconsistencies by distinguishing different layers of composition' is well represented by Lucas: 'The scope for disagreement here is certainly not less than in more usual forms of textual criticism' (*Aristotle: Poetics*, p. xxv). Jaeger too was suspicious of 'rationalizing interference' by philologists (*Aristotle*, p. 6). For a test case – the status of ch. 12 – see Lucas, *Aristotle: Poetics*, pp. 135–6; and Else, *Argument*, pp. 360–3, and *Translation*, p. 94. That there are disparate elements in the *Poetics* there can be no denying. The crucial question, in the absence of reliable internal evidence for dating, is: on what basis is the disparateness to be judged? See also n. 21 below.

18. The larger problems come after ch. 14, concerning the status of part of ch. 15, of chs. 16–18, 21, 24, and part of 22. But there are questions about ch. 12 too, and its relation to 16–18 (ch. 18 being evidently a group of notes).

19. Primarily, one imagines, the 'look' of the actors, whatever strikes the eye – their masks and costumes – often splendid no doubt. Aristotle says that Sophocles introduced scene-painting, and the *deus ex machina* must have been quite a sight; yet 'spectacle' throws the emphasis where the Greek theatre can least support it. In any case, Aristotle says that the poet had little control over this 'aspect' and does not discuss it further in detail.

20. Here a passage, long suspect and subjected to much emendational ingenuity, is athetised by Kassel: 'a happiness; and the end [? of tragedy] is a certain

action, not a quality. The persons [in the drama] are of certain kinds because of their characters, but they are happy or unhappy because of their actions.'

21. Jaeger, *Aristotle*, p. 384.

22. Cf. *Metaphysics*, 1041^b 6–9: 'Since we must know the existence of the thing and must be given, clearly the question is *why* the matter is some individual thing . . . Therefore what we seek is the cause, i.e. the form, by reason of which the matter is some definite thing; and this is the substance of the thing.'

23. Plato too; see *Phaedrus*, 264C: 'Every *logos* [discussion] should be like a living organism [*zōion*] and have a body of its own; it should not be without head or feet, it should have a middle and extremities which should be appropriate to each other and to the whole work.'

24. *The Notebooks of Samuel Taylor Coleridge*, ed. Kathleen Coburn (New York and London, 1957–72) III, 4397, f. 53; *variatim* in *Literary Remains* (1836–9) I, 225, and *Biographia Literaria*, ed. J. Shawcross (Oxford, 1907) II, 259. Cf. G. M. Hopkins on observing the form of sea-waves: 'it is hard for [the eyes] to unpack the huddling and gnarls of the water and law out of the shapes and the sequence of the running' – *The Journals*, ed. Humphry House and Graham Storey (Oxford, 1959) p. 223. See also *Metaphysics*, 1050^a 21–4.

25. Jaeger, *Aristotle*, p. 384, where he also states that 'The meaning of "entelechy" is not biological; it is logical and ontological.' Marjorie Grene follows D'Arcy Wentworth Thompson in proposing that Aristotle's biology 'may have provided the cornerstone for his metaphysics and logic' and that seems to complement rather than contradict Jaeger's position. See *A Portrait of Aristotle*, p. 32; and for a general critique of the 'genetic' method advocated by Jaeger, see ch. I.

26. *Metaphysics*, 1072^b 27–8. Jaeger uses this phrase as motto on his title-page.

27. *Poetics*, 1448^b 4–5.

28. Ibid., 1449^a 15.

29. Ibid., 1449^b 28. *Katharsis* occurs again in 1455^b 15 but in a neutral-referential sense.

30. For a conspectus, see Else, *Argument*, pp. 225–6, n. 14. See also Lucas, *Aristotle: Poetics*, pp. 97–8 and Appendix II.

31. H. D. F. Kitto, 'Catharsis', in *The Classical Tradition*, ed. L. Wallach (Ithaca, NY, 1966) pp. 133–47.

32. George Whalley, 'The Aristotle–Coleridge Axis', *University of Toronto Quarterly*, 42 (Winter 1972–3) 93–109.

CHAPTER FOUR: 'SCHOLARSHIP', 'RESEARCH' AND 'THE PURSUIT OF TRUTH'

1. The now-standard threefold division of university departments and 'research' allocations into science, social sciences and humanities (with mathematics hovering somewhere overhead and geography somewhere underfoot) – how did this scheme get established, and why is it not

vigorously challenged? A scheme based on discipline and method rather than on subject-matter and intended sphere of influence would certainly invigorate learning and might help to draw discovery into a specifically human (rather than social and economic) dimension.

2. The crude trade-classification into 'scientist' and 'humanist' has the serious disadvantage of separating two groups who are primarily concerned with imaginative activity, and of allowing the 'pure' scientist to be mistaken for a technologist. Could a less tendentious scheme be based upon the 'ways of mind' which, though engaged by everybody, occur with varying prominence in various kinds of study and activity? To delineate the 'ways of mind' would be a matter for a study called 'heuristics', a conceivable branch of epistemology which has so far received little systematic attention. (See also n. 16 below.) Psychological studies of 'creativity' seem to be limited by their reluctance to gather appropriately complex evidence.

3. S. T. Coleridge, *Biographia Literaria*, ed. J. Shawcross (Oxford, 1907) I, 107. It would follow from this proposition that the only way to be pedantic in such learned company as the Royal Society of Canada would be to talk at a very trivial level.

4. Spokesmen for the government of Ontario recently (May 1970) announced that the investment in undergraduate education had proved 'unproductive', and the investment in graduate education 'counterproductive'.

5. I have used the word 'poem' several times here as standing for 'highly developed writing'. The language of the best prose is often more highly developed than the language of much verse – see, for example, Sir Charles Sherrington's *Man on his Nature* (Cambridge, 1946); and some of the best verse is strikingly translucent and direct rather than obscure and difficult. Poetry is the only way of saying certain kinds of things; the difficulty is to let the mind grasp what poetry is saying in its own very direct way.

6. Greek is particularly well provided with processive nouns that have almost the force of verbs. *Mimēsis* is such a noun, prominent in Aristotle's *Poetics*. When it is translated as 'imitation' the energy and processive inflection have gone from the word. Even a person who knows neither Greek nor Latin seems able to sense the static quality of the noun 'imitation' – as though he could tell directly that a noun formed from a past participle could hardly imply process. Existential philosophy and phenomenology have encouraged philosophers to turn away from abstract nouns (static 'ideas' or 'absolutes') in order to secure suitable verbal form for their thinking. Modern translations of Aristotle use a direct un-Latinistic English that would have seemed uncouth or improper to philosophers less than a century ago.

7. In poetry, however, a word that is normally abstract can become vivid and concrete in the hands of a particular writer. Wordsworth's use of 'things' and the verb 'to be' deserve close study; but only a person who looked at the world the way he did could get such an effect.

8. Surely Keats's thinking – remarkably vigorous, original, and fearless – bespeaks a mind uncluttered by most of the furniture of advanced formal education. It took such a man to say, 'I am certain of nothing but of the holiness of the heart's affections and the truth of imagination.' Yeats's invincible sense of the integrity of words and verbal rhythms similarly was grounded in his insensitiveness to music.

9. In *Poetic Process* (London: Routledge and Kegan Paul, 1953; Cleveland and New York: Meridian Books, 1967) I used the word 'vector' in discussing language, thinking the image was new. I am now informed that one or two contemporary American writers have (or had) also used it as a suggestive analogy. The coincidence is reassuring.

10. For example, I am so acutely aware that the word 'poetry' comes from the Greek verb *poiein* (to make) that I cannot refrain from pronouncing it 'poi–ētry'. A listener, whether or not aware of the Greek reasons for this, will hear the pronunciation as odd or pedantic; to a person aware of the reason for the pronunciation, however, a complex point is made instantly.

11. In my view language is radically metaphorical, its structure not logical but paratactic – words being placed side by side, or rather face to face, and allowed to work out their relation without the identities of words being destroyed. Logical or propositional structure has supervened upon metaphorical structure but need not be allowed to supersede it; yet educational emphasis since the eighteenth century has tended to damage, and even obliterate, the metaphorical sense. In highly developed language the logical and metaphorical principles are usually in strong, but not destructive, tension.

12. Cf. a marginal note of Coleridge in Tetens's *Philosophische Versuche* (Leipzig, 1777): 'What are my motives but my impelling thoughts – and what is a Thought but another word for "I thinking"?'

13. A single utterance may usefully be regarded as a 'trajectory', a complex vectorical function implying an end and amplitude as well as direction. The internal structure of such a trajectory consists of the vectors of words and phrases, sounds, variations in accent, pitch and duration – a rhythm energetic and shapely enough to impart, imply and satisfy the feeling of just completion. The trajectory of human utterance is like the trajectory of a physical missile in the sense that it declares energy released in a certain direction; it is unlike a physical trajectory in two senses: (1) in a utterance there is no missile to trace the trajectory, unless we infer an abstract 'meaning' or 'intention' that is inseparable from all the components of the flight, and anyway the missile makes itself as it goes; (2) the flight is not determined simply by the aim taken and the energy released – it can be, and usually is, modified from moment to moment 'in flight' and will not necessarily fall on an expected target. One of the fascinations of listening to language is the tension between expectation and realisation, the interplay of remembering, immediately perceiving and anticipating which can provide not only in the end a sense of the utterance as a whole but an exquisite appreciation of the way things get said. The imaginative use of language encourages us so to enter into the life of language. Listening to language, like listening to music, is enriched by an informed intelligence.

14. T. S. Eliot, *The Use of Poetry and the Use of Criticism* (London, 1933) pp. 118–19.

15. *The Notebooks of Samuel Taylor Coleridge*, ed. Kathleen Coburn (New York and London, 1957) I, 950 (early 1801). What seems to us an inversion of terms was probably intentional, since the note shows signs of being thoughtfully written; it confirms my feeling that 'invent' produces a more vivid image than 'discover'. Later Coleridge takes 'discover' as the higher term, probably

reflecting current usage. In 1802 he noted, 'We imagine ourselves
discoverers & that we have struck a Light, when in reality we have only
snuffed a Candle' (I, 1315); and more than ten years later: 'To invent [as
distinguished] from to discover – H. Invents the Time Piece – A. discovers
the Longitude' (III, 4181).

16. Unfortunately English has no verb to match the Greek *heuriskein* – a busy,
seeking word for which 'pursue' is no substitute and of which 'research'
gives no inkling. Coleridge catches well the heuristic spirit not only by his
description but by the way he writes:

> There is no way of arriving at any sciential End but by finding it at every
> step. The End is in the Means: or the Adequacy of each Mean is already
> its End. Southey once said to me: You are nosing every nettle along the
> Hedge, while the Greyhound (meaning himself, I presume) wants only
> to get sight of the Hare, and Flash – strait as a line! he has it in his mouth! –
> Even so, I replied, might a Cannibal say to an Anatomist, whom he had
> watched dissecting a body. But the fact is – I do not care two pence for
> the *Hare*; but I value most highly the excellencies of scent, patience,
> discrimination, free Activity; and find a Hare in every Nettle I make
> myself acquainted with. I follow the Chamois-Hunters, and seem to set
> out with the same Object. But I am no Hunter of *that* Chamois Goat; but
> avail myself of the Chace in order to a nobler purpose – that of making a
> road across the Mountain in which Common Sense may hereafter pass
> backward and forward, without desperate Leaps or Balloons that soar
> indeed but do not improve the chance of getting onward.

– BM MS Egerton 2801, f. 126; printed in *Inquiring Spirit*, ed. Kathleen
Coburn (London, 1951) pp. 143–4. Southey and the Greyhound sound
rather like the Science Council's notion of a curiosity-motivated researcher.

CHAPTER FIVE: 'RESEARCH' AND THE HUMANITIES

1. The third definition (late seventeenth century) is much more general:
'Investigation; inquiry into things.' Certainly the word is now often used in
that indistinct and comprehensive sense – as when some humanists assert in
desperation that when they are reading a book they are 'doing research'.
Other humanists are implicitly using the first two definitions when they say
that, whatever they do, 'research' is not the name of it. Neither of these
extreme positions helps us much to understand what humanists typically do.
The *OED* also records a use that may deserve wider currency than it has so
far enjoyed: 'Research knee-jerk: a knee-jerk requiring special means to elicit
it.'

2. The phrase 'the humanities' seems to have come into use as recently as the
beginning of the eighteenth century (*OED* 1702), referring to the area of
activity of the 'humanist' – that is, a person learned in the Greek and Roman
civilisations. 'The humanities' seems to be a corruption of the word *humanitas* –

a term of strong and honourable implication which originally meant the cultivation befitting a man. Classical writers, with characteristic fastidiousness, seem never to have used *humanitas* in the plural. The plural *humanities* may have occurred by the same process of haphazard inflation that has produced 'science*s*', 'technique*s*', and 'discipline*s*' (more 'thinginess'?), reinforced perhaps by an ignorant mishearing of the singular word *humanitas*; or it may have come through an attempt to anglicise the name of the distinguished Oxford School of *literae humaniores* ('Greats') – 'those branches of literature [literature being presumably anything excellently written?] which tend to humanise or refine, such as the ancient classics, rhetoric, and poetry' (*OED*. The phrase *literae humaniores* does not appear until 1691; the study embraces literature, philosophy, history, and social and political institutions). The late emergence of the word 'humanism' is interesting: Coleridge used it in 1812 (? coined it) to refer to a belief in the humanity of Christ; in 1836 it refers to a devotion to human interest; by 1860 it could mean (as in a vague way it tends to do now) 'the religion of humanity'.

3. To ascribe to Bacon the proposition that 'Knowledge is power' is not only not what Bacon said or meant but is the unashamed apotheosis of a prevailing desire for power and control that is open to serious question and that Bacon – even with his scabrous public record – would surely have deplored. What Bacon actually said was '*Scientia et potentia in idem coincidunt*' 'Knowledge and power come together (coincide) in a single point' – (*Novum Organum*, 1, 3). By '*potentia*' he did not mean the power to technological manipulation but the power of the mind to participate in natural process. To use knowledge as an instrument of power is no less corrupting than the deliberate use of any other kind of power. The true end of knowledge in a civilised society is *awareness*; from refined and sensitive awareness alone springs the quality of action and decision that is its own argument.

4. Current analysis of university work that depends upon the assumption that 'teaching' can be separated from 'learning', and that 'research' and scholarship can be separated from teaching-and-learning is a prime example of the 'thingy' nominalism discussed at the beginning of this paper. The implied aggressiveness of the verb 'to teach' may have a certain appeal to persons whose habit is to seek to exercise power; but no aggressive term or analogy is proper to the delicate and dynamic personal relations that a self-realising education depends upon. The complex of teaching-and-learning (education), like the fear-of-God and the pity-and-terror of tragedy, is not exhausted by analysing the component words of the phrase one-by-one; indeed such an analysis turns the notion into a parody of itself. If we had an *Académie* it could serve us well at present by placing a one-hundred-year embargo, in discussions of education, upon the separate terms 'teaching' and 'learning', and upon those two curious abstractions beloved by schools of education, 'the learning-process' and 'the learning-experience'. These last two terms are opaque fantasies that seem to have been introduced in order to give full rein to sentimental voguishness and to preclude intelligent inquiry into radical educational issues in quarters where, it is alleged, such matters are kept under careful and continuous study.

CHAPTER SIX: PICKING UP THE THREAD

1.   Since writing this essay I have noticed in the writing of educationists a
     sudden eruption of the word 'numeracy' – which, I suppose, by loose
     analogy means the ability to add and subtract (a mystery that even
     navigators by tradition seldom master). In such grand vestments now creep
     the three Rs, under a new name, with added bleach.
2.   Cf. *The Letters of Mercurius* (London, 1970) p. 46: 'Dr Chadwick is held by
     all to be a man of sense and learning . . . as also an excellent preacher,
     able to put together an English sentence, with subject, verb and syntax,
     which is rare enough in these illiterate days, and would doubtless do much
     good to the young, were they not artfully discouraged from hearing him.'
3.   In my family, my mother was fond of reading aloud to us when we were
     children. In the summer, on an island on Devil Lake, a favourite place to
     read was a little glade by the water. Sometimes an old groundhog who
     lived at the edge of the glade would clamber out of his burrow and listen
     'motionless and still' as though, even in a world haunted by the white-
     throated sparrow, the whisky-jack and the loon, the sound of my mother's
     voice reading was a marvel not to be missed.
4.   A pianist can learn agility at the keyboard by practising scales and
     arpeggios with increasing precision and velocity; he can work at *études*,
     preferably those of Chopin, Brahms and Bartok, which combine musical
     interest with concentrated technical difficulty; he can work at compositions
     of high musical quality and sort out the technical difficulties as they turn
     up. In writing (except in some kinds of verse) we cannot 'practise' in so
     direct a way, and it is very difficult to contrive technical exercises that will
     develop competence in writing. Probably the nearest we can get is in a
     patient study of the dynamics of any writing we admire, and an attempt
     to match the quality of it. But writing will come to life only if the writer
     cares about what he is writing; and parody is too subtle a matter for weak
     heads.

CHAPTER SEVEN: JANE AUSTEN: POET

Quotations from the writings of Jane Austen are identified in the text. The
abbreviations used are as follows:

E   *Emma*
MP   *Mansfield Park*
MW   *The Minor Works of Jane Austen*, ed. Chapman.
NA   *Northanger Abbey*
P&P   *Pride and Prejudice*
S&S   *Sense and Sensibility*

1.   *Jane Austen: The Critical Heritage*, ed. B. C. Southam (London, 1968) pp.
     127, 130.
2.   M. Lascelles, *Jane Austen and her Art* (Oxford, 1939) p. 106.

3. *Austen: The Critical Heritage*, pp. 87–105, 122–3, 148–66.
4. Ibid., pp. 130, 243, 157, 243.
5. Edwin Muir, *The Structure of the Novel* (London, 1928) pp. 42–6.
6. Lascelles, *Austen and her Art*, p. 109.
7. Ibid., pp. 32–3.
8. Muir, *Structure of the Novel*, p. 42.

CHAPTER EIGHT: BIRTHRIGHT TO THE SEA: SOME POEMS OF E. J. PRATT

1. I am grateful to George Story for drawing my attention to this important refinement of Newfoundland idiom. It defines, at one stroke, as perhaps nothing else can, the closeness of the horizon from a small vessel – the immediacy and scale of what has to be done expertly and promptly in dories and small boats, and in schooners and trawlers. Since nautical idiom is as remarkable for understatement as for precision, the word 'sea' is used to refer to waves, particularly those brainless great lumps of water that come at you at unexpected angles; otherwise it refers to something over the horizon, imagined, almost literary, and is not much used by Newfoundlanders.

2. This distinction happens to be nicely illustrated by an intersection of the actual and the imaginatively real in connection with Coleridge's 'Ancient Mariner' – a landlubber's poem that, within a few months of first anonymous publication, the editor of the *Naval Chronicle* strongly recommended to professional seafaring men. Coleridge wrote his poem before he had ever made a sea voyage. Whatever gave it maritime verity came from his reading of the detailed reports of seafaring men, especially in the great collections of Hakluyt and Purchas, and from talking with seafaring men when he lived in and about Bristol, the second seaport in the kingdom. (It's clear that he did not 'research' that poem.) We recall how parts of the poem are pervaded by the immensity of the sea, the infinitude of the ocean:

> We were the first that ever burst
> Into that silent sea!

and

> Alone, alone, all alone,
> Alone on a wide wide sea!

On his first voyage, from Yarmouth to Hamburg, in September 1798 after 'The Ancient Mariner' had been published – the same voyage on which the Wordsworths were sea-sick and Coleridge says he was not – he noted down what he saw in his first afternoon at sea: 'At four o'clock I observed a Wild Duck swimming on the waves, a single solitary wild duck. It is not easy to conceive, how interesting a Thing it looked in that round objectless Desart of Waters.' Once out of sight of land on the voyage to Hamburg he was thinking of the sea in 'imaginative' terms. But when he came to revise his letter for publication about ten years later, he added,

> I had associated such a feeling of immensity with the Ocean, that I felt exceedingly disappointed, when I was out of sight of all land, at the narrowness and nearness, as it were, of the circle of the Horizon. So little are images capable of satisfying the obscure feelings connected with words.

By then he had made a voyage from Portsmouth to Malta and had sailed back from Leghorn, fifty-five days at sea on each voyage, and had paid attention to what you actually *see* from the deck of a ship and what it feels like: how *near* the horizon is – from the bridge of a destroyer only seven or eight miles, from the deck of a sailing-vessel rather closer; and the sense of standing not at the centre of an expanse of water that stretches out to infinity but rather of being inside the rim of a shallow saucer, the sea a hollow of no great extent curving upward toward the horizon, or sloping away gently downwards as though to flow over the near horizon. Yet, if the sailor knows that he has a few hundred leagues, or a thousand miles of open ocean to cross before his landfall, his feeling of the immensity of the sea is heightened, not by what he can see but by what he imagines, his premonitions, his calculation of how long it will be before anything rises above that bounding horizon. (Cook's astronomer Green, on 29 June 1770 near Cape Tribulation in Australia, thinking how far he was from home set down his longitude as $214° 42' 30''$ West.) The confinement of his vision may well give him a sense of enclosedness rather than of freedom, of obsessive fixture rather than of unlimited movement through space.

3. The day I was flying to St John's to give this lecture, a notable winter storm had blown up, and a similar drama was working itself out around the small, top-heavy, listing, uncontrollable *Gabriella* some distance off Cape Race. No less skill or resolution (over a shorter period) was brought to the crisis, but the outcome was more sorrowful: only two survived out of thirteen. Seven days after the ship was abandoned, a life-raft was washed ashore at St Shotts with the bodies of six men and a woman in it.

Bibliography of the Works of George Whalley

BOOKS

No Man an Island (Toronto: Clarke, Irwin, 1948) viii + 72 pp.

Poetic Process (London: Routledge & Kegan Paul, 1953) xxxix + 256 pp. Reprinted in paperback (Cleveland & New York: Meridian Books, 1967) xxxix + 256 pp.; reprinted in hardback (Westport, Conn.: Greenwood Press, 1973). Ch. 3, 'The Artist and Reality', first published in *Cataraqui Review*, vol. I, no. 2 (Summer 1951) pp. 5–31.

Selected Poems of George Herbert Clarke, edited and with Foreword by George Whalley, and with a General Introduction by W. O. Raymond (Toronto: Ryerson, 1954) xxvi + 54 pp.

Coleridge and Sara Hutchinson and the Asra Poems (London: Routledge & Kegan Paul, 1955; Toronto: University of Toronto Press, 1955) xxi + 188 pp. with plates. The poems are included in *Coleridge Poems*, ed. John Beer (London: Everyman, 1963); the text of 'Letter to Asra' (pp. 154–64) is included in *Major British Poets of the Romantic Period*, ed. William Heath (New York: Macmillian, 1972).

Writing in Canada: Proceedings of the Canadian Writers' Conference, Queen's University, 28–31 July 1955, edited, and with a Preface by George Whalley, and with an Introduction by F. R. Scott (Toronto: Macmillan, 1956) xii + 147 pp. (hardback and paperback editions).

The Legend of John Hornby (London: John Murray, 1962; Toronto: Macmillan, 1962) xiv + 367 pp. with maps and illustrations. Reprinted in paperback (Toronto: Macmillan, 1977, Laurention Series). Extracts reprinted in E. Waterston and Munro Beattie, *Composition for Canadian Universities* (Toronto: Macmillan, 1964) pp. 10–11; in Pierre and Janet Berton, *The Centennial Food Guide* (Toronto: McClelland & Stewart, 1966) pp. 94–5; and in *Canadian Writing Today*, ed. Mordecai Richler (Harmondsworth: Penguin Books, 1970) pp. 127–36.

A Place of Liberty: Essays on the Government of Canadian Universities, edited, and with an essay 'Further Proposals' (pp. 154–75) by George Whalley (Toronto: Clarke, Irwin, 1964) xii + 224 pp.

Death in the Barren Ground: The Diary of Edgar Christian, edited, and with an Introduction by George Whalley (Ottawa: Oberon Press, 1980) 192 pp. and illustrations.

The Collected Works of Samuel Taylor Coleridge, Marginalia I: Abbt to Byfield (first of 5 volumes), edited by George Whalley, being no. 12.1 of the *Collected*

263

Works (Princeton: Princeton University Press; London: Routledge & Kegan Paul, 1980) clxxiv + 879 pp. and illustrations.
Christopher Pepys 1914–1974: A Remembrance by his Friends, edited, with contributions by George Whalley (Oxford: privately printed, 1980) xvi + 84 pp.

SCHOLARLY AND CRITICAL ESSAYS
'The Poet and his Reader', *Queen's Quarterly*, 54 (1947) 202–13.
'Romantic Chasms', *Times Literary Supplement*, 21 June 1947.
'The Mariner and the Albatross', *University of Toronto Quarterly*, 16 (1947) 381–98; reprinted in part in '*The Rime of the Ancient Mariner': A Handbook*, ed. R.A. Gettmann (San Francisco, 1961) pp. 83–8; reprinted, with omissions, in *Coleridge: A Collection of Critical Essays*, ed. Kathleen Coburn (Englewood Cliffs, 1967) pp. 32–50; reprinted with references revised, in *Twentieth Century Interpretations of 'The Rime of the Ancient Mariner'*, ed. James Boulger (Englewood Cliffs, 1969) pp. 73–91; reprinted, with references revised, in *Coleridge: The Ancient Mariner and Other Poems*, ed. A. R. Jones and W. Tydeman (London: Macmillan, 1973) pp. 160–83.
'Coleridge and Wales', *Times Literary Supplement*, 16 Aug. 1947.
'The Metaphysical Revival', *Yale Review*, 37 (1948) 434–46; reprinted in German translation as 'Zum Verständniss moderner Dichtung' in *Die amerikanische Rundschau*, no. 19 (June 1948) 69–78.
'The Great Canadian Novel', *Queen's Quarterly*, 55 (1948) 318–26.
'The Bristol Library Borrowings of Southey and Coleridge, 1793–8', *The Library*, ser. 5, 4 (1949) 114–32; reprinted in Paul Deschamps, *La Formation de la Pensée de Coleridge (1772–1804)* (Paris: Didier, 1964) Appendix I, pp. 545–52 (annotated list only).
'The Dispersal of S. T. Coleridge's Books', *Times Literary Supplement*, 28 Oct. 1949 (special article, anonymous).
'Two Undated Coleridge Letters', *Notes and Queries*, 15 Oct. 1949, p. 454.
'Coleridge and Southey in Bristol, 1795', *Review of English Studies*, new ser., 1 (1950) 324–40.
'The Pathetic Fallacy', *Queen's Quarterly*, 57 (1950) 521–9.
'Coleridge and John Murray', Quarterly Review, no. 588 (1951) 253–66.
'Coleridge on Classical Prosody', *Review of English Studies*, 2 (1951) 239–47.
'The Integrity of *Biographia Literaria*', *Essays and Studies 1953*, new ser. 6 (London: John Murray, 1953) pp. 87–101.
'Coleridge, Southey, and *Joan of Arc*', *Notes and Queries*, 1 (1954) 67–9.
'A Library Cormorant', *The Listener*, 52, no. 1332 (Sept. 1954) 396–7, 400; text of BBC Third Programme talk, broadcast 23 Aug. 1954.
'Preface to *Lyrical Ballads* – a Portent', *University of Toronto Quarterly*, 25 (1956) 467–83.
'Coleridge's Sheet of Sonnets', *Times Literary Supplement*, 23 Nov. 1956.
'Coleridge's Debt to Charles Lamb', *Essays and Studies 1958*, (London: John Murray, 1958) pp. 68–85; based on 'Charles Lamb and Coleridge's *annus mirabilis*', *Charles Lamb Society Bulletin*, no. 136 (May 1957) pp. 156–7: abstract of an address to the annual meeting of the Charles Lamb Society, Salisbury.
'The Fields of Sleep', *Review of English Studies*, 9 (1958) 49–53.
Bibliographical entries for: S. T. Coleridge, James Hogg and Samuel Rogers,

in *Cambridge Bibliography of English Literature V* (supplementary volume), ed. George Watson (Cambridge: Cambridge University Press, 1958) pp. 557–65, 852.

'Yeats and Broadcasting', Appendix III to Allan Wade, *A Bibliography of the Writings of W. B. Yeats*, 2nd edn, revised by Rupert Hart-Davis and George Whalley (London: Rupert Hart-Davis, 1958) pp. 409–18. Reprinted in Allan Wade, *A Bibliography of the Writings of W. B. Yeats*, 3rd edn revised and ed. by R. K. Alspach (London: Rupert Hart-Davis, 1968) pp. 467–77.

'Henri Bergson', *Architects of Modern Thought, 3rd and 4th Series* (Toronto: CBC, 1959) pp. 33–44; a talk contributed to a series of broadcasts by various authors.

'Scholarship and Criticism', *University of Toronto Quarterly*, 29 (1959) 33–45; address delivered to the first plenary session of ACUTE, Edmonton 9 June 1958. Reprinted in *Academic Discourse*, ed. John Enck (New York: Appleton-Century-Crofts, 1964) pp. 150–62; reprinted in *The Practice of Modern Literary Scholarship*, ed. S. P. Zitner (Glenview, Ill.: Scott, Foresman, 1966) pp. 1–13.

'English at School', *Journal of Education* (University of British Columbia), 4 (1960) 63–73.

'The Humanities and Modern Science', *Proceedings of the NCCUC 1960*, pp. 45–54; reprinted, with small revisions, as 'Humanities and Science: Two Cultures or One', *Queen's Quarterly*, 68 (1961) 237–48; reprinted in *Current* (New York), no. 19 (1961) 58–64.

'Coleridge on the *Prometheus* of Aeschylus', *Proceedings of the Royal Society of Canada*, 54 (1961) Section II, pp. 13–34.

'Portrait of a Bibliophile: Samuel Taylor Coleridge 1772–1834', *The Book Collector*, 10 (1961) 275–90.

Introduction to Stephen Leacock, *My Discovery of England* (Toronto: McClelland & Stewart, 1961) pp. vii–xiv.

'Coleridge Unlabyrinthed', *University of Toronto Quarterly*, 22 (1963) 325–45; a public lecture delivered at the University of Wisconsin (spring 1962).

'Revolution and Poetry', *Centennial Review*, 8 (1964) 371–90; address to the Foster Poetry Conference, Oct. 1963. Reprinted, with small revisions, in *English Poetry in Quebec: Proceedings of the Foster Poetry Conference, 12–14 Oct. 1963*, ed. John Glassco (Montreal: McGill University Press, 1965) pp. 65–87.

'Sheet-Anchors and Landfalls', *Humanities Association Bulletin*, 15 (1964) 17–24; address to the annual Banquet of the Humanities Association, Charlottetown (17 June 1964).

'Late Autumn's Amaranth: Coleridge's Late Poems', *Transactions of the Royal Society of Canada*, 4th ser., 2 (1964) 159–79.

'Metaphor' and 'Simile': articles in *Encyclopedia of Poetry and Poetics*, ed. Alex Preminger (Princeton: Princeton University Press, 1965) pp. 490–5, 767–9.

'Literary Romanticism', *Queen's Quarterly*, 72 (1965) 232–52; a contribution to a seminar on Romanticism (Feb. 1965).

'The Wisdom of the Body', *Canadian Medical Association Journal*, 93 (1965) 603–6; address to the Osler Society, London Ontario (spring 1965).

'Coleridge's Poetical Canon: Selection and Arrangement', *Review of English Literature*, 7 (1966) 9–24.

'Literary Computing', *Proceedings of SHARE XXVIII* (1967); paper delivered to SHARE conference, San Francisco (16 Feb. 1967). Reprinted, revised, in *Quarterly Bulletin of the Computer Society of Canada*, 7 (1967) 9–13.

'Samuel Taylor Coleridge', article in *The Catholic Encyclopaedia* (New York, 1967) vol. III, pp. 988–90.

'Celebration and Elegy in New Zealand Verse', *Queen's Quarterly*, 74 (1967) 738–53; paper delivered to Commonwealth division of MLA, Chicago (Jan. 1966).

'Coleridge Marginalia Lost', *The Book Collector*, 17 (1968) 428–42, 2 plates; addendum, note 315, *The Book Collector*, 18 (1969) 223.

'Coleridge and the Royal Society of Literature', *Studies by Divers Hands*, new ser., 35 (1969) 147–51; part of the Tredegar Memorial Lecture entitled 'The Unseen Coleridge', delivered in London (23 May 1968).

'The Harvest on the Ground: Coleridge's Marginalia', *University of Toronto Quarterly*, 38 (1969) 248–76; public lecture delivered at Oxford (17 May 1968).

'The Publication of Coleridge's *Prometheus* Essay', *Notes and Queries*, Feb. 1969, 52–5.

'Wordsworth Library Catalogue: Harvard MS Eng 880', typescript xeroxed, 51 pp.; and 'A Checklist of Books in Wordsworth's Library', typescript xeroxed, 110 pp.; transcribed and arranged (?1958); copies presented to Dove Cottage Library (spring 1969); to Cornell Wordsworth Collection and Victoria College Library (spring 1971).

'Coleridge and Vico', *Giambattista Vico: An International Symposium*, ed. Giorgio Tagliacozzo and Hayden V. White (Baltimore: Johns Hopkins Press, 1969) pp. 225–44.

Bibliographical entry for S. T. Coleridge, in *The New Cambridge Bibliography of English Literature*, vol. III: 1800–1900, ed. George Watson (Cambridge: Cambridge University Press, 1969) col. 211–54. Items by George Whalley include those: on Wordsworth, col. 205; on Coleridge, col. 212, 215, 225, 244; on Southey, col. 261; on Shelley, col. 343; on Lamb, col. 1230; on Yeats, col. 1929.

'On Translating Aristotle's Poetics', *University of Toronto Quarterly*, xxxix, no. 2 (1970) pp. 77–106; revised version of paper delivered to ACUTE, York University (11 June 1969).

'On Reading Coleridge', *Writers and their Background: S. T. Coleridge*, ed. R. L. Brett (London: Bell, 1971) pp. 1–44, 271–81.

' "Scholarship", "Research", and "The Pursuit of Truth" ', *Transactions of the Royal Society of Canada, 1970*, ser. 4, 8 (1971) pp. 290–322; paper to Royal Society of Canada, Division II, Winnipeg (3 June 1970).

'England/Romantic–Romanticism', *'Romantic' and its Cognates: The European History of a Word*, ed. Hans Eichner (Toronto: University of Toronto Press; Manchester: Manchester University Press, 1972) pp. 157–262.

' "Research" and the Humanities', *Queen's Quarterly*, 79 (1972) 441–57; commissioned for the Corry-Bonneau Commission on the Rationalisation of Research; distributed with the report – *Quest for the Optimum* – in duplicated typescript.

'On Editing Coleridge's Marginalia', *Editing Texts of the Romantic Period: Papers Given at the Conference on Editorial Problems, University of Toronto, November 1971*, ed. John D. Baird (Toronto: A.M. Hakkert, 1972) pp. 89–116 and plates; paper delivered at the University of Toronto (6 Nov. 1971).

'The Aristotle–Coleridge Axis', *University of Toronto Quarterly*, 42 (winter 1972/3) 93–109; paper delivered to the Classical Association, Memorial University, St John's, Newfoundland (27 May 1971).

'Some Complex Functions of Language', *The Structurist*, no. 12 (1972–3) pp. 9–16.

'Thomas Gray: a Quiet Hellenist', *Fearful Joy: Papers from the Thomas Gray Bicentenary Conference at Carleton University*, ed. James Downey and Ben Jones (Montreal: McGill-Queen's University Press, 1974) pp. 146–71; see also pp. 258–9; paper delivered in the National Library, Ottawa (19 May 1971).

'Coleridge's Poetic Sensibility', *Coleridge's Variety: Bicentenary Studies*, ed. John Beer (London: Macmillan, 1974) pp. 1–30; paper delivered at Cambridge University (9 Oct. 1972).

'Lend Your Books to Such a One', *Charles Lamb Society Bulletin*, n.s., nos 10–11 (Apr/Jul 1975) pp. 55–60.

'Picking Up the Thread', *In the Name of Language*, ed. Joseph Gold (Toronto: Macmillan, 1975) pp. 46–70; paper delivered to ACE/ACTE Conference, Glendon College, Toronto (15 May 1973).

'Where are English Studies Going?', *In the Name of Language*, ed. Joseph Gold (Toronto: Macmillan, 1975) pp. 131–60; revised and extended from a paper delivered to ACUTE annual meeting, Queen's University, Kingston (29 May 1973).

'Jane Austen: Poet', *Jane Austen's Achievement: Papers Delivered at the Jane Austen Bicentennial Conference at the University of Alberta*, ed. Juliet McMaster (London, New York, Toronto: Macmillan, 1976) pp. 106–33; revised paper delivered to the Centennial Conference, Edmonton (6 Oct. 1975).

'The Place of Language in the Study of Literature', *Indirections* (OCTE), II, no. 2 (winter 1977 [Feb.]) 13–31; paper delivered to OCTE annual convention, Toronto (15 Oct. 1976), entitled 'The Imprint of Man's Mind'.

'Poetry as Education of the Senses', *The Structurist*, no. 17/18 (1977/8) 37–46.

'Birthright to the Sea: Some Poems of E. J. Pratt', E. J. Pratt Memorial Lecture, St John's Newfoundland, Memorial University (20 Oct. 1976); reprinted in *Queen's Quarterly*, 85, 4 (winter 1978/9) 578–94 (Preface revised).

'Teaching Poetry', *The Compass*, no. 5 (winter 1978/9) 1–15; address to ACUTE, University of Western Ontario (24 May 1978).

'Literature: an Instrument of Inquiry', James Cappon Inaugural Lecture, Queen's University (28 Nov. 1977), in *Humanities Association Review*, 29, nos 3/4 (summer/fall 1978) 243–59. French version 'La Littérature: un instrument de recherche', *ibid.*, pp. 223–42.

'The Humanities in the World at Large', keynote address to conference on 'The Humanities in Society: Towards a New Coalition', Carleton University (20–22 Nov. 1978). Address delivered in the auditorium of the Ottawa Public Library (20 Nov. 1978); draft circulated before the conference, typescript 21 pp. Final version, as delivered, and submitted to the Conference for publication, duplicated for distribution to the Council of Queen's University (June 1979) 23 pp. Published in *Queen's Quarterly*, 86, no. 1 (1978) 1–15.

Index

Index